SAMUEL BUTLER

S. Butler. taken Nov. 19 1901

To Grant Richards Esqr with S. B's very kind regards Dec. 18. 1901

SAMUEL BUTLER
AUTHOR OF EREWHON:
THE MAN AND HIS WORK

BY

JOHN F. HARRIS

LONDON
GRANT RICHARDS LTD.
ST MARTIN'S STREET
LEICESTER SQUARE
MDCCCCXVI

PRINTED IN GREAT BRITAIN BY THE RIVERSIDE PRESS LIMITED
EDINBURGH

PREFACE

I HAVE first of all to thank Mr H. Festing Jones for help and suggestions on many points in the pages that follow. My thanks are due also to Mr R. A. Streatfeild, Samuel Butler's literary executor, and Mr A. C. Fifield, the publisher, for permission to make quotations from Butler's works; and to Mr Bernard Shaw for kindly lending me the manuscript of an unpublished paper on Charles Darwin which I have made use of in Chapter IV. The Bibliography at the end of the book has been compiled with the help of " The Biographical Statement " in *The Notebooks of Samuel Butler*, and revised and enlarged by Mr Festing Jones and Mr A. T. Bartholomew of the Cambridge University Library, both of whom I have to thank for permission to insert it.

J. F. H.

June 1916.

5

CONTENTS

TO

HENRY FESTING JONES

INTRODUCTION

In one of the most vivid chapters of his *Physics and Politics*, Walter Bagehot, that alert critic of the mid-Victorians, puts forward a theory to account for the way a different character or *ethos* distinguishes different ages. Indeed, like national character, the character of an age or society is an incalculable thing; yet Bagehot draws an interesting analogy with literature, which in some measure may explain its origin. He notes that certain historical periods, not only in our development but in that of practically all Europe, are notable for a definite, predominant type of literary production. The Elizabethan age, in the light of the forces liberated by the Renascence, was an age of drama; in Queen Anne's time the noisy pamphleteers and the quiet, respectable writers of the periodical essay vied with one another in claiming public attention; while in our own day it seems that the novel, which has so woefully declined from its early, English excellence, is the most important literary form.

So, in a literary sense, the age hangs together, and "men catch the words that are in the air." Yet too often the traditional style cramps the innovator; and, as Bagehot says, he writes his own words at the risk of contemporary neglect. Wordsworth is quoted as an instance. And Wordsworth is an interesting example, because, above and beyond his own originality, it was in no small degree the external circumstances

9

of the time which made him what he was—leaving aside the fact that in Blake, much more interesting as a personality, he had an important forerunner. At any rate Wordsworth, certainly an innovator, succeeded in impressing himself on his generation. He was the central figure of the Romantic Revival so largely fed by the new, often disturbing " ideas " that bubbled across the Channel after 1789. The movement that he represented coloured the literary history of a large part of the nineteenth century; and its influence, unlike most literary influences, became a real factor in social life. Thus the two phenomena which Bagehot tried to explain, in this case touch and meet.

Apart from this broad tendency at the opening of the last century there are others which, beginning a little earlier, worked under cover of it. At the end of the eighteenth century we may trace a very definite movement against so-called indelicacy. Fielding's *Tom Jones*, interestingly foreshadowing the action of a modern Town Council, was practically put upon the Index; the stage was ruled by artificiality; Mrs Sherwood, a little later, wrote her amazing *History of the Fairchild Family*, which exerted so deadly an influence on succeeding generations of English children; Mr Bowdler was to exercise his busy blue pencil with satisfying effect on the works of Shakespeare. So the forces of nineteenth-century sentimentalism— forces which were to swell to an unnatural size—were already mustering themselves, even if below the surface. The age became more and more acquiescent, more and more complacent—traits which are to be recognised in almost every department of national life. Material prosperity, increasing with the progress of the

Industrial Revolution ; national satisfaction after the successes in the Napoleonic wars ; a blunt, adventurous type of prose writing, which gave no heed to any of the deeper problems of life, supplied the environment in which men found themselves. It sufficed for them. They were quite content it should remain as it was.

In the political thought of the age we may trace a similar tendency. The first half of the century, it is true, so far as theory of government was concerned, was dominated by the old Benthamite utilitarianism —the " greatest happiness principle," according to which the prospect of pleasure and the fear of pain are the guiding influences in any course of action. It was a convenient and unanswerable theory which Bentham worked out with the utmost psychological minuteness ; and its importance for us lies in the fact that it was a stepping-stone to the typically Victorian attitude of *laissez-faire*, the distinctive political creed of the second half of the century. Individualism was thus enthroned, and State interference became anathema. So Victorian complacency was nourished and fostered by the political circumstances of the time.

One might, perhaps, have expected that such a view would bring into play a sturdy independence of opinion, a dislike of humbug, an unwillingness to worship the conventionally accepted gods of literature, art or science. But this was not so in fact. The Victorians were never happy unless there was someone on a pedestal to worship. To be a " great man " it was necessary to contrive for oneself a social vogue. It is interesting to watch the way these illustrious people of the age kept their celebrity by a stupid, pompous affectation of superiority. The great men became

fashionable—fashionable just like blue china or pre-
Raphaelite pictures.   And in an age of fads and crazes
it could hardly be otherwise.   George Eliot, the cold,
arrogant, successful woman, is a good illustration.
One reads about her absurd Sunday "at homes," in
St John's Wood, with nothing but amusement.   They
became a sort of ritual; women, apparently, were
admitted only in exceptional circumstances; the conversation was of the loftiest intellectual character.
The new-comer, the visitor of the week, was permitted
the place of honour by George Eliot's side, as described
in a reminiscence of one of these tea-parties.   It must
have been a forbidding ceremonial, enlivened only by
the genial presence of George Henry Lewes, who, we
cannot doubt, was silently amused at the melancholy
affair.   Indeed the posing silliness of it all in a small
way is an illustrative feature of the period.

In his brief study of Victorian literature,[1] Mr
Chesterton, writing from quite another point of view,
speaks at some length of what he calls, perhaps a little
obscurely, " the Victorian compromise "—which compromise he finds to be one of the most strongly marked
traits of the middle and later decades of the century.
He represents the Victorian school as showing its
distinctive spirit in a series of revolts against that
particular and prevailing tendency which drifted across
the Channel after the French Revolution.   Thus,
according to him, " rationalism triumphant " was the
peculiar temper which distinguished what may roughly
be described as Victorianism—or at any rate its be-
ginnings—and against this background one can trace
fairly easily the successive attempts—whether it be

[1] *The Victorian Age in Literature.*

Carlyle, or Ruskin and the pre-Raphaelites, or Newman, or Matthew Arnold standing somewhat apart—one can trace the successive attempts to discredit this solidly scientific school. This generalisation is as roughly accurate as such things often are; and it must not be forgotten that the so-called scientific school, no less than the men and movements in revolt against it, was made up of individuals possessing, much more than they possessed anything else, the vices and virtues of their time. Chiefly they all managed to acquire a degree of professional dullness which alone would have fixed them unmistakably, so far as chronology is concerned.

To return, however, one might accept Mr Chesterton's formula, good enough for our purpose, as a sort of *point d'appui*. The question may then occur : How is it possible to fit a man like Butler, the subject of this study, into any system, however wide and comprehensively, or uncomprehensively, vague; how are we to classify one who, above all others, belonged to no school, was traceable, it may fairly be said, to no influence at all *direct* in character, looking back to, and fitting in with, none of those particular habits of thought at any rate in the age just preceding and merging into his own ? On an external view, of course, it might be maintained that Butler harmonised with the solid, scientific background of Victorian thought— harmonised with it, yet was not of it. Again, as we have already hinted, one might quite easily say that Samuel Butler stood outside the Victorian system. And this would be the truest description of him. He did not stand outside it in the sense that he neglected it, gave it no attention. It always interested him;

if it had not been as it was Butler's work could never
have been what it is in character and outlook. Butler
was outside the Victorian convention in that his
sympathies ran directly counter to those of his age and
also because, temperamentally, he was able to see the
deceits and weaknesses of the society around him. So
he defies the labellers, the people whose delight it is
to fix a man's precise position in the letters of his day.
Indeed of all amusements, perhaps, none is more futile
than this attempt to pigeon-hole and classify genius.
Genius can admit of no classification.

One might mention half-a-dozen writers—Voltaire,
Fielding, Defoe, Swift and Nietzsche, perhaps, in an
indistinct way—whose work has some similarities to
that of Butler. But the comparisons serve very little
useful purpose; they do not bring us much nearer to
understanding him. And it must inevitably be so in
a man who went his own way, thought for himself, and
wrote his own words, not those of other people. On
every subject that engaged his attention he came to
an independent decision. His was a life, in a mental
sense, hindered by no useless encumbrances; things
which he knew to have no value or meaning for him
he discarded, whether they were doctrines, dogmas,
books or people. In one case, however, there is evidence that he had studied carefully and wisely: Swift
was a writer whose work Butler, quite early in life,
read and assimilated; indeed the mental attitude of
the greatest English satirist must have appealed to
him as none other could do—with the possible exception of Fielding. Fielding's personality interested
Butler much more than his work, whereas with
Swift it was the quick terseness of the writing which

particularly claimed his attention. Yet here also he must have felt the strong personal presence—which he always looked for behind the written word—giving life and force to the whole. There are points of contact, too, between Butler and Defoe, that great master of realism. On many occasions Butler's *vraisemblable* method reminds us of this eighteenth-century writer. The successful affectation of reality, as opposed to fiction, which Butler practised once at least with complete success, is in the best tradition of Defoe—Defoe so bluntly described by someone as " perhaps the greatest liar who ever lived."

So Butler's literary position is indeterminate. A classic by training, he was also a man of science, novelist, philosopher and art critic. And in addition to these literary interests he composed music and painted pictures. To everything he undertook, provided it interested him—and all these things interested him—he gave the completest attention, working with a conscientious care quite unusual in those who find that they can obtain attractive results with little labour. He never traded upon his own great natural abilities. He was, in one important aspect of his character, a marvel of industry and thoroughness. It is his general position, however, as a satirist and ironist that constitutes his greatest importance. We have already, in a vague and inadequate way, tried to point out some of the characteristics of Victorian society, the society into which Butler was born. An attempt to catch the *ethos*, the tone of such a society, must be very much of a failure. And yet there are a few external marks which serve to indicate what the later-Victorian age was like. The gibes at its expense, like the gibe at the middle classes, are old and threadworn ; perhaps they are none the less justified for that. The important thing is that Butler was born into that age, and more important still, what he said about it has no small meaning for us at this present time. He was the one great writer, the social satirist, who saw through the humbug and deception of contemporary life. In his freshness and freedom he stands as the completest counterweight to the foolish sentimentalisms of certain of the Victorians. And in a period which produced more useless things—and this in a wide sense—than almost any other, a cheap age of false values and mis-placed enthusiasms, unaccountable prejudices, aston-ishing deficiency in artistic perception and yet with it a bewildering lack of real practical efficiency, in such an age it was a thing of incalculable value to possess one man who could hold up the follies of his day to the light of common-sense—and behold that they were very stupid follies. And just because Butler was in advance of his own time—there was much of the wide, prophetic spirit in his work—what he wrote has a very real value to-day.

Mr Gilbert Cannan, in his study of Butler,[1] has, in the opening chapter, described him very well against the background of his unfortunate age. He would have us consider what the England of that time was like : it was, as Mr Cannan sees it, the age of com-mercialism and the Great Exhibition, when Shake-speare was considered "not altogether proper, and had a greater successor in Tennyson"; a gloomy age of antimacassars and family prayers. And, indeed, the disease of complacency had eaten so far into English

[1] *Samuel Butler.* A Critical Study by Gilbert Cannan, 1915.

vitals that a satire like Butler's *Erewhon* was admitted
to be valid, but of no importance. Butler himself, of
course, was convinced of the importance of the things
satirised in his book no less than of the legitimacy of
his satire. In this first-published book he did not
quite realise what he was after; but it swept together
many of the vagrant ideas that had been worrying him
to get themselves expressed; it enabled him, also, to
see where he stood in relation to the society in which
he had to live. We shall return to *Erewhon*, for a
completer analysis, in a subsequent chapter.

It was thus that Butler made his first tilt at conventionally accepted windmills. He was testing his
powers, he was using up old material. And he must
have been gratified at the time if he was aware that he
had written something that no other living man could
possibly have written. The merits of the anonymous
book were recognised; and it was only later, when its
true authorship was revealed, and when also the
revealed author was discovered writing other quite
different books of a somewhat puzzling character, it
was only then that the decision went forth—the reviewers and literary men decided it—that Butler was
much too dangerous and unrestrained as a writer and
must be left severely alone. It is to the credit of
Butler's age at any rate that it discovered so early the
dangerous quality in his work. Its instinct was protective, and, as shown in the sequel, it had marked down
its man and eliminated him fairly successfully from
the number of people who " really mattered." So
the conspiracy of silence continued, and Butler worked
quietly away on the lines he had laid down. The
contempt, the neglect of people who, like himself, were

presumably engaged in a search for truth was certainly bewildering; the conspiracy, however, only served to vitalise his powers; his ideas became clearer to himself, and in his writing he forged a perfectly plain and adequate instrument to express them. In this respect again he is in the completest contrast to the rest of his age, with its talk of "style," its affected "illustrations," its polishing of sentences to the necessary "exquisite" point.

Butler, in any case, could never have identified himself with those people from whom he was so successfully cut off. His aloofness was the attitude of a man who must criticise what is around him because there is so much to criticise. And one of the chief interests about Butler, to us who can get some bird's-eye view of his life, is the spectacle of a comparatively lonely man— as we reckon loneliness—doing his work and publishing his books at his own expense, on which, counting the whole output, the loss was little short of one thousand pounds. Reckoned by modern monetary standards, his life work was a failure. Yet it is only necessary to cast an eye over recent scientific research, or observe the tendencies of the younger school of creative writers, to see how wide Butler's influence has been since his death, in 1902. Indeed the emergence of Samuel Butler into the light of day has been a literary event of the last thirteen years; and it has now become possible to see the splendid sense of what he wrote—on all those diverse topics which interested him, so long obscured by the men of the age last past, who did their work so effectively. We speak here of Butler's common-sense, fully aware of his theory of the female authorship of the *Odyssey*, which has been a

stumbling-block to many; to this subject we shall
return in a later chapter.

Butler's literary position in his own time is well
summed up in one of his notes, called "Myself and my
Books." He confesses himself to be quite aware of
the reasons which contributed to making his work
unsuccessful; he was prepared for its failure, but in
no wise deterred from the course he had prescribed.
"I attacked people," he says, "who were at once unscrupulous and powerful, and I made no alliances. I
did this because I did not want to be bored and have
my time wasted and my pleasures curtailed. I had
money enough to live on, and preferred addressing
myself to posterity rather than to any except a very
few of my own contemporaries. Those few I have
always kept well in mind. I think of them continually
when in doubt about any passage, but beyond those
few I will not go. Posterity will give a man a fair
hearing; his own times will not do so if he is attacking
vested interests, and I have attacked two powerful
sets of vested interests at once. [The Church and
Science.] What is the good of addressing people who
will not listen? I have addressed the next generation
and have therefore said many things which want
time before they become palatable. Any man who
wishes his work to stand will sacrifice a good deal of
his immediate audience for the sake of being attractive
to a much larger number of people later on. He cannot
gain his later audience unless he has been fearless and
thorough-going, and if he is this he is sure to have to
tread on the corns of a great many of those who live
at the same time with him, however little he may wish
to do so. He must not expect these people to help

him on, nor wonder if, for a time, they succeed in
snuffing him out. It is part of the swim that it should
be so. Only, as one who believes himself to have
practised what he preaches, let me assure anyone who
has money of his own that to write fearlessly for
posterity and not get paid for it is much better fun
than I can imagine its being to write like, we will say,
George Eliot, and make a lot of money by it."

This passage was written in 1883, and it explains
quite sincerely, we believe, Butler's position. It may
seem at first sight to be either a naïve utterance or
the complaint of a disappointed man. It is, however,
much more a piece of genuine sincerity, one of the remarkable features about Butler's writing. Always he
faced problems squarely and said so exactly what he
thought as to be even, at times, somewhat disconcerting. He speaks here about attacking people
because he did not want to be bored ; and we fancy the
meaning of this is that insincere people who subscribe
to doctrines in which inwardly they do not believe
will have to submit to them *ad nauseam* all their lives,
and so sink deeper and deeper into the slough of boredom and self-deception. The passage is interesting
also because it shows Butler's realisation of his position
as a writer, and his faith in a later generation. The
value of his work he was quite willing to leave not
proven. And this faith in a posterity is characteristic
of Butler ; it appears again in his notion of immortality
—that the dead can only live by their work, vicariously,
in the thoughts and deeds of others. Lastly, the note
just quoted refers more than once to the two audiences
which, mentally at any rate, Butler always opposed to
each other. He felt strongly that the majority of his

contemporaries could take no interest in his work; he wrote therefore for a much smaller select audience, and a later generation, both of which would recognise the value of his achievement. This dual element in Butler's hearers is essential and worthy of special emphasis.

We have said that Butler's study of English society was an interested one; it was, also, much more than that—it was an amused study. In a sense he stands for civilisation looking at itself and laughing in the realisation of how funny it all is. It is funny because of its inconsistencies, its unreasonableness, because of the utterly anomalous laws, conventions, institutions which man, a reasonable animal, has built up. Measured by his own standards of common-sense, man's practice tallies very ill with his reasoned theory. Many of his institutions admit of no justification; attempt on his part to justify them spells failure. Butler recognised all this and his curiosity drove him on to examine the strange phenomenon. He examined it, and as a result told his generation many unpalatable truths about itself. So, in one way, he reminds us of the Wise Youth in *Richard Feverel*—although it is a comparison, we are sure, he would have disliked and repudiated. For it is true that Meredith's character is more of a symbol than a person; about Butler there is nothing bloodless or inhuman. Yet both of them in their aloof, amused attitude, their laughter at the capers of mankind—the laughter, perhaps, of modern and rather pagan deities—represent a type sufficiently rare to demand attention.

There is a further feature of Samuel Butler's work which must not go by unnoticed in a general introduction. This feature is the remarkable interdependence of thought shown in everything he wrote. He was never a pedant nor a specialist. He had the gift of seizing the vital connection between varieties of, at first sight, unconnected things, focusing and showing the material relevance between widely different points of view of thought and life. The classics, science, music, painting, philosophy jostled each other in claiming his attention ; but between each one of these studies he had established a real and vital connection. It is just in this that one may see the differences between what is called genius and talent. Genius is not in the least an intensified, a sort of superlative, talent ; it is simply the capacity for showing the wide meaning of apparently isolated experiences, for correlating the various ideas and aspects of life so that each one of them may throw a new light from its own particular angle. Walter Bagehot—with whom, as the sane critic of the mid-Victorian period, Butler has some points of similarity—has pointed out, in his famous essay on Shakespeare, the value to a writer of that " experiencing nature " which enables him to bring his knowledge of affairs into intimate relation with his written work, to write not *in vacuo* but with everything tested by his acquaintance with human life as he has observed it. " His mind," says Bagehot of Shakespeare, " did not form in early life a classified list of all the objects in the universe, and learn no more about the universe ever after. . . . What truly indicates excellent knowledge is the habit of constant, sudden, and almost unconscious allusion, which implies familiarity, for it can arise from that alone . . . a species of incidental, casual, and perpetual reference to ' the

mighty world of eye and car.' " These passages, as
well as anything we know, explain also Butler's peculiar
gifts. His work carries with it, pre-eminently, the
sense of having lived the things he wrote.

And Butler's " constant, sudden, and almost unconscious allusions," his illustrations, in other words,
have a real relation to their context. These illustrations are not embroideries, pieces of prettiness, inserted
to fill out the text, or because the writer liked the look
of them. Butler's illustrations indeed differ from those
of the Tennyson school in that they do actually
illustrate. Open a book of his almost at random—
Alps and Sanctuaries, for instance. Notice there his
remarks on the individuality of the Italians—the
Italians above all things must be *themselves*. The
surest sign of national decadence among them is a
desire for German life and German traditions. " I
will not say," he remarks, " that priggishness is absolutely unknown among the North Italians; sometimes one comes upon a young Italian who wants to
learn German, but not often. Priggism, or whatever
the substantive is, is as essentially a Teutonic vice as
holiness is a Semitic characteristic ; and if an Italian
happens to be a prig he will, like Tacitus, invariably
show a hankering after German institutions." Here
the illustration is perfectly natural and adequate.
We know, even without the bias of schoolday recollec-
tions, that Tacitus was as Butler describes him. And
Tacitus was an Italian.

This is just a slight example of Butler's illustrative
method so conspicuous in all his work. His mind was
a well-filled storehouse of ideas and references, each
one of which had its own particular relevance. In his

written work we frequently come across the same idea
or allusion, clothed in a slightly different form, which
reveals a mental compactness, yet with it a width of
range and vision, unequalled in any recent writer.
So these ideas and fancies, theories and thoughts about
life—"the wise, beautiful, and strange creatures that
were continually winging their way across the field of
his vision," as Mr Festing Jones aptly described them
—constantly recur throughout all his books. Very
little, as we have said, was isolated. In *Erewhon*, for
example, we have that notion of the World of the
Unborn, a world peopled by disembodied beings who
could only gain admittance to this other world we know,
by taking a drug, losing their memory and importuning
two married people to get them born. Incidentally
this is a comment on death and the question : What
happens at that, the other, end of life ? We meet the
notion again, however, in the *Notebooks*, where he writes
about an imaginary son who was always begging him
to bring him into the world, and whose pleadings he
sometimes could hardly resist. And so it was with
each one of his books : when painting or writing music
or what not they came to him, forced themselves upon
him and pestered and worried till they got themselves
written.

Such an intimate and original relationship of ideas
shows, at any rate, independence. There was no conscious striving after consistency ; it was much more
that, with Butler, the very composition of his temperament made everything he studied fit systematically
into his general outlook. His quarrel with Darwin,
for instance, was over something fundamental in his
own point of view and in the Darwinian teaching.

Has intelligence a place in the evolutionary process ? Butler, of course, was quite convinced that it has; and he felt himself bound to criticise vehemently anyone, no matter what his prestige or his position, who would oust intelligence from the universe. He expressed the difference between himself and Darwin quite shortly in the title of one of his scientific books, *Luck, or Cunning ?* And Butler's scientific theories, which are finding such startling justification to-day, may be considered as among his most important intellectual contributions : not quite his ultimate conclusions, however, for out of them grew a distinctive philosophy which is the real apex of his work, linked on to all else that he did through these scientific opinions. Thus of these opinions his novel, *The Way of All Flesh*, is, in one point of view, a practical illustration. The book was true enough to the life that he knew, and, as Mr Salter points out in his *Essays on Two Moderns*, it is interesting to notice the discrepancy which here appears between one aspect of his scientific theory and the practical side, the real life dealt with in the novel. That was a working out in practice, and in one particular case—his own—which could not endanger the position he had taken up.[1]

There is a further most vital part of Butler's intellectual equipment which, in respect of his immediate contemporaries, led more than anything else to distrust and misunderstanding—namely, his humour. As Mr Festing Jones remarks, in his short " Sketch of the Life of Samuel Butler," which forms the Introduction to *The Humour of Homer*, Butler, to veil his own earnestness, " turned most naturally to humour, employing

[1] See *post*, p. 227.

it in a spirit of reverence, as all the great humorists
have done, to express his deepest and most serious
convictions." Hence his contemporaries for the most
part—and Butler knew that it would be and was
actually so—could not believe that a man writing thus
humorously could have any serious, sincere opinions
about anything either in heaven or earth. This view
was natural after all, for the writers to whom they had
become accustomed used their humour rather as an
excrescence, or veneer, perhaps, than as something
fundamental, containing and concealing the things
most important to them. To humorists humour is so
real and vital that it colours all their conceptions ;
they cannot separate it—why should they ?—from
the sacredest things they know ; they live with it and
in it as an intimate part of themselves. For humour
is not an incidental thing but something ultimate,
inseparable from the temperament of him who possesses
it. We realise this perhaps vaguely when we speak
of being able to tell a man almost anything, except that
he has no sense of humour. For about this quality
there is a social element ; to be without it one is an
outcast, cut off from a large, vivid side of life and
human intercourse.

It is only, then, looked upon as a humorist, with
humour an integral part of his make-up, that we can
hope to understand Butler. On every page he wrote,
this element is present, and in *Alps and Sanctuaries* he
justifies its obverse in a dissertation on earnestness—
or rather the attitude of *surtout point de zèle*. "This,"
says Butler, "is not the saying of a cynic, but the
conclusion of a sensible man ; and the more deep our
feeling is about any matter, the more occasion have

we to be on our guard against *zèle* in this particular respect. There is but one step from the ' earnest ' to the ' intense.' When St Paul told us to be all things to all men he let in the thin end of the wedge, nor did he mark it to say how far it was to be driven."

After speaking of uncertainty as an element in belief, and quoting Mr Tennyson on faith and doubt, the writer continues :

" Faith was far more assured in the times when the spiritual saturnalia was allowed than now. The irreverence which was not dangerous then, is now intolerable. It is a bad sign for a man's peace in his own convictions when he cannot stand turning the canvas of his life occasionally upside down, or reversing it in a mirror, as painters do with their pictures that they may judge the better concerning them. I would persuade all Jews, Mohammedans, Comtists and free-thinkers to turn high Anglicans, or better still, down-right Catholics for a week in every year, and I would send people like Mr Gladstone to attend Mr Bradlaugh's lectures in the forenoon, and the Grecian pantomime in the evening, two or three times every winter. I should perhaps tell them that the Grecian pantomime has nothing to do with Greek plays. They little know how much more keenly they would relish their normal opinions during the rest of the year for the little spiritual outing which I would prescribe for them, which, after all, is but another phase of the wise saying —*Surtout point de zèle*. St Paul attempted an obviously hopeless task (as the Church of Rome very well under-stands) when he tried to put down seasonarianism. People must and will go to church to be a little better, to the theatre to be a little naughtier, to the Royal

Institution to be a little more scientific, than they are in actual life. It is only by pulsations of goodness, naughtiness, and whatever else we affect that we can get on at all. I grant that when in his office, a man should be exact and precise, but our holidays are our garden, and too much precision here is a mistake."

He mentions then the " spiritual pleasures " to be derived from those temporary truces so valuable to intellectual opponents if they can enter upon them. " It is a great grief to me that there is no place where I can go among Mr Darwin, Professors Huxley, Tyndall, and Ray Lankester, Miss Buckley,[1] Mr Romanes, Mr Allen, and others whom I cannot call to mind at this moment, as I can go among the Italian priests."

These passages show very well the wisdom of Butler's contention that it is bad for a man to be always hearing the words he wants to hear—the words he heard last time. In his own case he made it a practice to view things from a new angle, not for the mere novelty of the process, but because it often led to some new discovery. Always he was " turning the canvas of his life upside down " in this search for criteria by which to measure it. He knew the inadequacy of so many of the old traditional standards : by thus using his humour he tested them and discovered unsuspected points of view. And such a use of humour, it must always be remembered, was serious and sincere—a voyage of discovery to find new and valuable truth. Mr Desmond MacCarthy put very clearly this aspect of Butler in a *Quarterly Review* article.[2] " Butler's sense

---

[1] Miss Arabella Buckley (Mrs A. B. Fisher), author of *The Fairyland of Science*, 1878, etc.

[2] January 1914.

of humour," he says, "often performed the same
service for him that the dove did for Noah in the Ark.
It flew out into the unknown, bringing back to him an
indication that he would soon find solid ground beneath
his feet." This adventurous quality, and his attitude
towards earnestness, "the last enemy that shall be
subdued," severally contribute towards that vivid
personality which appears in all his work. It might
be supposed that with such a creed there could not be
left much room for enthusiasms. This, however, was
not the case. He may have deprecated the attitude
of extravagant and promiscuous enthusiasms, because
he saw that it was blinding so many people to reality,
destroying all selective and critical judgment; but
ne quid nimis cannot be called a maxim of his. Butler's
love of music, especially Handel's music, his love of
drawing, and of Italy, his "second country," make up
three great enthusiasms of his life. Had it not been
for them, he would never have been the man he was,
but a purely cynical being out of touch with his fellow-
creatures, with nature and with art, entirely negative
in outlook.

It was following some such line of thought as this
that a writer in *The Times*, in a review of the *Notebooks*, after quoting the note, "Nightshirts and Babies,"
in which Butler confesses that he would like "a *Santa
Famiglia* with clothes drying in the background,"
spoke of Butler's love of the beautiful and the comic
in the same picture—which is but another aspect of
his own remarks about twisting round the canvas of
life, mentioned above. The writer in *The Times*
aptly compares him, in this, to a gargoyle looking down,
as it were, amid the Gothic : for "he made his jests

about everything in heaven or earth, not because he thought nothing serious, but because he tested the seriousness of anything by its power to survive the ordeal." He laughed, in fact, at the triumph of the mechanical over life, and he delighted in a thorough-going burlesque of human life, taking up usually an unexpected position, not merely, as we have said, out of perversity, but in order to obtain that different point of view from a new and original angle.

To Butler the humorist, says Mr Gilbert Cannan, the " greatest figure of the time, Charles Darwin, loomed like a bogey." And to Mr Cannan it appears almost like a miracle that his humour was able to escape destruction in the long contest with Darwin. Thus he implies a sense of effort in this side of Butler's genius ; it was, he says, " driven to the last gasp and gave it in a chuckle. . . . He succeeded in saving his humour for its *Blüteperiode*, but only at the cost of acquiring a habit of aggression." But was this actually so ? Did Butler, in the real sense of the word, *fear* Charles Darwin ? It seems not. He knew that by reason of his prestige and his position at the head of one of the great vested interests in England he was dangerous ; he criticised him, in the first place, on an essential point which Darwin did not make clear in his work—whether fortuitous variation or intelligence is the real origin of species. So far as one could see, Darwin favoured " small fortuitous variations," and it was on this question that Butler criticised him. Later he may be said to have attacked him, quite justifiably, over a personal matter on which it is unnecessary to enter here. But Butler never feared Darwin. As the mis-understanding between them deepened he developed his position with even greater clearness, stating his case with a terse vigour and straightforwardness of attack unequalled in any modern controversy—for it was, indeed, a controversy of principles, though Darwin took small part. Not even then, we think, did Butler's old, native humour desert him. It may have assumed the guise of satire or irony, as indeed it so often did in its most characteristic form, but it was none the less humour for that. Contrast the attitude of Darwin— we admit the contrast is unfair—and one may then really see what a humourless mind is like. The amount of thought and labour which Butler brought to bear upon him was rather in proportion to the influence he exerted and the godlike position he held in England— a similar position to Ruskin's dictatorship of the artistic world—than because of any particular respect for his opinions, or for the ability with which they were put forward. Indeed, in one of his notes, " Personified Science," which may sound offensive to many minds —it does not matter for that, being, from Butler's point of view, a true statement of the facts—he says : " Science is being daily more and more personified and anthropomorphised into a god. By and by they will say that science took our nature upon him, and sent down his only begotten son, Charles Darwin, or Huxley, into the world so that those who believe in him, etc. ; and they will burn people for saying that science, after all, is only an expression for our ignorance of our own ignorance." This may be an extreme way of putting it, but there it is.

It must appear in all this that Butler takes a place as moralist—only natural in one so independent, who had considered moral questions without the bias of religions, traditions or social customs. More than anything else, perhaps, it was Butler's sojourn in New Zealand, in the early, most important years of his life, that cut him loose from established conventions. He got away from people to Nature, his sheep, and his own thoughts. And although he confessed to finding few "intellectuals," and men interested in the things of the spirit, he liked the rough vigour of the life there, the sturdy common-sense of the people, the sense of adventure and possibilities in the new country. It was the memory of this New Zealand he had known and loved that helped him in the vigorous reaction against the materialism of English thought and life. He recognised the humbugs and deceits which were as the bases of that life; so, as an anonymous writer has remarked, in respect of the new ideas which have changed the complexion of our moral values, he was the first prophet. "His satire was directed against law-abiding people who made others unhappy." For law is not an end in itself but only a convenience. In this matter we perceive some connection with Nietzsche's notion of the absurdity of the "thing in itself"; nothing in itself can be absolutely and mechanically determined; circumstances alter cases, and a rigid, inflexible code of law or morality—ancient and not seldom obsolete—is quite unreasonably taken as the standard or norm by which to measure conduct. Butler would have been strongly opposed to sweeping away all law; what chiefly he desired was a finer, more reasonable appreciation of its functions. And here it was individuals that he criticised rather than the collective body making up the State. Individual self-reliance, the "right judgment in all things" prayed for in one of the Church collects, were among his ideals in this life. Parents, educators, people set in authority over youth were those he chiefly attacked, partly because, in his experience, they were so lamentably out of touch and sympathy with the young generation, partly because they did not even know their own silly business. We laugh nowadays at the meaningless eighteenth-century catechism which to the question, Why did God make the gentle swallows in their nest ? " answers : " To show children what they are to imitate," and accounts for the existence of the pig by calling it an example of what not to imitate. We laugh at this facile nonsense ; but, as Butler would have agreed, in the teaching of the young with regard to natural phenomena there has not really been much reasonable progress from that day to this. He speaks in one place about the dangerous discretion and reserve surrounding sexual questions : " The best opinion of our best medical men, the practice of those nations which have proved most vigorous and comely, the evils that have followed this or that, the good that has attended upon the other should be ascertained by men who, being neither moral nor immoral and not caring two straws what the conclusion arrived at might be, should desire only to get hold of the best available information." Here the ultimate desideratum with Butler is vigour and comeliness, good breeding, which are the aims and ends of all morality as of all religion. It is, in fact, the happy position of being under Grace and not under the Law that he would insist on ; to reach such a position there must be no prepossessions or initial assumptions ; only those who discard such things can hope to reach the place of grace, where love is not far distant.

c

And as with sexual matters in the education of the young, so it is in money matters, the second most important affair that touches us in this world. There is a dim, religious mystery about it, which parents preserve as long as they are able; boys are told that they will have to " get their own living," but they are usually as ignorant of the whole process—though not so analytical about it—as the little introspective Ernest Pontifex (*The Way of All Flesh*), waiting in the matron's room on his first night at school, was ignorant of the true meaning of that " awful and mysterious word ' business ' " which he had heard so often. And so it is with too many of these spiritual pastors and masters; hypocritically or deliberately they teach what at the best is inadequate and imperfect, and often useless.

Thus to Butler the best morality is that which may best ensure the getting of all those things which " work together for good to them that love God "; they are, in his own words, " good health, good looks, good sense, experience, a kindly nature and a fair balance of cash in hand." He here gives a list of physical and personal possessions which will see a man through life with the minimum of discomfort. They are the few things needful, and a religious or moral system that fosters them has no cause to fear attack.

There is another point, however, which crops up in Butler's remarks on " Elementary Morality " : the question of the family. And his attitude here was very largely determined by the circumstances of his own life. This originating cause of his embitterment was a joyless upbringing in narrow evangelical surroundings, which undoubtedly had a certain souring

effect on his temperament. From his father there
was little real appreciative sympathy of his aims and
efforts and difficulties; and that kind of imagination
which enables its owner to put himself in the position
of others and realise their point of view was one of the
gifts Butler's relatives do not seem to have possessed.
The Christianity, too, that he knew was that attenuated,
soulless, unlovely type from which, with his love of
comely happiness, it is small wonder that he broke
loose. He discarded these old beliefs altogether; and
although it was over a fundamental point of Christian
dogma that he broke away, he perhaps hardly realised,
at any rate in those days, that Christianity was not
entirely of that gloomy character in the midst of which
he had been brought up. The uncomfortable feeling
about his family lent a distinctive colour to his
thoughts. He says: " I believe that more unhappiness
comes from this source than from any other—I mean
from the attempt to prolong family connection unduly
and to make people hang together artificially who would
never naturally do so." Indeed one might apply to
the young Butler, in his relations with his family and
his father, the words of the motto which Oliver Wendell
Holmes found attached to the mechanical toy:
" *Quoiqu'elle soit très solidement montée il ne faut pas
brutaliser la machine.*"

It is necessary, lastly, to include a few words on
Butler's philosophy of good and evil. "God and the
Devil," he said, " are an effort after specialisation and
division of labour," for " the bad are just as important
an element in the general progress as the good, or
perhaps more so." We may trace here some interesting parallel with William Blake's *Book of Urizen* and

the later symbolism which grew out of it; in Blake's story of the Fall it was not Satan who fell, but God, the author of the moral codes ; he represents Urizen, cast out into chaos, as the "negation of all creative activity," and in a later work identified him with Jehovah. Without any of these elaborate festoons of imagery Butler's thought about good and evil contains the same idea. "Every discovery and, indeed, every change of any sort is immoral, as tending to unsettle men's minds, and hence their custom and hence their morals, which are the net residuum of their ' mores ' or customs. Wherefrom it should follow that there is nothing so absolutely moral as stagnation, except for this that, if perfect, it would destroy all mores whatever." The revolt of the angels, therefore, is the record of the first innovators who broke loose from the stagnating influence of the moral code ; and in an ethical sense they may be regarded as those who wished for some progressive movement beyond the systems they already knew. But the two sides, as Butler saw, are necessary to each other ; their struggle means life, and we cannot reasonably have it otherwise. It was characteristic of him that he carried the idea to its logical conclusion.

CHAPTER I

EARLY YEARS

SAMUEL BUTLER was born at Langar Rectory, Nottingham, on 4th December 1835. He was the son of the Rev. Thomas Butler, and grandson of the famous Dr Samuel Butler, headmaster of Shrewsbury School and later Bishop of Lichfield. When eight years of age the young Butler went with his family to Italy, and spent the winter there—this being the first introduction to his "second country," as he afterwards came to describe it. Two years later he proceeded to a preparatory school at Allesley, near Coventry. Even at this early date he showed a considerable faculty of observation—just as later on he observed and noted the life of the Italians as recorded in *Alps and Sanctuaries*. Butler the schoolboy must have stored up in his mind many things which only saw the light of day, perhaps, when he began to write his novel, *The Way of All Flesh*, or to keep that little notebook in his waistcoat pocket in which he recorded old memories or quickly flying thoughts or chance scraps of conversation. In his sketch of Samuel Butler's life Mr Jones has included a note which humorously describes how the dreadful tedium of early morning prayers—they were longer then than now—at Allesley was relieved by a boy, kneeling opposite, who was able to blow saliva bubbles off the tip of his tongue which sailed away for a foot or so before bursting. It must indeed

37

have been a fascinating distraction, and one he would
not be likely to forget.

In 1848, the year of revolutions, he left his preparatory school and went to Shrewsbury under
Benjamin Hall Kennedy, the author of the famous
Latin grammar painfully well known to later English
schoolboys. In Butler's novel the character, Dr
Skinner, may be looked upon as a portrait of Dr
Kennedy, of whom, with the uncanny perceptive gift
common to most boys, he had formed so vivid an
estimate. In this same year, also, he went to Italy
for the second time with his family, and it was about
this period that he first heard the music of that com-
poser who was the most powerful influence in his life
—the music of Handel.

In 1854 Butler went up to Cambridge as an undergraduate at St John's College. At first he intended
to read mathematics, but afterwards changed his
mind and took his degree, in 1858, in classics, being
bracketed twelfth in the First Class of the Classical
Tripos of that year. The chief evidences of his literary
ability are to be found in a dozen or so " skits " which
he wrote during these years. They remained unpublished until recently, and have now been included
in the new edition of *A First Year in Canterbury Settlement*. All of them are interesting pieces, especially
in the light of his later work, which show the peculiar
bent of Butler's mind at this period ; as Mr Streatfeild
has remarked, in spite of their faults and deficiencies,
they are valuable " as documents illustrating the development of that gift of irony which Butler was
afterwards to wield with such brilliant mastery."

The first of the miscellanea, a " Translation from an

Unpublished Work of Herodotus," is a description, in
the manner of that writer, of the Johnians rowing :
" . . . they do not call them by their names but by
certain numbers, each man of them having a number
allotted to him in accordance with his place in the boat,
and the first man they call stroke, but the last man bow ;
and when they have done this for about fifty miles
they come home again. . . ." It is good undergraduate parody, as also is " The Shield of Achilles,
with Variations," an Homeric itinerary of Cambridge.
Another piece, the " Prospectus of the Great Split
Society," was evidently written at the expense of those
who formed narrow cliques and parties within the
College—a thing almost inevitable in a large community. The aim of Butler's Society was to foster
strife of all kinds " whereby the society of man will be
profited much." Monthly suppers are to be held, at
which it is expected " that much latent abusive talent
will be developed." But everything is to be done
" with an air of great politeness, sincerity, and good
will, at least at the commencement, for this, when
evidently fictitious, is a two-edged sword of irritation."
One sees here how early Butler had understood the use
and deadliness of irony, this two-edged sword of
attack.

Perhaps the most interesting item in the collection,
however, is a piece entitled " Powers," an amusing
example of ironical Nietzscheanism. He points out
that to be powerful it is by no means necessary to be
excellent. " When thou goest to chapel talk much
during the service, or pray much ; do not the thing
by halves ; thou must either be the very religious
power, which kind though the less remarked yet

on the whole hath the greater advantage, or the thoughtless power, but above all see thou combine not the two, at least not in the same company, but let thy religion be the same to the same men." It is a fine defence of high-handed, unscrupulous behaviour; and Butler must have laughed pleasantly over the self-consciousness of these various Powers. They were the Swells in the College at that day. Much later he wrote a note on Swells, more serious in intention. "People ask complainingly what swells have done. . . . The good swell is the creature towards which all nature has been groaning and travailing together until now. He is an ideal. He shows what may be done in the way of good breeding, health, looks, temper and fortune."

In addition to these, Butler's undergraduate sketches number among them an examination paper set to a gyp, poems, and a dialogue in the Court of St John's College between the Junior and Senior Dean on their way to chapel. To the former's remark that he is much pleased with Samuel Butler—

> " I have observed him mightily of late ;
> Methinks that in his melancholy walk
> And air subdued whene'er he meeteth me
> Lurks something more than in most other men "—

the Senior Dean replies :

> " It is a good young man. I do bethink me
> That once I walked behind him in the cloister ;
> He saw me not, but whispered to his fellow :
> ' Of all men who do dwell beneath the moon
> I love and reverence most the Senior Dean.' "

The above may serve as an example of Butler's private fun at the expense of the two academic dignitaries.

Certainly he never thought that the piece would at
any time be published.

In addition to the music of Handel there was
another rather different influence which touched Butler
—though probably only momentarily—when at the
University : this was the teaching of the Cambridge
Simeonites, a body founded by the evangelical divine,
Charles Simeon. As described in the early pages of
J. H. Shorthouse's *Sir Percival*, the personal influence
of this man and his work lasted long after his death,
and during the earlier decades of the last century was
prodigious—as extensive, it is said, as that of Newman.
His labours were continued by the Simeonites, or
" Sims," as they were irreverently called, and in *The
Way of All Flesh* Ernest Pontifex is described as
coming under their sway for a brief period. In the
novel there is an account of a prayer meeting and
address in St John's, given by a Rev. Gideon Hawke,
a prominent London evangelical preacher. The entire
description is written, of course, with all that force
of delicate irony which Butler could command when
desiring to satirise shams and humbug. Yet it is
impossible to convey the sense of fear and spiritual
unworthiness that is made to sweep across Butler's
hero as the speaker warms to his text an thunders
denunciations upon the wicked. As an awe-inspiring
being Gideon Hawke—though we have only one glimpse
of him, preaching that memorable sermon—is com-
parable to Dr Skinner, another of the remarkable
minor characters of the book. The conclusion of this
Simeonite sermon is dramatic :

" And now Mr Hawke, who up to this time had

spoken with singular quietness, changed his manner to one of greater warmth and continued—

" ' Oh ! my young friends turn, turn, turn, now while it is called to-day—now from this hour, from this instant ; stay not even to gird up your loins ; look not behind you for a second, but fly into the bosom of that Christ who is to be found of all who seek him, and from that fearful wrath of God which lieth in wait for those who know not the things belonging to their peace. For the Son of Man cometh as a thief in the night, and there is not one of us who can tell but what this day his soul may be required of him. If there is even one here who has heeded me '—and he let his eye fall for an instant upon almost all his hearers, but especially on the Ernest set—' I shall know that it was not for nothing that I felt the call of the Lord, and heard as I thought a voice by night that bade me come hither quickly, for there was a chosen vessel who had need of me.' "

The effect of this harangue was, of course, considerable—there was scarcely one of his hearers who did not believe that he was the vessel for whom God had sent Mr Hawke to Cambridge. The sermon is valuable, too, as showing the kind of religious society in which Butler found himself. It is interesting to speculate about it. Did such a man as Hawke really come to St John's while Butler was up ? It is more than probable.

Thus the Simeonites were a religious body of a markedly evangelical type. And it must be remembered further that when Butler, nurtured in a gloomy age of Sundays and boredom, went up to Cambridge, in 1854, he was intending to be ordained. Unlike

most of the Simeonites, it is true, he did not consider
that he had received any very particularly "loud call
to the ministry "; but his father, at any rate, felt quite
assured of his future vocation. So it was only natural
that he should, like Ernest Pontifex, identify himself,
if only in a vague sense, with this phase of religious
life—the only religious phase that showed any signs
of activity while he was at Cambridge, as he himself
says—"connected with the name of Simeon," the
ultra-Protestant divine. If the Simeonites did nothing
else for Butler they at any rate stimulated him at the
age of nineteen, in his second term of residence, to
write an amusing parody on one of their tracts. Like
Ernest, Butler dropped a copy of his tract into the
Simeonites' letter-boxes as a counterblast to their
uncouth utterances, thrust " by night into good men's
letter-boxes while they were asleep " (*The Way of
All Flesh,* cap. xlvii.)

Butler's squib was discovered recently by Mr A. T.
Bartholomew among the Cambridge papers of the
late Mr J. W. Clark. One or two quotations from the
Simeonite manifesto will help to explain Butler's
parody :

" When a celebrated French king once showed the
infidel philosopher Hume into his carriage, the latter
at once leaped in, on which his majesty remarked :
' That's the most accomplished man living.'

" It is impossible to presume enough on Divine
grace ; this kind of presumption is the characteristic
of Heaven. . . ."

" The *one* thing needful is Faith : Faith = $\frac{1}{4}$

(historical faith) $+ \frac{3}{4}$ (heart-belief, or assurance, or justification) $+ \frac{5}{4}$ peace; and peace $= L^n$ trust $-$ care $+$ joy^{n-r+1}."

"At the present time the trial of the Church is peculiar. . . . '*While men slept* the enemy sowed tares'—he is now the base hypocrite—he suits his blandishments to all—the Church is lulled in the arms of the monster, rolling the sweet morsel under her tongue. . . ."

The above extracts, incredible as it may seem, are genuine items taken from the Simeonite screed. Butler's parody kept close to the original and was pointed in the extreme.

"There are only ten good men in John's," he says. "I am one; reader, calculate your chance of salvation."

Further on he comments: "A great French king was walking one day with the late Mr B., when the king dropped his umbrella. Mr B. instantly stooped down and picked it up. The king said in a very sweet tone, 'Thank you.' "

He proceeds, in admirable burlesque of the Simeonite remarks, to discover mathematically the recipe for the leaven of the Pharisees, to compare the River Cam with the River Jordan, to warn his hearers, in no uncertain voice, of the wickedness of Barnwell, "a place near Cambridge," and to show that the nursery rhyme "Rock-a-bye-baby" is nothing less than a thinly veiled religious parable. Nor does his parody end before he has included a little allegory about Faith and Works, who did not see quite eye to eye with each other,

and eventually got drunk and fought lustily. These
pages contain indications of that delightful humour
—though more extravagant because the Simeonites
must have been the most extravagantly impossible
group of people with whom Butler even came in
contact—which is scattered through his later work.
They are interesting, too, as showing a type of religious
observance and religious instruction common in
Cambridge sixty years ago and now almost extinct:
not entirely, however, for we remember within the last
few years listening to the harangues of an American
worthy, delivered in American, who, under the ægis
of some religious body, was converting undergraduates
very briskly in the large room at the Guildhall. The
scene would indeed have been after Butler's own heart!

Probably the first article of Butler's that ever
appeared in print was an essay " On English Composition and Other Matters," contributed to the first
number of *The Eagle*, the magazine of St John's
College. This was published in the Lent Term of
1858. " I think," he says, " the style of our authors
of a couple of hundred years ago was more terse and
masculine than that of those of the present day,
possessing both more of the graphic element and more
vigour, straightforwardness, and conciseness." Which
shows that even at this early date he preferred to look
back to those writers of the later seventeenth century
—Dryden, Defoe, Halifax and the pamphleteers, and
Swift further on—who were successful in conveying
their meaning in a prose and verse as direct and forcible
as one could wish to read. Here, indeed, were those
virtues of vigour and straightforwardness which Butler
found so singularly absent from the literature of his

own day. This is a good instance of one of those early judgments to which he remained continuously faithful; his praise of that clear-cut, bright, diamond-like quality of prose-writing foreshadowed the quality of his own work, which he afterwards revealed as one of the completest harmonies of matter and treatment in nineteenth-century literature. Elsewhere in this same paper Butler mentions Handel, one of those geniuses in whose art there can be no " rule "; and he adds that in writing we must never hunt after a subject. " Unless we have something which we feel urged to say, it is better to say nothing."

A further contribution to *The Eagle*, " Our Tour," is the record of a twenty-five-pound holiday trip through Normandy, Brittany, Paris, the French Alps, Italy, Switzerland, Strasburg and " home to dear old St John's, cash in hand 7d." At the close of the piece, in an unaccustomed explosion of fine writing, he describes the view from his windows in New Court as the night draws on, over Trinity Library and the " umbrageous chestnuts that droop into the river." " I say to myself then," he concludes, " as I sit in my open window, that for a continuance I would rather have this than any scene I have visited during the whole of our most enjoyed tour, and fetch down a Thucydides, for I must go to Shilleto at nine o'clock to-morrow."

It is difficult for us to get much idea of Butler's social life at Cambridge; he seems to have mixed chiefly with public-school men—Shrewsbury men, perhaps. He must always have been a welcome figure in any " circle "; in hall, where his portrait, painted by himself, now hangs—how surprised he would be

to see it there !—he was doubtless an admirable table
companion. But there was nothing obtrusive about
him—rather, perhaps, a shyness and uncertainty of
himself. With the tutors and authorities generally
he seems to have been on good terms—certainly he
attended chapels with a sufficient regularity—though
they must often have amused him, as we know the two
deans did. Dr T. G. Bonney, fellow of St John's
College, a contemporary of " Sam " Butler, as he was
called at Cambridge, has given us an interesting description of him at this time. He was always very
good company, " rather above the middle height,
rather thin and pale, dark hair, a slightly sardonic or
saddened expression, but with a strong sense of humour
and witty in phrase." The portrait we have referred
to, which hangs in the College hall, was painted by
Butler twenty years later. It is decidedly dark in
tone, as Butler's painting generally was, but having
regard to the lapse of time, it is considered to be
a good likeness of him and supports the description
given above.

In addition to his other activities at Cambridge,
Butler was a useful member of the College Boat Club.
He coxed the first boat when head of the river in 1857,
and also did some coaching. On the last night of the
Lent races in this year, a mishap occurred which nearly
resulted in a disaster. At the start Butler got the
bung rope, or chain, involved with the rudder lines,
and his boat was nearly bumped by Second Trinity,
but he succeeded in getting away and Second Trinity
was bumped by First Trinity at the next corner.
A letter to his mother describing the event opens thus :
" My foreboding about steering was on the last day

nearly verified by an accident which was more de-
plorable than culpable the effects of which would have
been ruinous had not the presence of mind of No. 7
in the boat rescued us from the very jaws of defeat."
He adds that a notable feature of the affair was the
" gentlemanly conduct of the crew in neither using
opprobrious language nor gesture" towards him.
This, we suppose, may be taken as a fair sample of
the kind of letter that he wrote home when at the
University.

During the whole of this period Butler was contemplating ordination, and on leaving Cambridge he
went to London and lived and worked among the poor
in a West End parish. Only then, apparently for the
first time, do we find any serious doubts creeping up
in his mind about his vocation to the ministry. The
rock on which he struck was, curiously enough, the
efficacy of infant baptism. Like John Pickard Owen,
in *The Fair Haven*, it occurred to him to inquire how
many of the boys, in the night school in which he
taught, had been baptized; he was surprised to find
that a large proportion of them had not, and more
surprised still to discover that he was unable to recognise by their moral behaviour, their good and bad dispositions, those who had and had not been cleansed
from sin in infancy. The position is curious, but it
must be remembered that Butler had been brought up
in a curious, intolerant religious environment. There
was no possibility of discussing questions of this kind:
they were taken for granted. And Cambridge was
little better; the Simeonites, so far as their religious
teaching was concerned, confined themselves to prayer
meetings and Bible readings—discussion of texts to

show their verbal truth, and minor matters arising entirely within their faith. So Butler had never before been brought face to face with a fundamental point of Christian doctrine—or at any rate if he had, he burked it. But now a new and arresting phenomenon presented itself. Why was it not possible by a straightforward process to recognise the difference between those who had and those who had not been duly received into the Church? To Butler's logical mind the difficulties seemed insurmountable; and these difficulties led on to the consideration of other theological questions held to be vital parts of a true belief.

But if he did not become a parson, what was he to do? He consulted his father, who at first was probably quite unable to realise his difficulty. A profession which was good and respectable enough for him and his father before him—who also had been a bishop— was surely good enough for his son. Later, however, he suggested various professions for this recalcitrant young man, and it was at length decided that he should emigrate to New Zealand, one of those satisfactory far-off places where unsubmissive people may best employ themselves. Butler himself, apparently, desired to become an artist, but this his family would not hear of. He sailed for New Zealand in the autumn of 1859.

Butler's New Zealand experiences are recorded in *A First Year in Canterbury Settlement*, compiled from letters home and articles published in *The Eagle*. There are fewer glimpses of the real Butler in this than in any other of his writings—which is perhaps to be accounted for by the fact that it was not entirely his own book. In a letter to a friend several years

D

later, he says, speaking of *Canterbury Settlement* : " My people edited my letters home. I did not write freely to them, of course, because they were my people. If I was at all freer anywhere they cut it out before printing it ; besides, I had not yet shed my Cambridge skin and its trail is everywhere, I am afraid, perceptible." There are several places in which we seem to detect restraint on the part of Butler, or else a revision of the text by his father. The probable effect of these two influences was to make his writing much more impersonal than it naturally was ; he dwells most on the birds, beasts and fishes of the colony, its natural scenery, its flora and the wild life he saw there. Although he was interested in all these things, it was naturally human people which interested him chiefly. The many anecdotes he must have had to tell, the little human touches, the rugged talk and manners of the colonists, on the whole he does not record, because he was writing for an unsympathetic audience. Over a good deal of the narrative, too, there is a feeling of restraint in other ways ; for the value that his father, the Rev. Thomas Butler, attached to the book, which he edited and bowdlerised, was purely utilitarian. To him it was the work of a rather inexplicable young man, who happened to be his son, and who had abandoned Holy Orders for a gamble in the Antipodes ; and in publishing his experiences the elder Butler published them chiefly as a hand-book useful to future emigrants. That the accounts of the young Butler's life and adventures lost a good deal in spirit and freshness under his father's blue pencil is shown by comparing them with the other written accounts which did not come under this careful parental scrutiny.

But as the book stands it gives a good picture of the kind of life Butler led for five years, working "like a common servant" in semi-solitude, devoting all his attention to sheep and "country." It was a life so different from that to which he had been accustomed in England that he must have come back home again with a very fresh vision of English society. New Zealand taught him to distrust the conventions of life ; she gave him also a strong robust, unwarped sense of values. Of his life in the Bush, he says :

"Yet, after all, it may be questioned whether the intellect is not as well schooled here as at home, though in a very different manner. Men are as shrewd and sensible, as alive to the humorous, and as hard-headed. Moreover, there is much nonsense in the old country from which people here are free. There is little conventionalism, little formality, and much liberality of sentiment ; very little sectarianism, and, as a general rule, a healthy, sensible tone in conversation, which I like much. But it does not do to speak about John Sebastian Bach's *Fugues*, or pre-Raphaelite pictures."

A First Year in Canterbury Settlement opens with an account of the voyage to New Zealand. Nothing very eventful happened, and he was extremely glad to reach his destination after a voyage of nearly sixteen weeks. "It seems as though I had always been on board the ship," he says, as they are nearing land, "and was always going to be, and as if all my past life had not been mine, but had belonged to somebody else, or as though someone had taken mine and left me his by mistake." Naturally, on his arrival, the people of the country interested him most—especially the shaggy men with "the rowdy hats"—and he was content to listen to their talk, soon becoming absorbed in their principal topic of conversation — sheep. Indeed, during the whole of his time in the colony Butler held no illusions about it, and he would have others do the same. There was not much poetry about the life there; visions of gold or fairy princesses were seldom realised. To Butler, as to all other serious emigrants, sheep were the only things that mattered. "You must remember they are your masters, and not you theirs; you exist for them, not they for you." They were, as he might have put it later, extensions, and most important ones, of his own personality.

It says much for his powers of adaptation that he entered into this new work with genuine energy and a desire to master the essentials of his business. This adaptive capacity of Butler becomes evident again and again in his after life. There was nothing insular about him; he never carried with him, as a sort of portable luggage, like so many Englishmen, an English standard by which to measure or depreciate everything he saw. It was partly that he knew how to behave; more, however, because he was willing to admit that there were other habits, other customs besides his own, and that other peoples might sometimes know what was best for themselves. We notice this later— especially in his Italian travels.

Thus to him New Zealand was a sheep country. He looked for nothing else, and so was not disappointed. One of the chapters of his book shows the thoroughness with which he had weighed the different methods of investing his money. He drew up one schedule to show what his ewes would amount to in seven years, and another calculating the yearly wool money. Within a very short time after his arrival he became an authority on these intricate, and, as one would suppose, uncongenial, matters. All this shows Butler's sound business common-sense and his shrewdness. He was determined to make what money he could and then return to England.

Accordingly he invested in a run—he called it Mesopotamia—built a V-shaped hut for himself, and settled down to an arduous life. And yet he did find it was a lonely life. In an earlier description of the character of the country, he says: " How one does long to see some signs of human care in the midst of the loneliness ! How one would like, too, to come occasionally across some little *auberge*, with its *vin ordinaire* and refreshing fruit." For Butler loved people, and particularly the people of a country, its natives; it was society people, with positions and reputations, famous in one way or another, whom he objected to, because he knew they were generally affected and unpleasant. Although the New Zealand country, the sheep, the bullocks, the tutu plant, the behaviour of the flies, with their hatred of untidiness, so much in advance of the English bluebottles, all engaged his attention, he never forgets to mention the odd characters he met—they did seem odd to him—the men with " the rowdy hats," the amusing Irishman at his hut who called everything that pleased him " beneficial," the old woman with corns who prophesied bad weather because they were so painful. He liked what was most various in human nature; and always throughout his life he seems to have had that gift of appealing

to simple people ; they gave him their confidences and
he sympathised with them. It must have been the
same in New Zealand, certainly it was so in London,
in his later Sunday walks round London, and in Italy.

Of all the animals with whom he had to do in the
colony, bullocks seem to have been those who caused
the most trouble, and with whom he was on the most
intimate, often unpleasantly intimate, terms. These
heavy, good-natured creatures had an unfortunate
habit of lumbering off in the night to a distance of five
or six miles. They had to be recovered first thing in
the morning. It was then advisable to drive the
bullock back as fast as possible, which he hated, but
which might cure him of his wandering habits. For
" he has played a very important part in the advance-
ment of civilisation and the development of the re-
sources of the world, a part which the more fiery horse
could not have played," and so is entitled to a certain
amount of respect. A most anxious moment was
when the bullocks were taking Butler's dray across a
river. Often they would pull the dray into the middle
of the river and refuse to pull it out again ; in the
manœuvres that follow the dray is in imminent danger
of being upset. On some such occasion as this—Butler
himself does not mention it in *Canterbury Settlement*—
he got his bullock waggons stuck, as one of his friends
describes, and was quite unable to extricate them.
Butler accordingly swore at the bullocks first in
English, and then, seeing it had no effect, went on to
Homeric Greek. Still no result. At last the bullock
driver came up and used some genuine Anglo-Saxon,
and the bullocks immediately went on their way !
Certainly an example of the triumph of the expert

over the mere amateur, which runs rather counter to Butler's own doctrines !

Before leaving these personal records of his life in New Zealand we may quote a passage which is full of admirable advice to a would-be emigrant. It shows the good sense with which he viewed his work of sheep-farming ; it shows also that a man must be prepared to rough it out in the colony. Butler himself went through many hardships in winds and snows and rains and all the unexpected varieties of New Zealand weather. On one occasion he and his party encamped in an unfinished roofless, doorless, windowless hut in the thick of a sou'-west wind, which in the night brought on a terrific snowstorm. In the course of the next day the snow inside the hut deepened to about six inches, and in the evening they preferred to sleep outside in a hole in the snow. This is only one of the many inconveniences which he suffered through inclement weather. It says much for the excellence of his constitution that he was able to stand it. And he warns insufficiently prepared gentlemen, proposing to emigrate, against entering too lightly on their new work :

" I should be loth to advise any gentleman to come out here unless he have either money and an average share of good sense, or else a large amount of proper self-respect and strength of purpose. If a young man goes out to friends, on an arrangement definitely settled before he leaves England, he is at any rate certain of employment and of a home upon his landing here ; but if he lands friendless, or simply the bearer of a few letters of introduction, obtained from second or third hand—because his cousin knew somebody who had a friend who had married a lady whose nephew was somewhere in New Zealand—he has no very enviable look-out upon his arrival."

It is useless to pretend that *A First Year in Canterbury Settlement* is not the work of a young man unaware of his own powers. It is less like the later Butler than his mildly revolutionary Cambridge pieces: he looked upon them, no doubt, as types of youthful indiscretion to which he would not revert; henceforth a serious attitude must be adopted towards the important business of life. Yet it is curious to note that later he did return very much to his old Cambridge point of view as revealed in those somewhat Swiftean writings. Or perhaps rather he never lost the attitude but obscured it in an active life in which there was little time or opportunity for the things of the spirit.

In New Zealand certainly religion cannot have troubled him much—at least other people did not thrust it forward for continual attention. He rejoices that there is so little sectarianism in the colony, one of the symptoms of its moral health. Yet there is evidence to show that religious questions were not entirely absent from his mind during the latter part of his three years in Canterbury. When still there he began a pamphlet on *The Evidence for the Resurrection of Jesus Christ as given by the Four Evangelists critically examined.* Thus it is clear that his beliefs had not remained stationary, presumably an ideal in religion. His doubts about infant baptism led on, by what steps we are unable to determine, to a questioning of that miracle which is the mainstay and backbone of the

Christian faith. The narratives of this important
event he found to be most difficult and discrepant
where they should be most clear. A consideration of
all this no doubt again led him to revise his position,
the results of which were the later embodying of his
pamphlet in one of the most curious and interesting—
interesting because of its very strangeness—of his books,
The Fair Haven. This, however, was not done until
some time afterwards. Butler was not by nature
introspective, yet he took very great trouble to determine his own point of view on one of the most important
problems that touches mankind.

His New Zealand period also gave Butler a new topic,
which lasted all through his life. It was while he was
still in the colony that Darwin's *Origin of Species*
appeared. For us to-day, who have grown up in the
midst of what is called the "Darwinian Theory," it is
difficult to realise the sensation caused by its original
appearance. Darwin and his book became society
institutions; their fame has been dimly paralleled
in the new century by that of M. Bergson, of whom it
has been boasted that he made philosophy a drawing-
room subject and influenced the modern ballroom by
his teaching. So it was with Darwin, on a much larger
scale, in respect of *The Origin of Species*. To the
Church it appeared as a dangerous scientific wolf in
their sheepfold; and, certainly at first, parsons felt
ill disposed to revise the Book of Genesis in the light
of it. As a story, the early chapters of the Bible are
much more attractive than a dissertation on geology
or the origins of variation; but to those who are on the
look out for a more certain knowledge, the latter may
be much more valuable. Yet at that time Genesis,

generally speaking, was treated pretty seriously, and
it was a hard saying that its supporters might have to
abandon it. The Church in these days has considerably changed its attitude and, to paraphrase the words
of a recent theological writer, she is not more greatly
concerned over the credibility of Genesis than the
edibility of Jonah. Speaking historically, both these
problems involve considerable difficulties.

The Origin of Species appealed to Butler profoundly.
It appealed to him in the first place because of its
wide application, the many interesting questions it suggested, and also because it was the work of a naturalist
with whom he felt a bond of sympathy through his
study of New Zealand natural history. The earliest
evidence of his appreciation was a dialogue discussing
the Origin and printed in a Christchurch newspaper.
This dialogue is a sufficient proof that even in those
early days he had a pretty clear grasp of what Darwinism amounted to and what it meant. The piece is an
imaginary conversation between an ardent supporter
of Darwin and one who is rather dismayed by the hard
logic of the book. The former, who is really Butler,
sums up the impression he has received from reading
the Origin somewhat as follows :—

Since all things in Nature, plants and animals, tend
to increase in geometrical progression, each of them
striving after what is necessary to its own existence,
it follows that there must be conflicts and collisions
between plant and animal life. So "struggle" is the
rule in Nature, and competition her law of progress.
Some are condemned to live, some to die. To the
suggestion that this may be subversive of Christianity
he answers : "I believe in Christianity, and I believe

in Darwin. The two appear irreconcilable. My
answer to those who accuse me of inconsistency is, that
both being undoubtedly true, the one must be recon-
cilable with the other. . . . The reconciliation will
never be effected by planing a little off the one and a
little off the other and then gluing them together with
glue." Did he write these words with tongue in cheek ?
Here, at any rate, there was to be no apparent compromise. One wonders what Butler would have
thought of the recent Oxford restatement of the
Christian religion entitled *Foundations*, which is perhaps the completest example of the planing and gluing
process, chiefly the planing, that anyone could wish
for.

This " Dialogue " from which we have quoted called
forth a sneering rejoinder; and the correspondence
that ensued shows Butler as Darwin's earnest disciple
boldly entering the lists against an Anglican
bishop who claimed that *The Origin of Species* was
nothing else than a slight and worthless variation of
the old tunes, occurring again and again, with scarcely
any change, played by worn-out barrel organs! The
bishop accused Butler of intemperance in replying to
his barrel-organ notion, and the little controversy
fizzled out. It seems, however, to have given Butler
his first taste for blood. Public controversy, like a
debating society, is indeed an admirable school for
clear thinking, especially if the opponent is of worthy
mettle. And Butler's mind was above everything a
controversial mind. He was at his best when conducting an attack—which, after all, is only another way of
saying he was a successful satirist. Each one of his
most important books, with the exception of *Alps and*

Sanctuaries, was an attack, either on hypocrisy, or Darwin, or religious England, or the conventional view of Homer. Always he required " stuff " on which to work, for he wrote nothing that did not of its own accord want to be written. Cambridge sharpened his wit—his intellectual keenness, that is—to some extent, and New Zealand and a bishop a little more ; but it was Charles Darwin himself who really did the most for Butler in this respect.

Before leaving New Zealand Butler wrote one further miscellaneous piece, " Darwin Among the Machines," the most brilliant of his occasional writings, probably the most brilliant individual piece that he ever wrote. Its argument is just this : that the increase in mechanical development, in proportion to the shortness of time involved, has been so immense that before long, as length of time is reckoned in the evolutionary process, the machines will have acquired a definite consciousness and will come to dominate man himself. It is true that they will always be dependent on man for their continued existence, just as the microbes in the human body depend on that body for their life ; but, unlike them, these Frankenstein monsters, the machines, will get the upper hand and rule humanity, with a cynical, unmoral, iron despotism. Butler's arguments are irrefutable ; the proofs he brings forward may not extravagantly be described as making one of the most remarkable pieces of exegesis in the language.

" Until the reproductive organs of the machines have been developed in a manner which we are hardly yet able to conceive, they are entirely dependent upon man for even the continuance of their species." He

adds that " these organs may be ultimately developed,
inasmuch as man's interest lies in that direction;
there is nothing which our infatuated race would desire
more than to see a fertile union between two steam
engines; it is true that machinery is even at this
present time employed in begetting machinery, in
becoming the parent of machines often after its own
kind, but the days of flirtation, courtship, and matrimony appear to be very remote, and indeed can hardly
be realised by our feeble and imperfect imagination."
Thus although the work of reproducing the machines
is done vicariously, there is no reason why they should
not eventually, of themselves, bring forth offspring
far healthier, more physically perfect, than could be
produced through any outside medium. For every
organism understands its own reproductive business
best. And to this rule the machines are no exception.

Later Butler elaborated a second view of the
machines as enlargements of the personality of him who
uses them. Personality he never defined as one and
indivisible, and so it is quite logical to conceive of
mechanical contrivances as a new side of man's
personality which may well get the upper hand. In
the first place the analogy between the adaptive power
of the machines, the displacing of inferior machines by
those more fitted for what they have to do, and the
upward struggle in the world of nature, is clear.
" Darwin Among the Machines," moreover, is a parody
of the actual present fact that thousands of men and
women have become slaves to moving iron and steel.
Butler's speculation is no less interesting to the
Socialist than to the philosopher. It is an apt
comment on the industrial age, in its own way quite

as instructive as anything the Maurices, Ruskins,
Kingsleys and Carlyles said about the forces let loose
by the Revolution. Butler, however, was not thinking of them when he wrote it, but was indulging in
one of those happy intellectual adventures—for its
own sake. There may, also, have been in his writing
a satiric note at the expense of Darwin, concerning
whom Butler may already have begun to revise his
opinions. This, however, is merely speculative. It is
sufficient to remark again that for brilliance of reasoning and statement Butler never surpassed these few
adventurous pages.

The last of his New Zealand writings was a brief
Note on *The Tempest*, in which he characteristically
shows what a " modern " young lady Miranda was—
as modern almost as the Nausicaa of the *Odyssey*. It
was always Butler's habit to interpret the older writers
in the language and point of view of his own day, for
he believed that human nature, at any rate since the
dawn of literature, has always been very much the
same. So he liked to translate the writers of another
age into a present-day idiom, because it helped him to
realise, and he hoped it might help others also, that
these writers were human people, with a personality
which he desired to appreciate to the full. The modern
tendency in literary criticism has been synthetic rather
than analytical—an attempt to reconstruct the character of the creator from his written work. Butler
to some extent sympathised with this view, but first
of all he wished the written word to speak for itself,
as best it could, in the vividest way possible. All this
becomes clearer in Butler's work on Homer and the
authoress of the *Odyssey*. And the little Shakespeare

note above mentioned is interesting as anticipating his later attitude.

Miranda, exactly like a young woman of to-day, knows that when serious love business is afoot her father may prove inconvenient. "My father is hard at study," she says to Ferdinand, who has been piling logs all day and must be very tired ; "pray now rest yourself—*he's safe for these three hours.*" A simple alteration. "Papa is safe " makes the sentence purely modern. And we cannot doubt that the inhabitants of a new country would appreciate this modern rendering.

On his return to England Butler settled in London in Clifford's Inn, where he lived for thirty-eight years, until his death. He now began life as a painter, one of his earliest pictures being *Family Prayers*, a bitter memory of his own childhood, and a pictorial comment on *The Way of All Flesh*, which he was yet to write. He also exhibited in the Royal Academy.

At this point Butler's " early life " may be said to come to an end. Considered as a whole, this period was one of germination, containing, however, not a few indications of what he was to become. Although he somewhere implied that it was necessary to slough off his Cambridge skin before he could write anything satisfactory, yet the University, in whatever other ways it may have deadened his perceptions, did certainly arouse in him a genuine love of the classics, and especially Homer, to which he returned enthusiastically later in his life. New Zealand, on the other hand, was of the utmost value in helping to lead him away from common and established conventions. She made him more practical, more self-reliant, less willing to trust to hearsay and accepted opinions. Always afterwards he studied at first hand, and on the spot, if possible, every subject which in any way interested him. More than this, his experiences in this new country supply a background of romantic adventure to the rest of his life. Yet to him, of course, there was very little romance about the New Zealand period; though to us, looking back to the earlier part of his career, there is a singular interest in picturing him on his run, Mesopotamia, busy with his sheep, yet still finding time to observe and record the natural conditions of the country. It was from these colonial days, too, that he got the nucleus round which *Erewhon* built itself up. Nothing less than all this was his New Zealand legacy.

And in respect of Butler's early writing one fact is particularly noticeable : there is little trace of immaturity; it is necessarily smaller in volume and intensity, but on the whole very much " of a piece " with his later work. More than any other writer of whom we are aware, Butler must be regarded in this light. It is impossible to isolate a part from the whole —and this is true of him almost from the first. And looking forward to the later books one finds very little of that " scrapping process " going on, where his ideas were concerned, which one might have expected in a rare, shrewd writer who has the courage of his opinions, keeping his eyes turned aside from what is shallow and popular and deceptive. He matured early. And in considering any particular part of Samuel Butler there is always a feeling of continuity. One must look forward and backward to see the whole Butler, for nothing is cut off from the main outline of his work. The early years are as vital as the later—

if less interesting—because although he saw things with the eye of maturity he probably did not realise that his vision of them was something rare and exceptional. Later—and only a little later—when he wrote *Erewhon* and *The Way of All Flesh*, he realised more intensely the breadth and depth of current self-deception. It was the England that he saw with new eyes, after his return, that awakened his restless satiric vigour. He reacted to the English scene as no one else in his century had reacted before. And towards this event, his early training at home, at the University, in a London parish and in New Zealand had conspired. Samuel Butler was one of capricious Nature's happy thoughts, whom she would not willingly suffer to escape; with wise care she made everything ready before admitting him back into the society which he had left so suddenly. In the result she was amply rewarded.

E

CHAPTER II

" EREWHON "

In coming to Samuel Butler's *Erewhon* period we reach a definitely new moment in his literary career. His departure from New Zealand, as already noted, led to a phase of art study in London which met with considerable success. "My study is art," he wrote to Charles Darwin about this time, "and anything else I may indulge in is only by-play." But painting pictures did not satisfy him for long, although a picture like *Family Prayers*, with its red-plush-backed piano, the parti-coloured thrum-work carpet, and the stolid-looking dependents of a country rectory sitting round, must have given him infinite pleasure.

Accordingly, as a sort of parergon to this principal work, he finished his pamphlet on the Resurrection, which was soon published. Its main conclusion is that the gospel evidence is not sufficient to justify a belief in Christ's death and resurrection from the dead. The year following the appearance of this little essay Butler was in Italy, and Mr Jones has described how in Venice he met an interesting Russian lady who was much impressed with him. His brilliancy and resource in conversation appealed to her as they did to almost everyone he met. On taking leave of him the Russian said : " *Et maintenant, monsieur, vous allez créer.*" She realised that so original a man must not be allowed to waste his time—although he could be most

66

entertaining to people in hotels if they interested him
—but must put his mind to some creative work. Her
words stimulated Butler, and he began to look round
and to consider what he could do. So far, he felt
bound to confess, he had not done very much. But
then he had been away from England for some time,
in a new country, doing manual labour and engaged in
such a way that little leisure or inclination was left for
creative effort. At any rate he now began to collect
his early articles in the New Zealand press, his
" Darwin Among the Machines " and " Lucubratio
Ebria," a further contribution on evolution, and to
examine them. These two pieces were the original
germs from which *Erewhon* grew, and round them, as a
sort of nucleus he built up the story, in his own haphazard fashion, covering up the joints with such literary
carpentry as he could command. The result was a
book rather incoherent in form, rather rambling in its
manner, a book of ideas rather than an adventurous
narrative, but which all the same established its author
as one of the most original and finely trained intelli-
gences of his generation. Its popular reception was
partly due to its anonymity, no doubt ; but beyond
that it interested people to see some of their familiar
institutions laughed at, just a little, for their own
amusement, as they considered it. Further, the writer
was following a difficult tradition, and following it
with success. Indeed in this " Work of Satire and
Imagination " Samuel Butler definitely emerges as
the satirist of his time—or, as Mr Bernard Shaw
has put it in one of his prefaces, defending himself
from a charge of foreign as against English influence :
" In his own department " — satire, that is — " the

greatest English writer of the latter half of the
nineteenth century."

We have seen, all through his early career, the
careful watch the capricious Fates kept over Butler.
This was so all his life, for they were determined not
to let him slip through their fingers. But especially
they took care that his view of English life should be
just and actual, seen without prejudice, with the
contrasted life of a newer country to illuminate and
set it off. In the few years between his return from
backwood wanderings and the appearance of *Erewhon*,
Butler's study of English society must have been a
very absorbed and interested one. Mr Cannan insists
on this, and goes even further. " Butler's mind," says
this writer, " was too inquisitive to be that of a great
artist. He was too conscious, too reasonable, too
desirous of knowing all the ins and outs of the community from which he had been expelled. He was not
content merely to imagine it and to take the good
there was in it and pass on, thankful to be rid of it.
He never was rid of it. He wanted not so much to be
avenged on it as to be amused by it." It was characteristic of Butler that he would never imagine anything if he could get to the thing itself. He became
intensely conscious of the community in which he found
himself, intensely aware of it. It saved him, no doubt,
from that *self*-consciousness which was developing
into a trick with his contemporaries. There is a rather
curious passage in *Alps and Sanctuaries*, which perhaps
throws some light in this connection. Butler is speaking of the two Englishmen whose appeal is most
universal—Handel and Shakespeare—and he remarks
of Handel that he is of a robuster, less introspective,

fibre. "Englishmen are of so mixed a race," comments
the writer, "so inventive, and so given to migration,
that for many generations to come they are bound
to be at times puzzled, and therefore introspective."
It is the man, therefore, who has not quite cleared his
mind—and who, indeed, has ?—that is most aware
of himself, most aware of his own probings to understand what at present seems so difficult. Contrary
to his own analysis, there is little trace of this with
Butler, who, equally with these two artists, belongs to
this mixed migratory race. Perhaps he did feel the
attractions of a life in some sort self-contemplative.
Had he succumbed to these attractions we should have
had no *Erewhon* in the first years of his real literary
life. Instead, may be, an intimate and indeed interesting personal revelation, from which, however, he
might never have got away. As a matter of fact, of
course, it was quite otherwise ; Butler had that rare
gift of saying what was true not only for himself but
for other people. The things that he said were not
particular, personal apologics, but wide general statements, for which he demanded recognition from those
who took the trouble to consider them. The fact was
that at first, and naturally, after his return, Butler was
much more absorbed by his fellow-countrymen than
himself, and although later on he wrote a semi-
autobiographical novel, it may be said quite fairly that
self-analysis and introspection were never distinctive
traits. His *ideas* always interested him—they were
like strange new people, and he wanted to know as
much about them as he could—but he always kept
them in their place. He did this in *Erewhon*, and with
his eye the whole time on the general satiric bearing of

his theme. For although the genesis of the book was his New Zealand article on the Machines, he kept everything as closely as possible in touch with the English community which had so fascinating an interest for him.

Butler's aim and intention in writing *Erewhon* appear rather interestingly in contrasting his book with some of the numerous other Utopias of literature. It must argue a reasonably high condition of civilisation that any man should imagine for himself an ideal state and write about it. The most famous of all such countries of the imagination is, of course, Thomas More's Utopia. It was written at a time when the New Learning had widened the European outlook, when the classics were being affectionately studied, and when, above all, the world had perceptibly grown larger in a geographical no less than in a mental sense. It was at such a moment that More wrote his *Utopia*. And his book contained, quite literally, the description of an ideal commonwealth as he conceived it. He was something of a philosopher, so therefore is his rather wordy Raphael Hythloday, the traveller whom he creates to tell his story. But although his narrative is of the perfect state as he imagined it, there are not a few references to the England of his own day : he speaks, in an Introduction, of the absurdity of punishing thieves by death ; he tells us of the agricultural pursuits of the inhabitants of Utopia, which his countrymen would do well to attend to in those times of enclosures and rural depopulation ; he describes the games of these rather priggish Utopians—one resembling a battle between virtue and vice—and how each does it ; further he recognises the value of good marriages and good births, and insists on the importance of the physical efficiency of those who intend to live together and produce children. Necessarily More's book is influenced by the later mediæval economics, and the thought of his own day. But it appears to have been little touched by the rather pagan side of the Renascence. One feels it might have been more human had it been more pagan, for his Utopia seems adapted only to people of a particularly stable character. It is not the ideal state suitable to ordinary men, but the ideal state of an idealised humanity.

Campanella, an Italian, who flourished a century after More, was another writer who conceived an interesting Utopia which he called the *Civitas Solis*. He belonged to an age touched by the scientific spirit to a greater extent than was More's. And in his ideal state he points out, like a modern scientist, that men and women must be so joined together that they produce the best offspring. Love there is the ruler, but love born of desire appears to be unknown ; only that arising from friendship : the breeding of the race is conducted according to philosophical rules, and male and female are accordingly paired off as their constitutions and dispositions seem to direct.

Passing over three hundred years, we may mention Mr H. G. Wells' very different *Modern Utopia*, which is an attempt to illuminate modern problems with the light of his own idealism. The writer tries to make his narrative as much in keeping with the matter-of-fact world as possible. Two new men of the new century carry the story along—one the Owner of the Voice and the other the Botanist, acting as stimuli to each other. His aim is to present a series of cinematograph pictures; often the apparatus jams, but he claims occasionally to succeed in showing on the screen "a momentary moving picture of Utopian conditions."

Now Butler's conceptions in *Erewhon* differ from these idealised societies we have mentioned in one important aspect : these latter are Ideal States— the best their creators could imagine at the time, and in the circumstances, in which they were writing ; but Erewhon is not Butler's Ideal State. He never intended it to be so. He was not in the least detached as they, on the whole, were. He was a satirist, while they were much more genuine Utopists. Butler's eyes, in fact, were the whole time riveted on the people he was satirising.

It is interesting to notice that, like two of the three writers mentioned above, Butler in *Erewhon* emphasised the importance of the physical qualities of the race. Disease with the Erewhonians was held as a crime. Indeed they drastically opposed, by their methods of treatment, physical and moral disease. Mr Salter [1] has summed up the moral teaching of *Erewhon* on these matters under three heads : In the first place, the State needs results in well-to-do healthy citizens. They are the best index of a nation's prosperity. Passing from physical to moral qualities, Butler would point out that crime is often to be remedied by improving social conditions, for although, like the modern Eugenists, he recognised the primary importance of nature in producing efficient men, he all the same would lay stress on nurture as a secondary element. In the account of the trial of a man for pulmonary consumption the judge,

---

[1] *Essays on Two Moderns.*

in his summing up, says : "You may say that it is not
your fault. The answer is ready enough to hand, and
it amounts to this—that if you had been born of healthy
and well-to-do parents, and been well taken care of
when you were a child, you would never have offended
against the laws of your country, nor found yourself
in your present disgraceful position. If you tell me
that you had no hand in your parentage and education,
and that it is therefore unjust to lay these things to
your charge, I answer that whether your being in a
consumption is your fault or no, it is a fault in you, and
it is my duty to see that against such faults as this the
commonwealth shall be protected. You may say that
it is your misfortune to be criminal ; I answer that it is
your crime to be unfortunate." Lastly, Butler wishes
to show, through the behaviour of the Erewhonians,
that in devoting ourselves to moral excellence—or
rather the pretence of moral excellence—we neglect
physical well-being. Indeed between these two most
important human qualities it is essential that a right
balance should be struck ; we tend to sacrifice one at
the expense of the other because of a series of precon-
ceived notions requiring revision in an age of scientific
development which has made clear things that before
were dark or obscured.

One of the chief charms of *Erewhon* is its realistic
narrative—and this is particularly true of the opening
chapters. The descriptions of the traveller's journey
into Erewhon, his passage over the mountains, the
descent of the watery chasm, the crossing of the muddy
glacier-fed river, and the final view of the Erewhonian
country, are made from certain parts of the New

Zealand country that Butler knew well. This part of
the book is wonderfully restrained and convincing, just
because it was so near to the reality; it shows also
Butler's gift for describing natural scenery and his
sense of adventure. It is a good framework, a setting,
for what is to follow, because of the very contrast
in the sequel. Henceforth Butler relies not on his
memory, touched by imagination—and indeed imagination is an element all through—but on his intellect.
Nature and outdoor adventure are left behind while
the author is concerned with the manipulation of his
ideas and fancies. We may add in parenthesis,
apropos these early pages, that there are at least two
places in New Zealand that claim to contain the great
stones or statues which the writer described as standing
at the entrance of the Erewhonian territory.

Butler once confessed that he regarded " books of
travel into supposed unknown countries " as one of
the most offensive forms that even literature can
assume. This may or may not be so. In reading
Erewhon, however, now and again one almost forgets
the satire—satire on religion, politics, ethics, education
and Mrs Grundy—so matter-of-fact is the narrative.
But satire is there, all through, and burlesque also at
times—as when the Erewhonians, on the death of a
friend of the family, send no letter of condolence, neither
do they wear mourning, but pack off little boxes
of artificial tears, the tears varying in number according to the degree of intimacy. Such ironical burlesque
justifies itself because in no human affair is our
behaviour quite so unnecessarily ugly and convention-
ridden as this necessary business of death.

The basis of Butler's book then is a wonderfully

complete and well-ordered topsy-turvydom ; and if we
admit the original premise all the rest follows naturally
and easily enough. This logical perversion of ideas in
Erewhon is, however, particular and selective. Butler
allowed the original objects of his satire to lead him to
his conclusions rather than any haphazard method.
Had it been otherwise he might still have got plenty of
fun out of his book, but not very much meaning. It
was the meaning and application contained in the
Erewhonian ethics and institutions that were his first
concern. So his book is paradoxical but never contra-
dictory : it is the creation of a system with this one
right granted to the author—the right to twist. As we
have seen, it was Butler's delight to be turning things
inside out, and examining them from a new point of
view, which, though almost an absurd one, may contain
valuable guidance in real life. *Erewhon* must have
taught Butler a great deal ; it eased his mind also by
providing a channel for some of the accumulated
material of nearly forty years. If he had not rid himself
of this he might never have got on to his other studies ;
particularly *Life and Habit* might never have been
written. It is impossible, however, always to separate
the satire from the beliefs held by Butler himself.
Behind very many of the perverted Erewhonian ideas
there lurked something stronger than mere perversion
—in the notion of the World of the Unborn, for
instance.

It was characteristic of Butler, whose mind was in
many respects the clerical mind, to make the hero of
his book a religious man. The hero can only suppose
that the people of Erewhon, partly because of their
lack of religion, are the lost ten tribes of Israel, and he

resolves to convert them. In this he had already had some experience, having reclaimed an old native chief, who, in spite of a rather sketchy theology which tended to confuse Adelaide the Queen Dowager and Mary Magdalene, showed signs of developing into "an earnest Christian." Thus a note is struck which becomes predominant in *Erewhon Revisited*. This latter is very much of a religious polemic, in which respect it differs from *Erewhon*, where, it is true, conventional religion is satirised in the Musical Banks, but not with the same directness of statement as in the sequel. The traveller into Erewhon was much puzzled by the Musical Banks, and he confesses that even after visiting one of them, and asking innumerable questions as to what they really signified, he was unable to come to any satisfactory conclusion about them. The fact is that in Erewhon, and this also is observable in other countries, there were two currencies. But, oddly enough, the officials of the Musical Banks were not paid in their own currency but in that of the ordinary mercantile banks (without music). Mrs Nosnibor, a prominent Erewhonian citizeness who supported banks of the musical variety, explained that the fewness of people in such places of business did not imply any lack of confidence. "The heart of the country," she said, "was thoroughly devoted to these establishments, and any sign of their being in danger would bring in support from the most unexpected quarters. It was only because people knew them to be so very safe, that in some cases (as she lamented to say in Mr Nosnibor's) they felt that their support was unnecessary. Moreover, these institutions never departed from the safest and most approved banking principles. Thus they never allowed interest on deposit, a thing now frequently done by certain bubble companies, which by doing an illegitimate trade had drawn many customers away; and even the shareholders were fewer than formerly, owing to the innovations of these unscrupulous persons, for the Musical Banks paid little or no dividend, but divided their profits by way of bonus on the original shares once in every thirty thousand years; and as it was now only two thousand years since there had been one of these distributions, people felt that they could not hope for another in their own time and preferred investments whereby they got some more tangible return; all which, she said, was very melancholy to think of." This is a good example of the satirical implication of Butler's book—a satire never dragged out into commonplace. The hero of the story also—who is a religious man—gives some hints of a religious significance in the transactions at the Musical Banks. For he is able to look on the system impartially as having no relation to any of the religious attitudes in his own country. This is exactly as it should be : Butler lets his narrative point its own moral, and adds to its interest by putting it into the mouth of a naïve, simple-hearted, earnest man who is far too eager to tell his story to waste his time in unnecessary comment. The author, in fact, allows his words to speak for themselves, and each reader must interpret for himself. All through, the story is told with an unshakable gravity, the serious air of a Cervantes or a Defoe. For the humour of it is not usually direct in character, but, as in the piece we have quoted above, a humour born of other absurdities reflected through Erewhonian behaviour.

Apropos the trial of a man for pulmonary consumption, we have noted a curious remark put into the mouth of the judge in the course of his summing up. The judge said to the prisoner : " You may say that it is your misfortune to be criminal ; I answer that it is your crime to be unfortunate." At first hearing this sounds like a mere piece of antithetical verbiage, but it conceals a very important side of the Erewhonian philosophy—their views on fortune and misfortune. What indeed is good fortune, and why should we reward it ? In order to answer this in the Butlerian view, we may first note another case brought into an Erewhonian law court. A youth, only just come of age, was accused of having been defrauded of a large amount of property by his guardian during his minority. The young man pleaded, as extenuating circumstances, that he was not of age, inexperienced, in great fear of his guardian and without independent professional advice. " Young man," said the judge, " do not talk nonsense. People have no right to be young, inexperienced, greatly in awe of their guardians, and without independent professional advice. If by such indiscretions they outrage the moral sense of their friends, they must expect to suffer accordingly." He was, therefore, condemned. In these proceedings we perceive the last fine shade of Erewhonian logic. Crime and immorality are diseases ; they are enemies and worries to the individual and a social enemy, since people do not always care to risk a marriage when there is embezzlement in the family, for instance. We do everything we can against immorality by providing moral straighteners, says the Erewhonian, but the whole process is painful and troublesome to the patient ;

ergo anyone who is foolish or unfortunate enough in any way whatsoever to put moral temptations in the way of his friends, or "outrage their moral sense," even though it is to his own disadvantage, deserves to be punished.

It is just here that the question of ill luck comes in. It is considered an offence against society and is punishable as such. And indeed, as Butler points out in another passage, there is nothing unfair in punishing people for misfortune. Here it is society which must profit at the expense of the individual. That is the reason why a man who is son to a millionaire is so richly rewarded—he is the most complex phenomenon so far produced, and society has every reason to be proud of him. But it is all luck and nothing else, and simply the old story: "To him that hath shall be given." And in believing, as Butler believed, that God cared not much for the individual but a great deal for the race, he put this element of good fortune on a new footing; society rewards good fortune—good looks, physical well-being, a good balance at the bank, whether the result of our own efforts or no—because they are of value to society. In a man who possesses all these things society sees its own ideal. We know, too, that ill luck is more often punished than not: the poor man born into vicious surroundings, with every incentive to wrong-doing and none of the happy fortune that keeps him away from it, starts inevitably with the dice of circumstance weighted heavily against him; in the long run probably Nemesis will overtake him. For the struggle against misfortune is most often a one-sided affair. As Butler remarks, we kill a serpent because it is unfortunate enough to be a serpent, in such and such circumstances in such and such a place, and because it is likely to be a nuisance to us. But the chief reason of our killing it is that it has not been lucky enough to be anything else than a serpent.

We have already seen that immorality treated as a disease and illness as a crime are the two fundamental points in which the Erewhonians differ most markedly from other civilised societies. It must be noted, however, in a few words supplementary to those in the earlier part of this chapter, that physical disease was not always detected in Erewhon and there were even some broader-minded people who were willing to excuse quite mild attacks, while in out-of-the-way places medical doctors and physicians did unmistakably exist. Not seldom there were cases of dissimulation. We have, for instance, the rather unpleasant young lady, Mahaina, who outwardly was a martyr to dipso-mania—though some of her friends shrewdly suspected it was indigestion. The more charitable of them were disposed to admit that perhaps she did tipple a bit, even if circumstances looked rather black against her. And there were a good many hintings and significant silences when poor Mahaina's case was mentioned in conversation. The supposed writer of the book seems to think that all this tends to make the Erewhonians rather hypocritical. He remarks, with wise common-sense, that if a person has a headache, he or she should be allowed to say so without producing long faces in everyone who is near. " As it was, even upon hearing it whispered that somebody else was subject to head-aches, a whole company must look as though they had never had a headache in their lives." Yet, as he admirably concludes, " even the best were liable to be out of sorts sometimes, and there were few families that had not a medicine-chest in a cupboard some-where."

Nor was this all.   The Erewhonians are not in reality less human than other people, and hence there are certain things that they have to condone in an illogical fashion.   Want of logic to them, as to others, is a "merciful provision of nature," a "buffer against collisions," a "blessed inconsistency" whereby they are enabled to do much that otherwise they might be prevented from doing—unless they could find some equally good means of excusing themselves. The birth of a child is one of the things thus condoned. It is true that the whole subject is painful to them. The mother's illness is carefully concealed, and it is only after the lapse of a considerable period that the offence is allowed to be forgotten.   Some of the strict-est moralists in Erewhon, we are told, insisted that it was wicked for a woman to have children at all, since her health suffered in the process : these writers made no allowance for the natural jesuitical tendencies of mankind, and were quite unwilling to admit that in so grave a matter, where illness (however short) was involved, the good that came out of the evil was any moral justification.   But children are born in Erewhon and no one takes much notice of these reactionary philosophers.

We have seen in an earlier section of this study how important to the Erewhonians was their mythology of the World of the Unborn.   To understand this it is necessary to examine their theory of time, and the relation of the small new-comers from the Unborn World to their older brothers and sisters in this.

F

They asserted in the first place that man, as it chances, is drawn through life backwards with his face to the past, instead of with his face to the future. They conceive of the future and past being, as it were, a panorama on rollers; to them the present exists only as one of the "minor compromises of which human life is full—for it lives only on sufferance of the past and future." Possibly this, in more comprehensible language, is what M. Bergson in recent years has been describing as his concept of time, substituting a cinematograph for the panorama on rollers. Into such a temporal world the denizens of the World of the Unborn are transferred from their own wide eternity. They are perpetually warned by their elders and betters, the spiritual pastors of the Unborn World, to stay where they are. If, however, they insist on leaving they must go before the magistrate, sign an affidavit and drink a potion which, as we have seen, causes them to lose their memories and sets them free as a kind of blind, disembodied principle or impulse to harass two married persons until they get themselves born. The married people do not in the least want them, for birth carries with it a decided sense of injury. Already the Unborn have been told by their own friends in their own world that they are in for a desperate gamble: they must draw lots for their dispositions, draw lots for their parents and enter into partnership with many people about whom they know nothing. And when they do get into this temporal world, even when quite young—indeed before they are able to speak—they are made to acknowledge that they were free agents in entering it.

And yet the Erewhonians felt a sense of duty to the

Unborn. They know very well that their ranks were
recruited only from the most foolish of them ; but they
were disposed to make the best of it. In the trial of
the *poitrinaire* the judge expressly states that the unborn must not be allowed to come near the prisoner.
Hence, although they rather dislike them, the
Erewhonians as potential parents are willing to give
them the best chance possible by maintaining their
own physical fitness—as indeed they are bound to do
by the law of the land. Here again we notice Butler's
insistence on the value to the state of material results
in the shape of healthy citizens ; if they are well-to-do,
also, so much the better. And it may be noted in
passing, that Butler's startling Erewhonian doctrine
of disease treated as an offence is not without its
parallel in modern legislation.

We have already spoken of the logical perversion
in *Erewhon*. This, on the whole, is a true description.
It is not, however, true to say that the people themselves were entirely logical, although at times they
were so—or could always logically justify their conduct.
They understood the value and use of compromise,
which, after all, is often the only course open in this
world whether it be the best of all possible worlds or
not. Few people, however, employ it so unashamedly
as the people whom Butler was satirising, and between
whose theory and practice there is so often so alarmingly wide an hiatus. So it is, therefore, with the
Erewhonians, and especially in their Colleges of Un-
reason, the intellectual centres of the country. They
pursued the practice of sitting gracefully on a fence with
great skill, and "a man must be a mere tyro in the arts
of Erewhonian polite society, unless he instinctively

suspects a hidden 'yea' in every 'nay' that meets him." All this was more than anything else fostered by their universities ; " hypothetics " was the principal study at schools and universities, and indeed the value of any course of learning seems always to have been precisely in inverse ratio to its practical usefulness. And here the author applies his irony directly to similar English institutions : perhaps he did this because his intimate acquaintance with them made him feel all the more strongly. At any rate, we know that in the words that follow he was saying what he said elsewhere about the priggishness of English academic communities, and what he felt to be the truest description of them :

" And yet perhaps, after all, it is better for a country that its seats of learning should do more to suppress mental growth than to encourage it. Were it not for a certain priggishness which these places infuse into so great a number of their *alumni*, genuine work would become dangerously common. It is essential that by far the greater part of what is said or done in the world should be so ephemeral as to take itself away quickly."

Leaving the universities behind, we may return for a moment to what is perhaps the most daringly original side of *Erewhon*—" The Book of the Machines." As already noted, this part of the work was expanded, with some modifications, from an earlier essay. We see here Butler's reverence for the material and mechanical to overcome matter, but there is also a lurking fear that the machines may come to mean too much, may be able to do too much, to the detriment of man. In *Erewhon*, in fact, there are two distinct views put forward on this topic : the first is the elaborated view of the machines, by a sort of physical symbiogenesis, getting the upper hand and acquiring a definite identity and consciousness ; the second view, that really held by Butler himself, was expanded from his article, " Lucubratio Ebria." The chief point in this second examination of the machines is that they are to be considered as " extra corporeal limbs " ; thus, as one writer has put it, to Butler " all contrivances and inventions are extensions of the personality of him who uses them " ; they are supplementary limbs which man can tack on to himself ; devices which alone raise him above the level of *ferae naturae* ; apparatus which, unlike the lower animals, he does not keep entirely within his own body.

In the course of an address (*La Signification de la Guerre*) to the Académie des Sciences Morales et Politiques on the European War, delivered in December 1914, M. Henri Bergson imagined a philosopher of the future who takes a wide view of recent developments. The passage immediately suggests Butler's conception of the machines.

The future philosopher will say, proceeds M. Bergson, that " the idea characteristic of the nineteenth century, of employing science to satisfy our material needs, had given an unexpected extension to the mechanical arts and obtained for man, in less than fifty years, more implements than were made in all the thousands of years he had spent on the earth. Every new machine being for man a new organ—an artificial organ which exists to prolong his natural organs—his body will suddenly find itself vastly extended without the spirit being able to enlarge itself sufficiently quickly to comprehend the whole of this new body. . . . What would happen if the mechanical forces which science has just brought to the point of using for the service of man, should make themselves master of man in order to convert him to their own material nature ? What would become of the world if this mechanism took possession of humanity entirely, and if nations instead of raising themselves of their own free will to a richer and more harmonious diversity, like living persons, fell into a uniform condition, like matter ? . . . What would happen, in fact, if the moral effort of humanity were to recoil upon itself at the moment of gaining its end, and if some diabolical artifice caused it to produce instead of a spiritualisation of matter the mechanization of spirit ? "

Having regard to these supplementary limbs, million-aires, in Butler's view, are the most highly organised creatures in our society—creatures who at will can tack on to their identity a special train or part of a P. & O. boat. The principal varieties of the race are to be found then, not in racial differences, but among the rich and poor, who are respectively examples of the most perfect human machinate mammal and the least perfect. Between the rich and the poor a wider gulf is fixed than between any other two human groups of which we are aware.

As a recognition of the value of a rich man to the community, the Erewhonians exempt from taxation anyone with an income of over twenty thousand pounds a year ; they are overcome by " so magnificent an organisation " ; they say : " How very much he must have done for society before society could have been prevailed upon to give him so much money." Money is one of the good qualities which in certain conditions a man finds it hardest to possess himself of ; he may have all the other good qualities, but most often this is lacking because his parents, guardians or masters have told him nothing, or at best but vaguely, about how he is to acquire this particular one; they tell him how to be good—honest, truthful, reverent, respectable in outward word and behaviour, deferential in his opinions, non-committal in conversation—but this last quality they wrap up like a religious mystery. If it were not so, children might begin earning money much earlier—benefiting society, that is—than they do at present. "Then the children will be independent early, and they will not press on the parents, nor the parents on them, and they will like each other better than they do now." All of which is probably a genuine conclusion from Butler's own experiences.

Before leaving *Erewhon* we may indicate briefly a curious and typically Erewhonian group of people, the Ydgrunites, who worshipped the goddess Ydgrun and had in many ways lost faith in the religion of the country. Conformity, unless absolutely intolerable, was, however, one of their principles. They did not talk much of the goddess whom they worshipped, but would do nothing contrary to her teaching. Possessing "a high standard of courage, generosity, honour and every good and manly quality," they were naturally the most considerable and influential body of people in Erewhon. Perhaps their counterparts in English life are disappearing; always, however, there must be left some supporters of "respectability with its thousand gigs," some fault-finders and busybodies whose sensibilities are being outraged.

Respectability for a long time yet, we fancy, will be the
most important religious creed in England. It insidi-
ously overrides everything that comes near it as if by
its own momentum. We remember recently hearing
of a young man intended for ordination, who found
himself at length unable, for various reasons, to take
the momentous step. One of his relations expressed
herself as surprised at this; she couldn't think what
objection there was to " going into the Church "; it
was quite respectable, she said. So respectability is
still the god that English people worship; faith, doubt,
sincere opinions, religious disabilities must all fall
before it. It is much more important that a young
man should enter the Church because it is respectable
than because of any particular aptitude—spiritual,
mental or physical—for that kind of work. And it is
the same in everything with which this strange
Ydgrunish habit comes into contact.

This, in outline, is a sketch of the chief philosophies
of the Erewhonians. We have endeavoured to give
some hint—Butler himself has done it inevitably and
completely—of their laws, their opinions, their behaviour; their parade of logical theory which in
practice so often had to collapse; the inconsistencies
which they generally managed to condone fairly
speciously; their panic fear of giving themselves
away; their views on money and machines; their
reckless study of " hypothetics "; their double
currency and the conduct of the Ydgrunites. All
this Butler sets out in his strange, grave, " future-
piercing" book. It is a book of ideas put forward
clearly and coherently; the ideas have been well
thought on, well digested. And there is nothing in

the book which has not a wide meaning and application for the people for whom it was written.

In *Erewhon Revisited,* written quite at the end of Butler's life, the story is undoubtedly much more coherent. The writer interrupts his narrative less often to interpolate an explanation of some particular Erewhonian theory. And though as a story it is better " pulled together," with better realised characters, the sequel is less spontaneous than the earlier book and has not the same novelty of presentation. *Erewhon,* in fact, was a series of discoveries ; *Erewhon Revisited* an endeavour to perpetuate the discoveries without their original freshness.

When contemplating a sequel it occurred to Butler to ask himself what would be likely to happen after his rather bourgeois hero, Mr Higgs, as he in future calls him, left Erewhon in the balloon along with Arowhena, as he did at the close of the earlier book. After considering the matter Butler came to the conclusion that the whole affair would become a miracle. He takes Mr Higgs and his readers, therefore, back to Erewhon, to show them the revolutionary changes which have come about through belief in this one supposed miracle. Higgs finds that he has become the unworthy centre of a complete religious system called Sunchildism ; and he arrives just in time to be present at the dedication of the new temple raised in his honour and to hear the sermon of Professor Hanky, Professor of Worldly Wisdom, who had been chosen to preach on that memorable occasion. All this, of course, gives Butler many satirical opportunities at the expense of established religions. And from this point of view the book is more a religious polemic than anything else. In his Preface, Butler disarms any criticism from self-conscious people by explaining his own position. "If I may be allowed for a moment to speak about myself," he says, " I would say that I have never ceased to profess myself a member of the more advanced wing of the English Broad Church. What those who belong to this wing believe, I believe. What they reject, I reject. . . . When I converse with advanced Broad Churchmen I find myself in substantial harmony with them." Mr Desmond MacCarthy has called this religion of Butler's a good, rollicking, Broad Church paganism. This description, as we shall try to show, is scarcely accurate, although it contains a good many of the ingredients which went to form his religious opinions.

Before examining these, however, we may turn to the earlier part of *Erewhon Revisited,* in which Mr Higgs realises with horror the misery he has brought upon the country in unconsciously providing it with events round which, although perfectly explainable by natural laws, a new faith might build itself. One miraculous occurrence, the balloon ascent, provided a nucleus round which others have accreted with considerable rapidity. Mr Higgs sees a religion in process of formation; the forces he has let loose he, or anyone else, for that matter, is quite powerless to check. He is greatly disturbed in mind as to whether he ought to speak out, seeing, as he did, a "whole people led astray by those who are merely exploiting them for their own ends." He realised that although the new religion was not firmly established it would be very difficult to destroy; time and circumstances and reasons of expediency were all against him. Nevertheless, he resolved to declare himself, which he accordingly did in particularly dramatic conditions.

It is small wonder that Higgs is appalled at the damage he has wrought in Erewhon. The straighteners—physicians whose duty it was to prescribe for the moral diseases of the people—have gone, their work being done by the Musical Banks, which have taken on a new lease of life and a new position as the trustees of Sunchildism. Nor was this all. As an indirect result of Mr Higgs' first visit the laws against the destruction of machinery had been repealed; consequently materialistic opinions were alarmingly on the increase. (This, in the first instance, was partly due to the fact that the Queen particularly wanted to have a watch.) Even in quite small matters there were changes; the old Erewhonian dress, for instance, had disappeared, being replaced, so far as the men were concerned, by modern European costume. Within these limits the people could wear their clothes as they liked, dress by an edict of the King being a matter of opinion, not of dogma.

Butler, in his narrative, intends that one should see the way a so-called miracle may be perverted for a practical use, and the way also that value is attached, not necessarily to the originally established things, but to the later accretions. It was to this vested-interest element, with its accompanying confusion of sincerities and humbugs, genuine believers and opportunists, time-servers and people on the make, their quarrels and persecutions and heresy-hunts, their jesuitical attitudes—it was to all this that Butler so much objected. Tolstoy, starting from a quite different point, had come to a somewhat similar conclusion:

in his rejection of Church Christianity in favour of what he imagined to be the original, unembroidered teaching of its founder, he was striving to get back to a simpler, less complex condition, uninfluenced by material motives and individual opinions. With this Butler, no doubt, would have agreed; but he would have questioned very searchingly—as we know he actually did—the fundamental premises, whether they be miracle or teaching, on which this belief depends. On these very subjects, indeed, he spent a considerable portion of his time; the conclusion that he came to, although definite enough in character, still permitted him to belong to the advanced wing of the Broad Church, with as good a claim to the title, probably, as any member of that body.

Dr Downie is Butler's model of a Broad Churchman. When he realises the position in which their religion stands, it is he who, as a sensible man of the world, is most anxious to consider what ought to be done about Sunchildism. Mr Higgs appreciates the Erewhonian difficulties and gives some sound, practical advice on the subject. "If you cannot abolish me altogether," he says, "make me a peg on which to hang all your best ethical and spiritual conceptions. If you will do this—if you will make me out to be much better than I was, or ever shall be, Sunchildism may serve your turn for many a long year to come. Otherwise it will tumble about your heads before you think it will." In other words, he tells them to drop the cock-and-bull stories—exploit his personal character if they like; relics and miracles and mystery-making must go by the board; and although, even then, their religion may be false in the letter, it may be true enough in

the spirit. He explains to them how much, at that
stage, they can do with Sunchildism in its still young
and plastic condition. It is the shrewdest advice that
Mr Higgs can give : and no doubt Gibbon meant
something like this when he spoke of the " utility "
of religions. Dr Downie is disposed to accept the
advice in a genuinely advanced-wing, Broad-Church
spirit. For it is, after all, the best counsel of
expediency.

And it will be in Erewhon as elsewhere. Two
parties will show themselves which are equally important, for neither can properly thrive without the
other. " Those who are at the head of science provide
us with the one party ; those whom we call our churchmen are the other. Both are corrupt, but we can spare
neither, for each checks as far as it can the corruptions
of the other."

Butler only once interrupts his story in *Erewhon
Revisited*. He does so in order to insert a chapter on
" Vicarious Existence," which is worth examining
because it was a belief that so largely coloured his own
thoughts as he grew older. He writes about it in some
detail in *God the Known and God the Unknown* ; but
here it is included as an instance of the many offshoots
from the Sunchild's teaching. The supposed writer of
the pamphlet which is the basis of this chapter began
by pointing out that life does not consist in bodily
organs, but in the power to use them—which means
ultimately in the work they do. He went on to show,
as Butler did in *Life and Habit*, that the more truly
living an agent is the less will he know of his own
actions. Hence the life after death is in many cases
the completer life—that existence we lead in others

that we know not of, and which is yet a more perfect life than we have ever consciously known. The work done, the force exercised by the dead is, perhaps, far greater than in their conscious life; they know nothing of their actions because they are more truly living than ever before. Certainly this is so with those great ones who have only reached their full power, vicariously, in the thoughts and deeds of others. " It seems, then," the writer continued, " that there is no such thing as either absolute life without any alloy of death, nor absolute death without any alloy of life, until, that is to say, all posthumous power to influence has faded away. And this, perhaps, is what the Sun-child meant by saying that in the midst of life we are in death, and so also that in the midst of death we are in life."

Through the writer of this pamphlet, then, Butler holds out no materialist's hope of resurrection from the dead, but instead a sure place, for each according to his merit, in " the heaven of men's thoughts." It is the only doctrine, as we shall see later, that Butler could consistently hold, believing as he did in a God so different from the conventionally accepted God. He explained his position as well as he was able in *God the Known and God the Unknown*. What then of faith, as that word is generally understood ? Butler's vicarious existence leaves no place for reward or punishment—reward or punishment, that is, which can be felt by those who have deserved them. Here faith raises its head—faith which consists " in holding that the instincts of the best men and women are in themselves an evidence which may not be set aside lightly; and the best men and women have ever held that death is better than dishonour, and desirable if honour is to be won thereby." Faith, therefore, is not a showy virtue; it resides in the hidden parts of us; it is something negative, and " though we can do little with it, we can do nothing without it."

This life of the world to come, which we all hope for, has, moreover, its parallel in the notion of the world of the unborn. Just as the inhabitants of this world have a right to pester and worry living people, so have those beyond the grave a right to thrust themselves in among the living, to secure the full measure of their posthumous life. For " life, whether before the grave or afterwards, is like love—all reason is against it, and all healthy instinct for it." The discussion of these matters, which rest on a fundamental human desire— the desire to be remembered—is best concluded by quoting an epitaph to an old lady mentioned in *Erewhon Revisited*. Epitaphs always interested Butler, and when writing this he was thinking of all that his belief in vicarious existence implied. Writers of epitaphs on modern tombs and gravestones might well emulate its dignity:

> " I fall asleep in the full and certain hope
> That my slumber shall not be broken ;
> And that though I be all-forgetting,
> Yet shall I not be all-forgotten,
> But continue that life in the thoughts and deeds
> Of those I loved,
> Into which, while the power to strive was yet vouchsafed me,
> I fondly strove to enter."

We have ventured this analysis of *Erewhon Revisited* out of its proper chronological place because it seemed to fit in consistently with the earlier part of the chapter,

and because, also, the book marks Butler's completion
of a system he had begun to build up in the first years
of his literary career. *Erewhon Revisited* is, as it were,
a clearing up at the end of his life, just as *Erewhon*
had been at an earlier moment. Between the writing
of the two books the widest gap yawns : the examination of the Christian miracles, all the scientific books,
the Homeric studies, the records of Italian travel, and
the novel are each landmarks which serve to punctuate
the intervening period. And yet, in spite of the lapse
of time, Butler did manage, in no small measure, to
recapture the spirit of the original book; not completely, of course, as it must always be with sequels.
Although the second book lacks the freshness and
originality of its predecessor, it is the best thing under
the circumstances we could have wished for. Regarded
in the special light in which the author regarded it, it
is a perfectly logical continuation.

Mr Shaw has spoken of Butler's particular vein of
wit which led him to " take familiar and unquestioned
propositions and turn them inside out so neatly as to
convince you that they are just as presentable one
way as the other, or even that the sides so unexpectedly
and quaintly turned out are the right sides. . . ."
Butler did this most conspicuously in the two Erewhon
books. He did it perfectly naturally, for it was a
characteristic habit to try and see ordinary things from
a different point of view. That is the reason why he
discovered so much that is new about quite ordinary,
everyday topics. And as he does this one is arrested
by his clear perception, his finely disciplined powers of
logical reasoning, his cool analytical faculty, and the
particular kind of imagination with which he coloured

what he had to say. Cold reasoning alone could never have revealed to him the idea of the machines as conscious beings; it required imagination in the first place to bring the thought into existence. Afterwards he developed it with all the sensible straightforwardness he could command. His thought was admirably disciplined; he kept it always in touch with facts and realities. He was never a visionary. For his ideas always have a tight hold on reality. And it is for this reason that everything he did is distinguished by such a refreshing common-sense.

It is part of Butler's achievement in the Erewhon books that he has written about an imaginary country without being romantic—without, that is, that sense of detachment and remoteness, as of people who don't much matter doing things, which positing their reality, they could never possibly do. This is not because the characters in *Erewhon* are so superlatively drawn. They are not. Yram and one or two others in the second book are the only ones with whom Butler seems really comfortable. It is because of the value of the *thinking* and the *twisting* that the writer put into the books that we are conscious of their importance. It is this that gives them their unique place in the Butler family. For it is no small merit to have compressed the foibles of one's generation into a volume. And this is what Butler contrived to do.

G

CHAPTER III

SATIRE AND IRONY

THERE is nothing in recent literature which offers so good an opportunity of studying these two closely related intellectual qualities—satire and irony—as the works of Samuel Butler. Although easily separable they are elements, nevertheless, not seldom closely allied ; the second intensifies the first, adds a new twist of meaning to it. Taken together they provide perhaps the deadliest weapon which man can employ : they have been used in all ages ; we find them in almost all literature in varying degrees of intensity. We have spoken of satire and irony as intellectual qualities. This is perhaps hardly an accurate description, because they belong much more to temperament than to practice. A man can discipline his satiric gift, but can never create it for himself; he can perfect it as a literary form ; but if he has not already the god-sent laughter, the sensitiveness to perceive the evils around him, the faculty of ridicule to communicate his inspiration to others, he beats with empty hands.

The function of the satirist has been described by Horace in two memorable lines :

"Detrahere et pellem, nitidus qua quisque per ora
Cederet, introrsum turpis." [1]

---

[1] "To strip off from everyone the skin, in which he, base at heart, passed contentedly before the eyes of the world."

98

Horace and Juvenal indeed may be taken as two universal types to which the company of satirists conforms. Horace was the man of the world, urbane, refined, who did not mind occasionally laughing at himself when he laughed at other people. He was, in fact, an example of the Epicurean whose own good taste is the measure of the stature of most things with which he comes into contact. " He was one of a class known in every age," says James Hannay, in his too little known book on satire,[1] " men, of whom it may be said, that they take a deeper interest in society than in mankind." Juvenal, on the other hand, is the completer master of invective; he reflects the coarse life, the voluptuous habits, the bloody vices of Rome under the empire. Yet each of them alike protests against luxury and love of show. Swift in our own literature comes nearest to Juvenal: both have that *saeva indignatio* always associated with Swift, the fierce scorn, the bitter laughing hatred of vice and folly.

Thus Horace and Juvenal are among the truest exponents of the old Roman spirit. They have their historical value, as all true satirists must, in catching the social tone, the manners and habits of thought of their age; reflected in their work are those more delicate lights and half lights, the contemporary character and temper, which the professional historian, partly because he has his eyes fixed on events rather than atmospheres, generally fails to reproduce. We know in our own time how the Du Maurier pictures— those happy Victorian satires of the crinoline age, marking the first invasion of the London drawing-room

[1] *Satire and Satirists*. By James Hannay. London, 1854.

by the industrial *nouveaux riches*—give a far completer
idea of the period than the actual historian could do.
It was the same with Horace and Juvenal on a much
wider scale, using a literary form complete in design
and intention. There was, indeed, something in the
Roman temper which made satire particularly congenial; the satirist must be a teacher, a critic and a
censor as well as an explorer of moral values. But,
above all, there belong to this form of art a vigorous
sense, a straightforward, curt intelligence which
especially recommended themselves to the practical
energy of the Romans. Satire, it has been remarked,
is an expression of public not of personal feeling
addressed to the practical understanding. Here lie
the reasons of its essentially Roman character.

" Satura tota nostra est "

wrote Quintilian, with the just pride of one who has
discovered a native art quite independent of Greek or
any other influence. He was paying a further com-
pliment to the Latin genius in a recognition of the fact
that satire is only present in a race possessing somewhere the will to live a full and vivid life. The satirist
keeps close to Life; his path is marked out for him
by the things and thoughts and habits of this world.
Practical common-sense guides him; if he deviates
from this he is a satirist *manqué* who had been better
employed in doing almost anything else.

So the word satire, in its derivation, is from the
Latin *satura*, a medley or mixture. It has no
connection with the Greek *Satyr*, though some have
contended that the goat-man of mythology is an
emblem of the varied character, grinning, half-human,

half-animal in form, of the later development. A
satire, then, is a mixed intellectual composition in
prose or verse where vice or follies are held up to
ridicule.

In passing from Latin satiric literature to that of
Europe in later times Hannay has noted important
elements in the pre-Reformation period which de-
scended with modifications after that event. Erasmus
was the first of the European satirists in the modern
sense. Yet satirists were found before his time in the
authors of the Latin rhyming-poems exemplified by
Walter Mapes. "And the minstrel, and even the
household fool (who has yet to be investigated, and
perhaps has never been thoroughly appreciated), were
all parts . . . of the representation of the thoughts
and passions of mankind, of which the priest was in
large measure the regulator." With the Renascence
there came a new satiric impulse which owed its rise
partly to the revival in classical study; between that
period and our own has flourished a by no means
undistinguished company, the chief of the modern
satirists, whom the world deservedly remembers.
France had her Boileau, and Voltaire, who in his finest
flight, *Candide*, ridiculed the eighteenth-century catch-
word travesties of common-sense; Spain her Cervantes,
who, if he did not laugh her chivalry away, at any rate
put out of court the maudlin, pseudo-romantic histories;
England her Pope and Swift, temperamentally among
the first of the satirists, and Samuel Butler; Germany
her Heine; Russia, too, whose literature is the creation
of practically one short century, has produced her
satirist in Gogol. A consideration of these writers
alone would supply material for a study of this

particular subject, which perhaps some day someone
will venture upon.

Swift seems to have realised very well the possibilities as well as the limitations of satire. In the
analytical table to his *Tale of a Tub,* probably the
greatest satire in English, he points out that there is
no profanity in his book; his severest strokes are
levelled against those who employ wit " in profaneness
or immodesty. Wit, the noblest and most useful gift
of human nature; and humour the most agreeable.
Those who have no share of either, think the blow
weak, because they are themselves insensible." It was
natural that Swift's irony should be misunderstood,
just as it was natural, only less so, that Butler's should
be—as is explained at the close of this chapter. Swift,
too, knew the value of satire as a weapon; he knew
that often it did not reach the mark at which it
was aimed; he was quite satisfied, however, to use
it as his most congenial method of attack. In the
" Author's Preface " to *A Tale of a Tub* he writes at
some length on panegyric and satire :

" For, as health is but one thing and has been
always the same, whereas diseases are by thousands,
besides new and daily additions; so, all the virtues
that have been ever in mankind, are to be counted
upon a few fingers; but their follies and vices are
innumerable, and time adds hourly to the heap. . . .

" But though the matter for panegyric were as
fruitful as the topics of satire, yet would it not be hard
to find out a sufficient reason why the latter will be
always better received than the first. For, this being
bestowed only upon one, or a few persons at a time, is
sure to raise envy, and consequently ill-words from the

rest, who have no share in the blessing; but satire, being levelled at all, is never resented for an offence by any, since every individual person makes bold to understand it of others, and very wisely removes his particular part of the burden upon the shoulders of the world, which are broad enough, and able to bear it."

He goes on to show that in Athens it was the privilege of every citizen to expose by name any person they wished; but the least word against society in general was severely punished.

" Whereas in England it is just the reverse of all this. Here, you may securely display your utmost rhetoric against mankind, in the face of the world; tell them, ' That all are gone astray; that there is none that doeth good, no not one; that we live in the very dregs of time; that knavery and atheism are epidemic as the pox; that honesty is fled from Astraea'; . . . Nay, further; it is but to venture your lungs, and you may preach in Covent Garden against foppery and fornication, and something else : against pride and dissimulation, and bribery, at Whitehall: you may expose rapine and injustice in the inns of court chapel: and in a city pulpit, be as fierce as you please against avarice, hypocrisy and extortion. 'Tis but a ball bandied to and fro, and every man carries a racket about him, to strike it from himself, among the rest of the company. . . ."

Elsewhere Swift describes satire as a kind of glass in which he who is looking discovers every face except his own. It was something, however, if people could even honestly detect vice in others—mankind as a whole does it easily enough in a chuckling malicious spirit—which might be the first step towards realising their own hypocrisy, and seeing their own distorted

face in the satiric mirror. It is difficult to believe that
quite everyone directly escaped the corrosive action
of Swift's satire ! In his pamphlets, where he attacked
with unexampled perfection of aim, we know they
did not. Although his satire may not have given
offence, the subject of it, in *A Tale of a Tub*, for instance, often did. In this and everything else he wrote
his very heat of indignation shows the sensitiveness
of his temperament. There is even, paradoxical as
it may sound, something sentimental about it. He
was tremendously aware of, tremendously sympathetic
with, wrongs and injustices of all kinds. This is clearly
seen in his Irish pamphlets—terrible, some of them, in
their satiric and ironic force. Swift's generation, probably, questioned his earnestness. How could such a
man be a serious priest of the Church ? He was earnest
enough, but like Butler, his successor, he contrived to
conceal this under an ironic mask. His strongest
feelings he hid away thus. And to an age which was
unacquainted with that vein of humour—we have
another direct, forcible evidence in Hogarth's pictures
of what the age was like—it may have seemed rather
queer and incomprehensible. As a preacher Swift
was sensible and direct ; he had, naturally, no
sympathy with " the moving manner of preaching."
His religion, no doubt, was a very proper affair,
filling a fit and reasonable place in his life. Here,
also, he seems to have veiled his earnestness pretty
successfully, for it is related that a friend had
stayed in the house with him for a quite considerable
period before he was aware that the Dean was in the
habit of conducting family prayers every morning for
the benefit of his servants.

Then there is Swift's undoubted misanthropy. The Yahoos and the Struldbrugs are two familiar peoples which embody his scorn and despair of mankind. He did despise it, and at the latter end of his life there came over him that consistent gloom which ended in mental collapse. Although he seems to have anticipated some such event, his madness was much more the breaking up of a mind tautened to the farthest stretch by work and disappointment than the destruction of a brain inherently weak and unbalanced. His fierce indignation, consisting in the knowledge that his genius was never fully recognised by his age, may have accentuated and hastened his collapse. But alone it does not supply an adequate reason. In the satirist, although Swift's work bears witness to the contrary, there need not necessarily be any spirit of misanthropy or even of pessimism. The satirist may well be an optimist who believes so much in the possibilities of the world around him that he wishes to change it; as a sane-minded man in a crowd he calls attention to new hopes by destroying first the old evils through the adventure of satire. But Swift could feel small hope for the society in which he found himself; its vices and gewgaws and hollowness were so immense, its pedants so powerful, its politics so corrupt, that he had no opportunity of seeing or feeling anything except the presence of the many-headed monsters. Early in his life Swift says in one of his letters : " A person of great honour in Ireland (who was pleased to stoop so low as to look into my mind) used to tell me that my mind was like a conjured spirit that would do mischief if I did not give it employment." The " person," whoever he was, seems to have gauged Swift's temper fairly

accurately; he did employ his mind to the finest
purpose to which it was adapted; had he not done so,
but allowed it to turn in upon itself, disaster might
have come much earlier. Perhaps the man who remarked these things to Swift would have considered
that as it was he worked damage and mischief
enough urged on by that untractable " conjured
spirit."

Leslie Stephen has asserted of Swift that in spite
of himself he was necessarily prejudiced. It so often
happens, he says, that when a person using satire sets
out to free himself from prejudices, he means the
prejudices of other people. This may be true; but
here it seems that the writer is using the word " prejudices " almost in the sense of " convictions." A
man must possess some of these necessary things, unless
his work is to be merely destructive. Moreover, if
Swift had prejudices, they were at any rate his own and
on the whole good prejudices. It is, in fact, almost
impossible to dogmatise on these points. Perhaps
Swift was prepossessed; perhaps by the accident of
his life and surroundings he was apt to see the worst
side of humanity.

There can be no doubt, however, about the merits
of his style. " Order, rule, sobriety," as one critic has
said, were his three principles of writing. And it was
his prose that so much appealed to Butler. Indeed we
have written of Swift at some length because it seems
that between him and Butler there are not a few points
of contact. Butler read him with attention quite
early in his life; but, curiously enough, his personality
did not greatly appeal to him. He says, in one of his
notes, that he bought a penny abridgment of *Gulliver's*

Travels and was enchanted by it. "What is it that makes one book so readable and another so unreadable ? Swift from all I can make out, was a far more human and genuine person than he is generally represented, but I do not think I should have liked him." He then speaks of Fielding, wondering why "the faults of his work overweigh its many great excellences, while the less great excellences of the *Voyage to Lilliput* outweigh its more serious defects. . . .

"Swift is terse, he gets through what he has to say on any matter as quickly as he can and takes the reader on to the next, whereas Fielding is not only long, but his length is made still longer by the disconnectedness of the episodes. . . ."

Satire and the satirists fill an important place in the history of literature. We have taken Swift as a particular example because in many ways he comes nearest to Butler. Satire, as we have seen, suggests many images. Mr Cannan, in a little book on this subject,[1] sets up Icarus, the typical figure with satire, "as a glass to concentrate the heat of the sun upon those who attempt to rise on wings of wax." The false flight inevitably must lead to a fall. In this view the satirist is, as it were, a testing agent to measure and estimate the capacity of his fellows ; we can imagine no better office, if he be allowed to fill it. Another recent writer maintains that satire is incompatible with deep convictions about right and wrong. There is not much truth in this. The satirist, unlike the moralist, does not set out with preconceptions in these matters : common-sense, the best instincts of normal people, if any can be found, are his touchstones

[1] *Satire.* By Gilbert Cannan. 1914.

of right and wrong. Slovenly, indecent thinking, superstitions, deceptions, the whole gamut of human folly are his wrong ; and though he parade no loud dogmas of good and evil, a criterion does exist somewhere, even if it is not being thrust continually forward in and out of season.

With Butler such a criterion was grace, the evidence of man making himself into a respectable human being. " And grace is best," he says,[1] " for where grace is, love is not distant. Grace ! the old Pagan ideal whose charm even unlovely Paul could not withstand, but, as the legend tells us, his soul fainted within him, his heart misgave him, and, standing alone on the seashore at dusk, he 'troubled deaf heaven with his bootless cries,' his thin voice pleading for grace after the flesh.

" . . . and there came a voice from heaven saying, ' Let My grace be sufficient for thee.' Whereon, failing of the thing itself, he stole the word and strove to crush its meaning to the measure of his own limitations. But the true grace, with her groves and high places, and troups of young men and maidens crowned with flowers, and singing of love and youth and wine —the true grace he drove out into the wilderness—high up, it may be, into Piora,[2] and into such-like places. Happy they who harboured her in her ill report."

This is not only a good piece of English, it is also a good piece of sense. It shows Butler's feeling about the comely virtues through which it is man's endeavour to perfect himself here on earth. He must be as one under grace, not as one under the law.

[1] *Life and Habit,* close of chap. ii.
[2] See the chapter on Piora, *Alps and Sanctuaries.*

The above, of course, is an expression of faith quite aside from any notion of satire. Before leaving finally this latter topic it is interesting to notice what James Hannay, writing in the early fifties of the last century, thought of the condition of satire in England at that time. At the end of his study of the satirists he says:

"In our own day we have plenty of Satire in our literature. But, for the most part, Satire does not bloom independently as a plant; it enters into the composition of literary productions, and gives a tone to them. We have not the satiric laurel. . . . We have novelists, and essayists, and journalists, who are satirical; but where is our Satirist?"

A new satirist *was* at hand in the person of Samuel Butler. That, of course, Hannay could not know. What he says about the position of satire in the middle of the last century is equally true now. There is satire but no satirist. Much water, however, has flowed under bridges since then. Butler, with cleansing force, has shown up the Victorian system as it actually was, and the falsities on which the nineteenth century built itself. His wit and irony flashed upon the age quite unexpected, quite unheralded. And the age left him alone with his condemnation of itself, although it did not altogether succeed in snuffing him out in the process.

We have described satire and irony as closely allied —so closely, often, that the two words are used indiscriminately as though the one were a modification or intensifying of the other. The satirist frequently uses irony—the deadliest weapon he knows—yet the two elements are separate and distinct. Irony is a subtler instrument of attack, and in proportion as it is more deadly so it is more dangerous. It is of the essence of irony that it is risky, just as it is liable to misinterpretation. It is part of the nature of irony, too, from which arises this difficult and dangerous element, that it expresses two meanings, appeals to two entirely separate groups of people at one and the same time. It requires the nicest manipulation, the most delicate handling lest it lose its native force and recoil on him who uses it. A writer employing irony must feel very sure of himself; he is playing with highly explosive material which does the work it is designed for only under treatment specially adapted to it.

The word irony is derived from the Greek εἰρωνεία, dissimulation. There are three distinct meanings of the word. Primarily it implies " saying the contrary of what is meant "; secondly, " a mockery of events," when circumstances dictate the wildest contrary of what was expected; and lastly there is that " dissimulation of ignorance " which Socrates waggishly practised when he personated an unlearned man admiring wisdom in others, and which is known as Socratic irony. The first two of these meanings chiefly concern us, and of these the first, irony in its fundamental sense, is the more important.

Mr Hilaire Belloc, in an essay, " On Irony," [1] where he deals with the original meaning of the term, explains its aim and function. "Irony," he says, "is that form of jest in which we ridicule a second person in the presence of a third." Nor is this third person, the audience, in any way restricted or confined : it may be the universe at large, it may be God, or it may be

---

[1] In the collection of essays, *On Anything*.

the ironist himself. He notes, too, that when used unworthily, irony will disappear; it flourishes best in societies which are military in temper, and is unknown in those societies where the love of ease dominates all men." The writer recognises its force, for when rightly used it is invulnerable and always reaches its mark; he speaks also of the deadliness of the weapon. "As it is called into being by evil things, it works in an evil light. It suggests most powerfully the evil against which it is directed, and those innocent of evil shun so deadly an instrument."

Gulliver's Travels is thus one of the completest ironies in English—so complete that it has become one of the favourite children's books, read by them without any suspicion of an ulterior meaning. Swift's *Modest Proposal for Preventing the Children of Poor People in Ireland from being a Burden to their Parents or Country* is another piece of irony, terrible in its statistical gravity. Here, as in Butler's *The Fair Haven*, irony sets out to turn its theme into absurdity. Swift's pamphlet is a *reductio ad absurdum*; it shows the immediate good that will come to poor Irish people by killing their babies for food. But the remedy is worse than the disease, which is an absurdity; and the fact that it is so indicates the grave nature of the disease. Better known, however, is the same writer's *Argument against Abolishing Christianity*, in which he shows that if it were done away with the only topic on which the wits could exercise their talent would be removed. Christianity must, therefore, be preserved. An earlier and elaborate ironical piece is to be found in the little-known pamphlet, *Killing No Murder*, directed against Oliver Cromwell by a certain Colonel Sexby,

in which the writer proves that since the Protector
has the interest of his country at heart he ought
quietly to submit himself to being murdered, since
undoubtedly that alone will remove from the country
the tyranny under which it is labouring. In this
document the author was tapping a vein of humour
that was to be used subsequently with persistent and
telling effect.

All these are examples of irony in its classic sense.
But there is the second meaning—the mockery of Fate
at the futilities of man, a theme Mr Hardy has so
successfully used in his Wessex novels. The uncon-
trolled freaks and caprices of circumstance are his
subject. "Incongruity" best describes such an
ironic situation. Fortune deals an insidious blow, or
shows her disregard of the propriety of things, or
smiles bitterly at unreasonable discrepancies : as when
a man receives a letter from the Front from one who
has subsequently died ; or suffers from an incurable
disease amid every refinement of luxury ; or when
the patchouli-scented draperies of a fluttering young
woman of the pavement suggest the immediate contrast. Machiavelli realised the effect of the unexpected
in creating his impression. Somewhere he describes
how an Italian tyrant had a certain minister sawn
asunder, while still alive, in the market-place. "But
to return to more important things——" he abruptly
adds.[1]

The greatest living master of this kind of irony, as
also the greatest living satirist, is M. Anatole France.
His is a laughing mockery of human life. He shows
the wide gulf between the expected and the actual ; he

[1] Quoted by W. L. George in his *Anatole France*, 1915.

demonstrates with a queer, amused smile the playful tricks of a sardonic Fortune ; he points to the riotous burlesques of Fate and Chance, and the wild, inconsiderate behaviour of the blind forces at work in nature. And so in his irony there is an appearance of acquiescence in the evils he records. This is not really so. He is much too interested, much too amused to take any too definite side—though now and again he cannot resist a sneer at the expense of a luckless victim.

Meredith, in his essay on the Comic Spirit, contrasts Satire and Irony in two sentences :

" If you detect the ridicule, and your kindliness is chilled by it, you are slipping into the grasp of Satire.

" If instead of falling foul of the ridiculous person with a satiric rod, to make him writhe and shriek aloud, you prefer to sting him under a semi-caress, by which he shall in his anguish be rendered dubious whether indeed anything has hurt him, you are an engine of Irony."

Meredith, while dealing with his specified subject, the idea of Comedy, thus gives a passing nod to these two particular forms of humour. He confesses that English people are very much in sympathy with one type of Aristophanic comedy, where irony and satire and the grotesque run together ; and this appeals to them because at bottom they have an esteem for common-sense. And although Meredith does not pause long over these two elements, as being quite subsidiary to his main topic, he recognises a moral agent in the satirist, and defines irony, rather obscurely, as " the humour of satire "—as if satire were not humorous by its own nature and from the character of the work

H

it sets out to perform.　He adds, in the same paragraph, distinguishing between the two kinds of irony he has conceived, that "the foppish irony fretting to be seen, and the irony which leers, that you shall not mistake its intention, are failures in satiric effort, pretending to the treasure of ambiguity." A certain ambiguity is no doubt always inseparable from irony itself.　Meredith's remarks on the whole do not make the matter much clearer—although in his novels not a few of the characters are conceived in a fine ironic spirit.

Samuel Butler's irony—he knew the value of the two separate elements used in their proper place—is best understood by a few quotations from *Evolution Old and New*, where he explains, in his own point of view, its intention.　He is writing of the ironical character of Buffon's work, in which he nearly always detects a note of subrisive humour.

" I am inclined to think," says Butler, "that a vein of irony pervades the whole, or much the greater part of Buffon's work, and that he intended to convey one meaning to one set of readers, and another to another; indeed, it is often impossible to believe that he is not writing between his lines for the discerning, what the undiscerning were not intended to see."　So there were two sides to his work, a scientific and a popular side, for he wished to speak to those who could understand him, and yet, like Handel and Shakespeare, wished to address the many as well as the few.　Therefore he used language " self-adjusting to the capacity of the reader."

The writer adds : " He would help those who could see to see still further, but he would not dazzle eyes that were yet imperfect with a light brighter than they could stand."

Further, " Even when ironical, his irony is not the ill-natured irony of one who is merely amusing himself at other people's expense, but the serious and legitimate irony of one who must either limit the circle of those to whom he appeals, or must know how to make the same language appeal differently to the different capacities of his readers, and who trusts to the good sense of the discerning to understand the difficulty of his position, and make due allowance for it."

Such is Butler's view of irony. There is about it an essentially dual element; it aims at two audiences; the surface meaning of the composition into which irony enters masks a second and deeper meaning which will be clear only to those who hold the necessary key. So humour belongs to the process; it is the author who gets the first smile out of his own cunning, and afterwards that second smaller audience which understands him and to which the true character of his work appeals. Or perhaps there is no separate second audience, so that the writer alone is left to laugh, rather bitterly, at his own unappreciated jest.

To Butler irony, like all his humour, was serious in intention. He used it for a legitimate reason, because only by that particular method could he say what he wanted to say. This high, serious, ironic purpose pervades not a little of his writing; though he knew quite well how to throw off the mask and descend with quick, mocking laughter upon bewildered, hide-bound people. There is no doubt about the stimulating quality of this " serious and legitimate irony," both to the writer and the reader who recognises its true character. The former must be continually alert to manipulate successfully this difficult double-edged instrument ; must always be on his guard lest he throw away his past labour by the indiscretion of a moment : it is the business of the latter to go to the furthest point his intelligence allows him, aided by the self-adjusting language of the author.

None of Butler's books is a completer illustration of this method than *The Fair Haven,* which was finished shortly after the publication of *Erewhon.* It is not so much that irony enters at times into the composition of the book ; the whole thing in aim and purpose is an irony. Its literary *vraisemblance* is as perfect as that of Defoe, and the effects which Butler is able to achieve by the complicated machinery of the book are far more telling than would have been possible in a straight-forward narrative. *The Fair Haven* remains at once one of the most unexpected and characteristic of his works. It is characteristic because it is so wonderfully an outcome of the particular kind of mind that he possessed. The Memoir of the supposed author and the book itself in one sense form the greatest contrast ; and yet Butler has succeeded fairly well in welding the two elements. The subject of the Memoir sets for the reader, though he may not be aware of it, the tone of what is to follow, and the book miraculously hangs together with some sort of completeness. For Butler, the whole thing was a final clearing up of the old question of the Resurrection and the evidence on which it is based. The fictitious gentlemen created to do the work for him were as screens to conceal him from whatever public there might be to read it. To have framed his polemic in any other way would have

destroyed the meaning he wished to suggest. In a
preface to the second edition revealing the true authorship, Butler explains this. He points out that
Erewhon had already aroused some suspicions in the
minds of certain ultra-orthodox Christians who appeared to find a parallel between the Christian Church
and the Musical Banks. So the "value of *The Fair
Haven* as an anchorage for well-meaning people"
might have been impaired if he had written it in his
own name, which now carried with it a satiric suggestion. By projecting his opinions through the personality of John Pickard Owen, the incredibly real
character whom he employed for the purpose, he
was able to make free use not only of satire, but also
to throw a veil of irony over the whole work.

Thus *The Fair Haven* is the most "hermetic" of
all Butler's books. He intended it to be so. Those
who had any inkling of the trend of his beliefs would
recognise its nature; but from others, like the reviewers
on *The Rock*, *The Record*, and similar evangelical
papers, who treated it as a genuinely orthodox defence
of revealed religion, its true character was hidden.
The editor of *The Rock* was so much impressed with the
book that he described it as "an extraordinary one,
whether regarded as a biographical record or a theological treatise." He considered the volume to be
so important that it was not reviewed with the usual
brevity. The merits of the posthumous production,
in fact, were discussed "in two consecutive numbers
of *The Rock*," a complete departure from the ordinary
custom. After this Butler must have felt that he had
not written in vain.

There can be no doubt, however, that *The Fair*

Haven did him harm.   It was after the publication of
the second edition of the book, disclosing the true
authorship, that the reviewers and literary men in
England who had shown any interest in his first
adventurous satire decided that Butler was far too
dangerous and unrestrained as a writer, and must be
left severely alone.   For it was part of his crime as a
literary man, a literary man in Victorian England, that
he refused to secure for himself and his work a label
by which both might be identified.   His position as a
literary outcast was consolidated later by the scientific
book, *Life and Habit*, which criticised the work of
Charles Darwin.   It is a commonplace in English
criticism that it expects from an author no new word,
but a repetition of what it heard last time, done more
or less in the same way.   Butler, in his first published
book, appeared as an amusing satirist ; therefore he
must remain a satirist and continue as he had begun.
He did not quite understand this argument, and even
if he had, he would not have appreciated the force of it.
It might be said, of course, that at the end of his life
he did so far submit to popular opinion as to write
a sequel to *Erewhon*.   But *Erewhon II.* was more a
return to an old problem which he wished to throw
into a satiric form than a return to the Erewhonians
for their own sake.

One result of *The Fair Haven*, then, was to surround
him with an odour of suspicion.   The book is described
in its sub-title as " A Work in Defence of the Miraculous
Element in our Lord's Ministry upon Earth, both as
against Rationalistic Impugners and certain Orthodox
Defenders, by the late John Pickard Owen with a
Memoir of the author by William Bickersteth Owen."

Such is the setting of the ironical Defence. The
volume, as we have said, falls naturally into two parts
—the Memoir and the discussion of the Resurrection.
The first of these is a select biography of the fictitious
author by his brother W. B. Owen. The two Owens
seem to have caused no less amusement to Butler than
to the readers who recognised their real character.
He, certainly, enjoyed them, though in the preface to
the second edition there is a whimsical half apology
for having created two such beings. " Is there not
enough actual exposition of boredom come over us
from many quarters without drawing for new bores
upon the imagination ? It is true I gave a single drop
of comfort. John Pickard Owen was dead. But his
having ceased to exist (to use the impious phraseology
of the present day) did not cancel the fact of his once
having existed. That he should have ever been born
gave proof of potentialities in Nature which could not
be regarded lightly." Butler clearly delighted in this
offspring of his imagination ; he created a character
and so found his aptitude for character-drawing which
was widened and developed in *The Way of All Flesh.*
So this Memoir, as Mr Streatfeild says, is a "trial trip
in the art of fiction." J. P. Owen was a person after
his own heart—a figure, that is, summing up everything he most wished to condemn—a figure which was
the immediate result of a narrow clerical environment
and its creator's revulsion from those surroundings.
About the elder Owen there is something mysterious,
even grotesque ; but having regard to the place and
time in which he lived, his early religious exercises—
ruthlessly and rigidly enforced—and the general character of his upbringing one feels no injustice in the

satiric presentation. There is an intensely disagreeable flavour about everything he did ; his amazing self-confidence, his certainty, his ridiculous familiarity with the plans God has seen fit to make in dealing with the world, his assumption of superiority coming from boldness to see other positions than his own, might have given some hint to the editor of *The Record* and others as to the nature of the biography. That it did not is proof at once of a certain affinity in religious temper, and of the accuracy of the satire.

John Pickard Owen was born in the early thirties of the last century, in Goodge Street, Tottenham Court Road. To us Goodge Street is chiefly a station in the Tube on the way to Euston, where no one *we* know ever gets in or out. The street upstairs, however, has a very definite atmosphere ; its drab ugliness seems especially congenial to a cruel and soulless drab religion. Altogether a very suitable birthplace at such a moment for such a person as Owen. He was brought up in the narrowest school of evangelical literalism, now happily almost extinct in England. It is difficult for us to realise the character and effects of this kind of fetichism. It was perhaps commonest among the poorer classes, but not by any means confined to them. And scientific progress in the last century at first did little to disperse it ; rather the bonds were tightened in the face of the new doctrines surely not of God but of the Devil. Butler knew the ins and outs of evangelicalism, and his work, therefore, has its historical value as the record of an important element in Victorian life. It was the lack of mental discipline from which he recoiled ; even at Cambridge, fresh from surroundings which encouraged spiritual extravagance,

the Simeonite teaching had disgusted him — at a
moment, too, when he was fully intending to take
orders. Religion is " a bold leap in the dark into the
arms of an affectionate father " ; Church Music brings
a man " not one iota nearer to Christ, neither is it
acceptable in His sight . . ." ; the peculiar subtlety
of the " adversary " in those latter days, sharpening
his wits, sowing tares, suiting " his blandishments to
all " ; these were the religious comforts with which
people were expected to refresh their souls. Butler
derived from them small spiritual or intellectual support. He shrank from such things with a violence of
disgust, although the very fact of their existence was
a hideous fascination. John Pickard Owen was an
immediate result of the reaction.

It is the pleasantest possible task to watch Butler
etching in this portrait. He is mainly concerned with
Owen's religious development because it was most
relevant to a proper appreciation of his remarks on
the Resurrection. Owen's brother, however, frequently
mentions his great intellectual gifts, his capacious
memory, his open-mindedness, his marvellous facility
of illustration, although he never mistook illustration
for argument. There was one trait in Owen, moreover, which he never seems to have overcome : this
was his tendency to take everything at its face value, no
doubt the outcome of his mother's teaching about the
verbal inspiration of the Bible. The Bible, it may be
added, seems to have been the only literature known to
the Goodge Street household in Owen's early years. It
was, of course, much more than literature also—a book
of reference in the affairs of everyday life, a prophetic
compendium of nineteenth-century history in which the

Owen family was to take a distinguished part. John
Pickard and his brother, in fact, were identified with
no less important persons than the two witnesses
mentioned in the Apocalypse, chap. xi.

It was, doubtless, this complete literalness in religious
matters which led to a surface interpretation of everything in life. " Everything with him was to be exactly
in all its parts what it appeared on the face of it, and
everything was to go on doing exactly what it had
been doing hitherto." As an illustration of this the
writer records a first childish disillusionment—in
respect of women. The incident is described with most
vivid realism ; many perhaps have felt just as Owen
did ; but no one has ever set it down with such humorous ease as Butler, anticipating the manner and style
of his later notebooks. It was a lady visitor to the
Owens, put to sleep in the nursery, who gave the first
shock to John Pickard's complacency. He was still
quite young, and when the lady began to undress was
surprised to find that the mass of clothing concealing
the female form was not " all solid woman " as he had
always thought ; woman, in fact, had legs just as he
had, and was in no degree more substantially built
than man. This was a shock, a first unexpected discovery that everybody and everything was not exactly
as it seemed. It may be remarked, too, that throughout her visit the lady only said her prayers when the
two Owen children were awake, and did not say them
when she thought they were asleep. All this was a
first stepping-stone to that later unhappy period of
scepticism through which Owen had to pass before he
could reach the Fair Haven where should be " universal
brotherhood in Christ."

The intervening years were full of vague spiritual unrest. Owen became a religious vagrant, wandering from one sect to another, and as such he gained that tremendous sympathy with other people's opinions and other people's business which enabled him to elaborate a scheme of reconciliation between believers and rationalists, on the basis of a reasonable examination of the evidence in favour of Christian miracles. These spiritual vagaries and a short period of profound scepticism led to his ultimately developing into " perhaps the widest-minded and most original thinker whom I have ever met," as his brother remarks. He had his evil moments, however, as when he condemned many of the Christian parables because they taught a doubtful morality, and because, practically, their application was difficult and sometimes unintelligible even from an Eastern point of view. Butler himself, later on, stated his objections in a note on " The Parables." But John Pickard, still in a wicked moment, has another Butlerian passage on lying and self-deception :

" That a man should lie to others if he hopes to gain something considerable—this is reckoned cheating, robbing, fraudulent dealing, or whatever it may be ; but it is an intelligible offence in comparison with the allowing oneself to be deceived. So in like manner with being bored. The man who lets himself be bored is even more contemptible than the bore. He who puts up with shoddy pictures, shoddy music, shoddy morality, shoddy society, is more despicable than he who is the prime agent in any of these things. He has less to gain, and probably deceives himself more ; so that he commits the greater crime for the less reward. . . .

" Oh ! if men would but leave off lying to themselves ! . . ."

But Owen at the height of his spiritual and intellectual power was as elusive and slippery as an eel ;
there was no sure means of catching him out. What
he would accept and what reject, no one could tell ;
nor was it possible to compass or comprehend the
wisdom of his inconsistencies, or to discover where the
logical side of him left off and the illogical began.
Certain parts of the Scriptures he was disposed wholly
to set aside—they might be valuable as giving comfort
to poor people, but by men of a rationalistic temper
like his own they must be discarded. Much that is in
St Luke's Gospel he is forced to reject as unhistorical ;
yet it has its use as going straight to the hearts of the
" lower " classes. Luke records many such words of
comfort : " Woe unto you that are full ! for ye shall
hunger. . . . Woe unto you, when all men shall speak
well of you ! for so did *their* fathers to the false
prophets." " Even the grammar of the last sentence,"
says Owen, " independently of the substance, is such
as it is impossible to ascribe to our Lord himself."

At the end of the Memoir there is a dark hint that he
may have recanted some of his beliefs. That, however,
was only when the cloud of mental disease came over
him. Except for this distressing condition at the
close, his self-satisfaction remained unimpaired ;
strangely enough the importance of the task entrusted
to him did not entirely overwhelm him ; he was
conscious of the magnitude of the work and bold in
his enthusiasm to carry it through. " Yet I know
well," he says, and here it is the true Pickard Owen
who speaks, " that the fire burneth within me, and

that day and night I take no rest but am consumed
until the work committed to me is done, that I may
be clear from the blood of all men."

The book which Butler so generously thrust upon
John Pickard Owen is chiefly a discussion, a sort of
Sherlock Holmes examination, of the Resurrection.
It is easy now to see in Owen's defence a caricatured
boldness in facing impossible issues ; perhaps in the
early seventies, an age of very serious religious controversy, it was less easy.   At any rate the exegesis begins
with a consideration of Strauss's hallucination theory
—the theory, that is, that the disciples only *imagined*
they saw Christ after the Crucifixion, and that on their
hallucination rests the whole fabric of Christianity.
This notion the writer rejects as untenable.   As being
of more importance, he passes on to the character and
testimony of the Apostle Paul : there can be no doubt
about his conviction of the reality of Christ's appear-
ances ; from Peter he obtained a coherent narrative
which established his certainty as to the truth of these
things.   Paul, then, was convinced.   The central part
of the book consists of " Difficulties felt by our
Opponents " ; Owen sets forth their position with the
extremest candour in order that his refutation of their
opinions may be the more thorough and convincing.
He takes upon himself the nature of an infidel, in fact,
in order that he may teach unbelievers to believe.
The volume concludes with a chapter on the " Christ-
Ideal " and a restatement of Owen's beliefs as set out
in the Memoir.

By piecing together the chapters on St Paul, the
criticism of Dean Alford's *Notes* on the New Testament,
and one particular difficulty "felt by our Opponents "

we arrive substantially at Butler's own position. It
is interesting to find him emphasising here the importance of St Paul's testimony. Paul's character and
personality no doubt puzzled Butler as it has puzzled
so many people ; he felt indeed how great was the
personal influence of the Apostle and that his enthusiasm was the result of intense conviction ; the strength
of character of one who could so impress himself upon
his age, and who could give a new twist to Christianity,
appealed to him also. But Butler never liked St Paul,
even though he did write the thirteenth chapter of the
First Epistle to the Corinthians. In *The Fair Haven*
he is simply cited as an evidence of the current conviction about the Resurrection. "From the first,"
says the writer, "he proved himself to be a man of
great strength of character, and like many such, deeply
convinced of the soundness of his opinions, and deeply
impressed with the belief that nothing could be good
which did not also commend itself as good to him."

From the matter which follows it is not difficult to
disentangle Butler's own views. He believed indeed
that Christ was placed upon the cross, but was unable
to accept His Resurrection ; there is no evidence, he
says, to show that Christ ever died upon the cross.
He was taken down by Joseph of Arimathea in a swoon,
and subsequently revived. In the New Testament
narrative that follows nothing is heard of Joseph, who
would naturally wish to keep in the background, considering the manner in which events had shaped themselves. "It is not probable," he says, "that a man
officially executed should escape death ; but that a
dead man should escape from it is more improbable
still ; in addition to the enormous preponderance of

probability on the side of Christ's never having died,
which arises from this consideration alone, we are told
many facts which greatly lessen the improbability of his
having escaped death, inasmuch as the Crucifixion was
hurried, and the body was immediately delivered to
friends without the known destruction of any organic
function, and while still hanging upon the cross."

In refuting arguments which deal with the objective
truth of what is recorded in the Gospels, J. P. Owen has
much to say of the particular methods by which
revelation is granted to man. He speaks of the
"incomparable chiaroscuro" of the New Testament
writings, which convey, in their often misty lights, a
potent truth and influence. One might point to the
whole edifice of Christian civilisation and Christian
art as a proof that there could be no fundamental mis-
conception; he prefers to realise for himself the position
of the Evangelists whose very innocence and *naïveté*
have become a cause of stumbling in a scientific age.
It is the *ensemble*, the general effect, the feeling—as in
a Turner painting—which are more important than
the detail, for "No combination of minute truths in a
picture will give so faithful a representation of nature
as a wisely arranged tissue of untruths."

There is such a thing, however, as too great a vague-
ness in detail and in evidence. Oral tradition might
lead to this; there was only one way of guarding
against it, at the moment when the danger presented
itself.

"*Precisely at that epoch the Gospels made their
appearance.* Not simultaneously, not in concert, and
not in perfect harmony with each other, yet with the
error distributed skilfully among them, as in a well-

tuned instrument wherein each string is purposely something out of tune with every other. Their divergence of aim and different authorship secured the necessary breadth of effect when the accounts were viewed together ; their universal recognition afforded the necessary permanency, and arrested further decay. If I may be pardoned for using another illustration, I would say that as the roundness of the stereoscopic image can only be attained by the combination of two distinct pictures, neither of them in perfect harmony with the other, so the highest possible conception of Christ cannot otherwise be produced than through the discrepancies of the Gospels."

This final quotation, a remarkable explanation of discrepancies, contradictions and difficulties, suggests the flavour of Butler's ironical method in defending Christian miracle. Particular points, particular conflicting evidences are left on one side ; he takes the theological bull boldly by the horns and justifies inconsistency as the only means by which a true and lasting image may be secured. John Pickard Owen summoned to his assistance in the formidable task sank into a mental decline. It was some satisfaction to Butler, no doubt, to be thus rid of him, although he had been faithfully at his hand for close on three hundred pages of well-sustained irony. Having in this way, however heterodox in a literary sense it might be, disposed of the Resurrection problem, Butler was in a position to deal with new and vital questions which were presenting themselves for consideration. His painting was again to be interrupted—this time by the first of his scientific books.

CHAPTER IV

DARWIN AND THE SCIENTIFIC BOOKS

Erewhon, as we have seen, had been for Butler a gathering together of many of the vagrant thoughts and theories which had come to him during the early part of his life. After completing it, and *The Fair Haven*, he again settled down to his painting, feeling this time pretty safe from interruption. A mind like his, however, so susceptible to new ideas or old ideas seen in an original light, so quick to follow up hints and clues which it had already suggested in the past, a mind so apt for reasoned speculation, inquisitive and alive, could not long remain aloof from new inquiries. And the problem which first of all at this time began to interest Butler linked itself on to the chapter in *Erewhon* dealing with the Machines.

We have noted already in that book two distinct theories of the Machines. The first was the Erewhonian theory of mechanical contrivances as socially danger-ous—a theory at once daring and picturesque, having a recognisable analogy with real conditions, which Butler made the central theme of his book. It was the second view of the Machines, however, that in which he had always believed, that now again began to assert itself. In *Unconscious Memory*, written some years later, he gives a few details as to how *Life and Habit*, the first of the scientific books, came to be written. "I proposed to myself," he says, "to see

not only machines as limbs, but also limbs as machines.
. . . The use of the word ' organ ' for a limb told its
own story ; the word could not have become so current
under this meaning unless the idea of a limb as a tool
or machine had been agreeable to common sense.
What would follow, then, if we regarded our limbs and
organs as things that we had ourselves manufactured
for our convenience ? "

Thus our limbs are to be considered as machines
which man and the animals carry about with them ;
they have been designed for the particular uses they
fulfil, just as man for his own purposes has designed
and modified and perfected those machines which exist
outside himself. So, in one sense, man's very body,
no less than the limbs he has added to it, may be considered as a machine which gradually he has adapted
to his own convenience. And at that point where the
capacities of his own body and limbs, the machines
which are part and parcel of himself, reach their limit,
he has made further contrivances which could not in
their nature be permanently attached to himself, and
which must be regarded as nothing else than extensions
of his own personality.

A consideration of these things and all that they
implied resulted in his book *Life and Habit*, in the
course of which he was necessarily led to examine
very many of the problems in evolution. His conclusions, always well reasoned and stated with singular
clearness, aided by illuminating illustrations and that
quality of humour which was nowhere absent from
his work, these conclusions go to form a particular
philosophy implicit in everything he wrote. *Life and
Habit*, moreover, is the most important of the scientific

books because it put forward his main view of heredity from which he never afterwards departed. *Unconscious Memory* is an amplification of that view dealing, among other things, with particular objections raised by his opponents. Often he himself had to create an opponent to criticise his own work, because at that time he had come very near to forfeiting whatever literary reputation he once possessed, his work being treated for the most part with contempt. Even if it had not been so, if he had never written *The Fair Haven*, the reception of such a book as *Life and Habit*, the work of a mere layman ignorant of the technique of any one branch of science, unpractised also in the use of magnificent scientific terminology, must have been discouraging. Here we may remark that Butler always suspected the involved scientific phraseology of people like Huxley, when it was equally possible to convey the meaning in English comprehensible to the man in the street, or at any rate the man in the omnibus. He suspected it, as being rather like the patter of the conjurer—intended to distract and mystify. He begs his reader not to be "too much cast down by the bad language with which professional scientists obscure the issue, nor by their seeming to make it their business to fog us under the pretext of removing our difficulties. It is not the ratcatcher's interest to catch all the rats; and, as Handel observed so sensibly: 'Every professional gentleman must do his best for to live.'" And as with the smaller issue, so with the larger : Butler was not a professional gentleman of science.

But because there were few opponents prepared to criticise his work, he did not allow it to go uncriticised.

Butler was one of that rare species who are capable
of exercising mental detachment, who are able to look
disinterestedly at their own theories and state the
arguments which militate against them. He did this
repeatedly and with remarkable mental fairness; it
was no mere setting up of foolish objections for the
pleasure of knocking them down again, but a valid
intellectual process of which few are temperamentally
capable. He waited patiently for objections to his
Memory theory of heredity, which is the chief subject-
matter of *Life and Habit*, just as later on he waited for
six years for criticism of his Odyssean theories; but
in neither case was any serious criticism forthcoming.
The only difference between them was that his
writings on Memory happened to be supported by a
German physiologist, and "in language far more
suitable to the persuasion of the scientific public,"
as Professor Marcus Hartog has remarked, which
may perhaps have secured them some measure of
recognition.

But, after all, recognition mattered very little to
Butler. He continued his work on the lines he had
laid down; he had no axes to grind, no party to subscribe to, no systematised series of doctrines which
any group of people could use for their own purposes.
And so, to the end of his life, he maintained that
detached attitude, which must never be confused
with indifference or lukewarmness. It must become
abundantly clear, in reading his scientific books, that
there was no Laodiceanism about *them*. Perhaps
what he said against earnestness may be taken here
as a warning more particularly addressed to himself,
because he felt how intense were his convictions in

each one of the four evolutionary books that he wrote.

In *Life and Habit*, then, Butler wished to show that living beings have made themselves what they are, purposively, from sense of need. " Growth," he said, " is only somebody making something." And he wanted also to explain how the machines or organs which the creature made for its own purposes came to be thus made. So complete an identification between means and ends could only have been realised intelligently; and for the outside intelligence, which is supposed to direct the progress of the race, he substituted an intelligence residing within the creature itself. The problem then confronted him : how could the descendants of the primordial cell—how could any of the creatures in the whole chain of descent—intelligently do their work when they knew nothing about it ? Butler answered that they did it by unconscious memory, which was able to assert itself by reason of the oneness of personality between parents and offspring. Thus the return of the associated ideas awoke the memories proper to the occasion, and the creature is able to do things about which otherwise it could know nothing.

One of the most interesting parts of the book is that in which Butler demonstrates how all the actions we do best we do unconsciously. To reach this height of unconscious proficiency it is clear that we must have done the action very many times before ; and this, we know, is exactly the case with all the things we do most easily—our breathing, the circulating of our blood, digesting and so on. Just in the same way the best thieves are those who are not aware of being thieves

—kleptomaniacs—and the greatest hypocrites of the world are the unconscious hypocrites. It is the same, too, with all the first-rate bores. And these classes of people are the least likely to be cured of their unpleasant qualities because they are completely unaware of any personal defect. Perhaps the kleptomaniacs may wait; certainly the other two can ill afford to do so.

The self-conscious scientific people who know what they know are also to be looked on with suspicion. They are a class of men living under the law rather than under grace, whose work is all governed by γνῶσις and very little by ἀγάπη. Butler criticised these men of science because he thought them dangerous; he feared that they would impose a worse despotism even than that of religion, since, in proportion to its size, they made the most powerful and influential group in the country. " It may well be we shall find we have escaped from one set of taskmasters to fall into the hands of others far more ruthless. The tyranny of the Church is light in comparison with that which future generations may have to undergo at the hands of the doctrinaires. The Church did uphold a grace of some sort as the *summum bonum,* in comparison with which all so-called earthly knowledge— knowledge, that is to say, which had not passed through so many people as to have become living and incarnate—was unimportant." Against this new menace Butler was determined to take a firm stand, although he knew his position to be quite anomalous and isolated.

The step from self-consciousness to introspection is not a very wide one; and Butler was well aware that people who suffered from this malady were generally no good. He would have nothing to do with David's maxim : " Commune with your own heart and in your chamber and be still," which is more than once insisted on in the Psalms. Introspection, after all, is attending to something that doesn't concern us ; it means also that we are not doing the business that lies before us. Often it has a religious origin, though it is not a necessary accompaniment to religion. To Butler, therefore, the best kind of religion is that which teaches us that ultimately we can know nothing about the universe, except that we are an integral part of it, and that we had better attend to our own affairs. Everything in the world, he saw, that did its work best did it just because it knew what that immediate work was, and gave no thought to the future, or to those larger processes of which it was but a single component part. What, for instance, could be more unpleasant than an introspective blood corpuscle—and doubtless they do exist, just like introspective men and women ? " If I were the being of whom such an introspective blood corpuscle was a component item," says Butler, " I should conceive he served me better by attending to my blood and making himself a successful corpuscle, than by speculating about my nature. He would serve me best by serving himself best, without being over curious. I should expect that my blood might suffer if his brain were to become too active. If, therefore, I could discover the vein in which he was, I should let him out to begin life anew in some other and, *quâ* me, more profitable capacity." The analogy with ourselves is simple : what is bad for the corpuscle is bad for us ; and we may be sure that when men and women are curious and self-inquiring and troubled about what is inside them, they are not making themselves into decent, successful, human beings at all, but are exhausting themselves in a manner that will interfere with all the proper functions of their life.

We have an instance of this in Tolstoy, whose life is so curiously divided into two distinct halves. Immediately before, very often after, his " conversion," as he called it, we find him in the most melancholy conditions of self-analysis. And so in the later life of Tolstoy there appears a certain inhuman callousness, a disregard of the claims of other people or even of his own family ; he is continually self-absorbed as he passes through successive moral crises, horribly intent on these interesting spiritual developments. He wrote no more " poetry," as the Russians call it—unless *Resurrection* can be classed with the great earlier creations of the *War and Peace* period. In this latter book, so wide in scale and conception and treatment, he created a piece of art which would have been utterly impossible of achievement to any self-conscious writer. It was something much bigger and wider even than himself, a theme which seized and worked its own will upon him ; but introspection closes the mind to all that, and renders it unsusceptible to the happy thoughts, the secret influences from without that come we know not whence. And it was with Tolstoy as with others : his conversion virtually brought his career as an artist to a close.

Human beings, then, and indeed all living creatures in a normal condition, will do their work best when they do it unconsciously, because they remember

having done it before in their ancestors. The best
proof that a creature remembers how to do anything,
and, therefore, knows all the ins and outs of its own
business, is that it does it so unerringly. Butler
could not see how hereditary instinct or Herbert
Spencer's "accumulated experience of the race" explained these things—how, indeed, anything but
memory would offer a satisfactory explanation. It is
true that the memories become more intense through
repeated experience ; yet the notion implies a sort
of *vicarious* experience. This statement of the case
appeared illogical to Butler : "The experience of one
person is not enjoyed by his successor, so much as that
the successor is *bonâ fide* but a part of the life of his
progenitor, imbued with all his memories, profiting by
all his experiences—which are, in fact, his own—and
only unconscious of the extent of his own memories
and experiences owing to their vastness and already
infinite repetitions." Butler would thus transfer the
experience of the race to the individual, although he
knew it was for the race rather than the individual that
Nature showed her most affectionate regard. In any
life-history there are passionate arguments going on
between the experiences of many countless ancestors ;
much has already been settled, as the shape of our
teeth, our nose and so on, but other questions are still
in debate. Professor James Ward has defined experience as " the process of becoming expert by experi-
ment." He points out, further,[1] that habit is acquired
by repeated trials and failures, until at length we
reach that stage where actions become "secondarily

[1] In *Heredity and Memory*. The Sidgwick Memorial Lecture at
Cambridge, 1912.

automatic "—or simply unconscious, as Butler would
have put it. This "mechanization of habit," in Professor
Ward's phrase, makes new advances possible, *natura
naturata* being necessary to further *natura naturans*.
"What is done, *natura naturata*," he says, "the decisions made, the habits formed, the customs fixed—
constitutes at any stage the routine, the general trend
of things within which future possibilities lie. What is
still to do, *natura naturans*, implies further spontaneity
and growth : new decisions to be taken, fresh experiments to be made."[1] Butler, on the whole, would
have agreed with this, though he knew that it was
impossible for any creature to depart very widely
from the doctrines taught by its forefathers. To him,
in fact, the unerring nature of our unconscious actions
is a proof of the force our past experiences exert within
us ; to Professor Ward the settling of these habits
makes it possible to move forward on new lines without
too much reference to what has been done before.

Further important links in the chain of Butler's
argument are to be found in his chapter on " Personal
Identity." Personality, as we have seen, he never
defined as self-contained and indivisible, but he found
that it was no more possible to deny identity between
the baby of ten minutes old and the old man of eighty
into which it developed, than to deny identity of
personality between the embryo five minutes or five
months before its birth as a baby and the baby of ten
minutes old. So the impregnate ovum itself must be
described as identical with the old man of eighty.
Birth and death, in fact, are nothing else than arbitrary

[1] Quoted by R. F. Rattray in "The Philosophy of Samuel Butler,"
Mind, vol. xxiii. N.S. No. 91.

divisions set up for social and legal purposes. They
are of the utmost use as practical expedients for conducting our affairs, but it is purely arbitrary to suppose
that what we call personality begins at birth and ends
off at death. Birth as a line of demarcation has been
made far too much of; it is, indeed, the beginning of
uncertainty, a quitting of the old best-remembered
paths of well-ordered behaviour, but a no more important event in our lives, though quicker and more
abrupt, than the passage from youth to age. Just as
the life before birth is an unconscious performing of
the routine we know best, so " infancy is as the dozing
of one who turns in his bed on waking, and takes
another short sleep before he rises." In spite of the
fact that there is no discontinuity between the embryo
and the human being of eighty, man is a creature made
up of countless personalities, countless souls, perhaps,
each one of which has its say in his actions and
behaviour. Our environment is, after all, often a part
of our personality. " To an embryo its mother is
simply environment," Butler wrote in *Erewhon Revisited*; undoubtedly the embryo is part of the personality of its mother, and vice versa it remains true also.

In the same way with certain people their relatives
and friends are the most important influences in their
lives. They do nothing without reference to them;
they have no will of their own; they depend upon
outside suggestions and outside advice. By long habit
they have become unable to determine for themselves
a course of action in the very simplest matters; they
are at the mercy of other people's opinions. Sometimes,
says Butler, we see people who have " become mere
processes of their wives or nearest relations." What

about their personalities ? Certainly they cannot be defined as a single, indivisible ego. We notice a similar state of things in our physical selves. Our bodies are made up of an infinite number of beings, parasites, which it is no exaggeration to describe as part of ourselves. Butler calls them " subordinate personalities," which may very well be unaware of our existence, but which must be counted nevertheless as parts of us. Personal identity, therefore, is manifold in its nature ; it demands extension both forward and backward ; it is not self-contained, as the whole of life bears witness. As " the myriads of smaller organisms " which inhabit our bodies, says Butler, anticipating the conclusions he reached in *God the Known and God the Unknown*, " are parts and processes of us, so are we but parts and processes of life at large."

But Memory, to which we must return as the keynote of *Life and Habit*, does not work continuously ; it may fall into abeyance and will only reassert itself with the return of the associated ideas. A hen does not remember anything about its past life as an egg, any more than we remember ourselves as embryos ; the hen possesses only the memories of its previous existences as a hen. Just in the same way a hen's egg remembers and knows the things it did before, when it was an egg, and sets to work accordingly. Butler gives many parallel instances of the reawakening of latent memories with the recurrence of the ideas or the environment associated with them. Every organism, when placed in a certain environment, remembers its own behaviour when previously in that environment ; if, however, it is placed in surroundings about which it knows nothing it must inevitably die. It has no memories proper to the occasion, and its memories alone constitute its life.

When considering the hen's egg we must try and look at these matters from the egg's point of view. " It has, I believe, been often remarked," says Butler, " that a hen is only an egg's way of making another egg." Four years later he wrote a note on Reproduction which bears upon this : " Its base must be looked for, not in the desire of the parents to reproduce but in the discontent of the germs with their surroundings inside those parents, and a desire on their part to have a separate maintenance." Weismann's theory of the germ-plasm—the germ-plasm which he opposed to the body-plasm as being immortal, " *in* the body," as Professor Hartog says, " but not *of* it "—throws light on this view. The immortal germ is continually striving to reproduce itself, though it is in no wise affected by, nor does it itself modify, the bodies in which it resides. To Butler, also, the germ was the all-important thing ; with Weismann, although unlike him, he could not believe in the non-transmission of acquired characters, or in the complete isolation of the germ cells, he would make the germ his starting-point. The idea developed in the World of the Unborn is of a piece with this doctrine as Mr Festing Jones has pointed out ; and in *Erewhon Revisited* the love affair of Mr Higgs and Yram is considered to be not so much their own fault as that of their son George, who was too insistent with his pleadings for a separate existence, and at length got what he desired.

It is clear that much that Butler wrote in *Life and Habit* is implicit in the teaching of Lamarck. Neither could believe in an origin of species which did not imply

" need, faith, intelligence and memory " ; both leaned
towards a teleological explanation of the evolutionary
processes. A continual striving, a trying, stimulated
by the will of the creature, was what Lamarck taught
as the basis of evolution. In the second and third of
his four laws this is directly explained :

" The production of a new organ in an animal body
results from the supervention of a new want (*besoin*)
continuing to make itself felt and a new movement
which this want gives birth to and encourages.

" The development of organs and their force of action
are constantly in ratio to the employment of these
organs."

Sense of need is the directing force in the Lamarckian
system ; and Butler felt convinced that the explanation of the eighteenth-century evolutionist was far
more satisfactory than the " small fortuitous variations " of Mr Darwin, for instance, and the haphazard,
unintelligent blindness of his " theory " of evolution.
Butler's criticisms of Darwin, which first appear in the
last pages of *Life and Habit*, are thus concerned with
a vital question in Darwin's teaching. " The weak
point in Mr Darwin's theory," he says, " would seem
to be a deficiency, so to speak, of motive power to
originate and direct the variations which time is to
accumulate. . . . Given the motive power which
Lamarck suggested, and Mr Darwin's mechanism
would appear (with the help of memory, as bearing
upon reproduction, of continued personality, and hence
of inherited habit, and of the vanishing tendency
of consciousness) to work with perfect ease. . . .

However we may differ from him [Mr Darwin] in detail, the present general acceptance of evolution must remain as his work, and a more valuable work could hardly be imagined. Nevertheless I cannot think that 'natural selection' working upon small, fortuitous, indefinite, unintelligent variations, would produce the results we see around us."

These criticisms of Darwin were further developed in *Unconscious Memory* and *Luck, or Cunning?* while *Evolution Old and New*, which followed *Life and Habit*, was designed to show how little justice had been done by Darwin to his intellectual predecessors, the eighteenth-century evolutionists. In later editions of *The Origin of Species* Darwin did give a brief résumé of the opinions of past writers on evolution ; but even then the writings of Buffon were dismissed contemptuously, Lamarck received only a short paragraph, and Dr Erasmus Darwin not even that.

Butler was quite unable to understand this attitude. He seems from the very first to have objected to the tone of the opening paragraph of *The Origin of Species*, which, in 1858, appeared "as a kind of literary Melchisedec, without father and without mother in the works of other people." There is about the paragraph in question, which gives a few personal details as to how *The Origin* was written, something of that curious Low Church spirit which, also, is inseparable from Darwin himself. It was this, we believe, that Butler so much disliked. And when the differences between Darwin and Butler led to a personal quarrel it is easy to see how entirely opposed their temperaments were and how little Darwin was fitted for controversy with "a clever and unscrupulous man like

Mr Butler " [1] With Darwin as a naturalist Butler
had no quarrel.   But in the naturalist trying to reach
wide, general conclusions, based upon his own observa-
tions, he expected to find something of the philosopher.
In this he was disappointed.   " Mr Darwin has generally gone to good sources," he says.   " The ground of
complaint against him is that he muddied the water
after he had drawn it, and tacitly claimed to be the
rightful owner of the spring, on the score of the damage
he had effected."

Mr Bernard Shaw has more than once described
Samuel Butler as the only Englishman who saw what
Darwin's Natural Selection really amounted to, since it
took him but six weeks to realise the worthlessness of
the mindless universe offered for public acceptance.
Mr Shaw himself, who is a Neo-Lamarckian, has done
justice to the " unbreathable atmosphere of fatalism
which is the characteristic blight of Darwinism," [2]
and which was only accepted because people did not
really know what it meant except that it made impossible a belief in the Book of Genesis, in special
creations, and in the universe typified by Paley's watch.
If you can realise, says the same writer, " how insufferably the world was oppressed by the notion that
everything that happened in the world was an arbitrary
personal act of an arbitrary personal god of dangerously
jealous and cruel personal character, so that even the
relief of the pain of maternity by means of chloroform
was objected to as an interference with his arrangements

---

[1] See Darwin's letter to T. H. Huxley, quoted in *Charles Darwin and
Samuel Butler : A Step Towards Reconciliation*.   By Henry Festing
Jones.

[2] In a paper on Darwin read to the Fabian Society, March 1906.

which he would probably resent, you will understand why the world jumped at Darwin." Unquestionably it did jump at him. *The Origin of Species* became a social institution, consequently very few people read it. Men and women, as a whole, were therefore unaware of the new despotism under which they were in danger of falling. There was no lack of good Darwinists. Every such one would, no doubt, as Mr Shaw suggests, run to the umbrella-stand for a stick, after the birth of his first baby, and, if he could circumvent the monthly nurse, test the clinging capacities of " the little arboreal creature." The Darwinian theologian, also, had equally important problems to consider. He wanted to know, for instance, quite innocently, at what precise point in the evolutionary process souls were given out ; animals, he believed, did not possess souls. For he had accepted Darwin, although it became thereby necessary to come to decisions about all sorts of new and troublesome questions.

The view, then, that Darwin's Natural Selection was much more important for what it saved people from than for what it gave them is certainly not without foundation. It was partly, of course, as we have said, that people were unaware what Natural Selection as against purposive Evolution really meant, and partly that in a short time Charles Darwin and a small scientific oligarchy were reaching a position of overwhelming influence throughout the country. Society was offering him an uncompromising allegiance, and even if there had been many sceptics British loyalty to a reputation must have overborne them. Samuel Butler knew quite well what Natural Selection contrasted with Evolution amounted to ; and when he found that

K

Darwinism was becoming a substitute for conventional religion, he attacked it just as relentlessly as he attacked religion in *The Fair Haven*. It was just because he had grasped so clearly the importance of the differences between Natural Selection and the older, and as he believed the truer, doctrines of the eighteenth-century evolutionists that he wrote his four books and numerous articles all dealing with the same question. Mr Cannan finds these books tiresome, and seems to detect within them evidence that Butler feared Charles Darwin. We must confess to being quite unaware of such an emotion in Butler; he attacked him so wholeheartedly because he was conscious of Darwin's prestige and the enormous influence he exerted. To Butler he was never a bogey. There seemed something inevitable, moreover, in their contest. As Butler, at the end of his life, said to Mr Shaw : " My grandfather quarrelled with Darwin's grandfather; my father quarrelled with Darwin's father; I quarrelled with Darwin ; and my only regret in not having a son is that he cannot quarrel with Darwin's son." Perhaps this did not occur to him when he felt bound to resist the importunities of that son, as described in *The Notebooks*, who was always coming to him and pestering to get born !

The quarrel between Darwin and Butler, in fact, was over a fundamental matter inseparable from the whole of Butler's thought and life. Mind, will, purpose and straightforwardness were what he stood for in everything he wrote and everything he did. He defended them fiercely when attacked. And it is of no use to ascribe to him a lack in sense of proportion, any more than the controversy can be dismissed as arising from wounded pride or an odd, unaccountable terror of Charles Darwin which gradually increased as time went on.

Butler's disagreement with Darwin, however, did not cause him to neglect his own important theory of Memory. As he was finishing *Life and Habit* he heard that a German physiologist, Professor Ewald Hering, had given an address in Vienna on " Memory as a General Function of Organised Matter." Butler purposely refrained from reading it until his own book was published, in order that he might not have to make any alterations or reconsider what he had said in the light of it. When he did examine the address on Memory he was delighted to find that Hering's theory was substantially his own.

Hering, in his address, sets out to discover what Memory is, whereas Butler had been satisfied to describe what it did, at the same time connecting it specifically with the phenomena of heredity. Hering asserted that Memory was due to vibrations of the nerve fibres ; occurrences, therefore, which have made small impression upon us will awake only faint vibrations ; whereas those characteristics which are common to many things will easily reproduce themselves, and the vibrations will be correspondingly more intense. Butler did not entirely commit himself to this hypothesis, though he leaned strongly towards it.

We may judge, however, of the importance he attached to Professor Hering's address by the fact that he translated it and included it, with notes and introductory comments, in his book, *Unconscious Memory.* He had already learnt German in order to examine an article on the Life and Works of Dr Erasmus Darwin

in a German scientific periodical. We have compared
Butler's version of the lecture on Memory with a later
translation made, we believe, in America ; as a clear
and direct piece of English the former compares with
the later version very much to Butler's credit.

Besides containing a translation of Hering's lecture
and of the chapter on Instinct in Von Hartmann's
Philosophy of the Unconscious—although he found it
for the most part unintelligible—there are some valuable chapters at the close of *Unconscious Memory*
dealing with possible objections to his own mnemonic
theory. It may be said that throughout the inorganic as well as the organic world like antecedents
are always followed by like consequents ; that there
is uniformity of action in atoms ; that with a little
ingenuity memory might be introduced into the inorganic world also ; and that memory cannot, for
instance, be connected with those diseases in the
cul-de-sac of old age which occur long after the time
for reproduction has gone by. Butler did not consider these criticisms valid. As we advance in life, he
said, we live less by inherited memory than by details
of memory gathered from personal experiences which
are pieced together by ourselves. And this is true of
all those actions which are new in their general scope,
but which in detail are not new. The second kind of
memory is " the memory of our own antecedents."

With regard to the atoms of inorganic nature " the
sameness of action of like persons placed under like
circumstances for the first time, resembles the sameness
of action of inorganic matter under the same combinations " ; so it is not remarkable that a son inheriting
his father's constitution should, as an old man, make

the same mistakes as his father. Gout, cancer and the diseases of old age are thus explained without the intervention of any sort of inherited memory.

We have dealt with these objections here, because they show the aptness of Butler's mind to criticise his theories searchingly and with that mental fairness which comes from a certain detachment. He liked to examine his theories from every possible side, in order that he might get to know as much about them as possible ; and in the same way with those other, less fully developed, thoughts that were continually coming to him. He wrote them down, to make sure that they would not escape him, and examined them from time to time in order to modify or add to them as he thought fit. He was exceptionally suited for exercising this kind of mental discipline over his ideas and fancies ; and hence it came about that the value of an idea, and so its truth, was in proportion to the number of points of view from which it would bear looking at. We have insisted already on the remarkable interdependence of thought which is everywhere in evidence in Butler's work ; this is a characteristic we cannot stress too strongly. As with his thoughts, so with his books. Outwardly, of course, nothing can seem more scattered and unrelated than the literary works of Samuel Butler. A satire, followed by an ironical religious polemic, a theory of heredity and three books on Darwinism, translations of Homer and a volume setting forth the female authorship of the *Odyssey*, together with an examination of Shakespeare's sonnets, a book of Italian travel, and finally a novel—these no doubt do sound at first hearing like a dissipation of whatever strength their author possessed over many scattered fields.

Yet the very centre of Butler's strength lay in his diversity. He saw the relation between things at first sight unconnected far more vividly than anyone else in his century. By temperament and training he was curiously a mixture of the synthetic spirit which enabled him quickly to reach a new point of view, and of the analytical habit by which he could examine objectively the position he had arrived at. He possessed this particular critical temper himself, and welcomed it from the outside when it had any valid criticism to offer.

The last of Butler's evolutionary books, *Luck, or Cunning?* sets in an even clearer light the position he held as against Darwin, shows how the very existence of evolution is bound up with it, and how the question at issue " affects the view we take of life and things in an endless variety of most interesting and important ways."

Luck, or Cunning, as the Main Means of Organic Modification? in its full title, is, however, not entirely concerned with Darwin, though it is an attempt to throw more light upon his " theory of Natural Selection." The plan of the book underwent changes while it was being written, and the original subjects, the intelligence of plants and trees, and protoplasmic continuity, were, in fact, only dealt with in a concluding chapter. Mr Herbert Spencer, Mr Romanes, Mr Grant Allen—especially Mr Grant Allen's book, *Charles Darwin*—and Professor Ray Lankester were mainly responsible for Butler's deflection from his original subjects.

In the chapter on Romanes' *Mental Evolution in Animals* there is a comparison between this writer and

Darwin. Butler found both of them obscure, and he notes in each a tendency to appear to differ from other people with whom they are really in agreement. Such a method gave a semblance of originality to their work. Yet Butler's own mode of procedure, for instance, had he been in Darwin's position, would have been first of all to state as precisely as possible the doctrines of the older evolutionists, then to say in what way he differed from them. Darwin never did this, partly, as Butler believed, because he felt so insecure about his own conclusions that all the time he had to be wrapping them in vague woolly sentences which should serve also as loopholes of escape should escape become necessary. His studied literary habit was showing itself, also, in his intellectual successors. And it was this painful obscurantism that Butler was concerned to attack. Indeed, the words of John Pickard Owen, who somewhere wrote of the " incomparable chiaroscuro " of certain of the biblical writings, recur in this connection. For there are masters of scientific no less than of sacred chiaroscuro.

We have seen already the willingness with which people in the sixties hopped across one more of the many Victorian *pontes asinorum* in accepting Natural Selection. And they did so quite ignorant whither the path they had thereby taken would lead them. The boom in Darwinism continued through the next two decades, and even now has not entirely died away. The reaction, led by Samuel Butler, was at that time a very small affair. But even if Darwin, as Butler remarked, was " the heir to a discredited truth " and " left behind him an accredited fallacy," he had other disadvantages, no less potent, to fight against. With

him, as with many others, it was a case of save me from
my friends. No reputation could emerge undamaged
from such a hail of fulsome adulation as was poured
upon it by Grant Allen in his *Charles Darwin*. And
the " contagious enthusiasm " which Darwin inspired,
" only equalled perhaps among the disciples of Socrates
and the great teachers of the revival of learning," is
seen in a curious and significant light in a quotation
from a review by Professor Ray Lankester written in
1881. " It is necessary to plainly and emphatically
state," says Professor Lankester, splitting the infinitive
with reckless unconcern in the warmth of his emphasis,
" that Professor Semper and a few other writers of
similar views are not adding to or building on Mr
Darwin's theory, but are actually opposing all that is
essential and distinctive in that theory, by the revival
of the exploded notion of 'directly transforming agents '
advocated by Lamarck and others." As Butler remarks, these writers were probably very well aware
that they were not " building on Mr Darwin's theory " ;
nor did they wish to do so. Professor Lankester
speaks of their " actually opposing " that theory ; and
he does so with pious horror, as if, says Butler, " there
were something intolerably audacious " in their conduct. The little incident at any rate shows the kind
of mental attitude of Darwin's ardent disciples ; to
them it seems to have been inconceivable that anyone
could seriously oppose the principles set forward by
their master. Professor Lankester took it for granted
that Professor Semper and the other writers were, or
at least wanted to be, good Darwinians, but had somehow been waylaid and led astray by an evil one among
them so that, in spite of themselves, their doctrines

became actually opposed to those of Mr Darwin, and showed unmistakable leanings towards the teaching of the discredited Lamarck. The sooner they realised how dreadful was the heresy they were introducing, and mended their ways, the better! This is the only interpretation that Professor Lankester's words admit of.

Apart from such criticisms as these, the title of this last book of Butler on the philosophy of Evolution classifies the two main schools of biological opinion each under a distinctive heading. Darwin is the apostle of luck, and his grandfather and Lamarck the apostles of cunning. On the title-page of *The Origin of Species* Darwin explains what natural selection is. It is there defined as " The Preservation of Favoured Races," which means " Fortunate " and therefore " Lucky Races." Design, on the other hand, and hence cunning, were held by Erasmus Darwin and Lamarck to be the motive power behind evolution. But when cunning is spoken of in this connection we do not imply all cunning and nothing else. There is a place for luck which must necessarily enter into design itself. The discovery of steam, as Butler somewhere wrote, was due to luck, but the modern Dreadnought is a thing of design. The question at issue, then, is which of the two elements is more important in organism : cunning, which on the whole knows what it is aiming at and makes every use of chance opportunities that come its way; or luck, which is continually turning up in the world, but which from its very nature can have no designed relation to the luck that has gone before it ? And it must be remembered again that when we speak of cunning " we do not mean that conscious attention and forethought shall have been bestowed upon the minutest details of action, and nothing been left to work itself out departmentally according to precedents, or as it otherwise best may according to the chapter of accidents." With cunning, therefore, Butler would connect memory as making a continuity throughout the life of the organism. Luck can have no such continuity since it is necessarily spasmodic, one phase being isolated from another. Otherwise it ceases to be luck.

The transition from a world governed chiefly by luck to one in which mind plays no part is not far to seek. In the seventies, as a direct result of the prevailing biological theories Butler noted the concurrent development of a mechanistic conception of the universe and what he calls a " protoplasm boom." Huxley was the prophet of protoplasm ; and the conclusion he and other eminent scientists arrived at was that the protoplasmic parts of the body are alone truly living, while the non-protoplasmic parts are non-living. So Huxley proceeded to show that men and women are nothing else than " conscious automata," thought and feeling being only " bye-products of cerebration," which have no material causative influences. Butler was in the keenest opposition both to the mindless conception of the universe and the protoplasm boom. He pointed out that if protoplasm was the only centre of life it must unite all life into a single body, and hence must itself be considered as " the life of the world." So protoplasm would become identified with God, who of all fleshly forms chose this by which to manifest Himself. " Our biologists, in fact, were fast nearing the conception of a God who was both personal and material, but who could not be made to square with pantheistic notions inasmuch as no provision was made for the inorganic world." Instead of allowing himself to be involved in such difficulties Butler preferred to assert—and the assertion was entirely of a piece with the conclusions he had arrived at from other observed phenomena of life—that the protoplasmic parts of the body are only *more* living than the non-protoplasmic. With this position is involved the whole of his philosophy of the inseparability of life and death, of degrees of death in life, and vice versa.

To people like Huxley, who were struggling to get rid of the Early Victorian notions of God and the Garden of Eden, and with these two would banish mind also, there was no doubt something anomalous and incomprehensible in a position like Butler's. Mind to them, no doubt, smacked somehow of spirit, and spirit of mystic, religious associations. And probably they could not get rid of the idea that to have design there must be an outside designer. Butler, however, explained quite clearly what he meant. The God he believed in was God in no mystic sense ; and the design that was in the universe was part and parcel of it. So at a moment when materialism and fatalism were rampant, when scientists and writers were approaching all sorts of delicate questions by the light of the crude method, opened up for them at the end of the fifties, it was perhaps not surprising that a man with Butler's clearness of vision, who saw where current tendencies were leading them, should be treated with unconcern. Probably no man in the latter part of the last century kept himself so well informed in the progress of biological opinions or made himself so well acquainted with the ins and outs of scientific hedging.

Certainly no one ever studied the different editions of *The Origin of Species* or collated them with such minute care—always, it should be noted, with the wish to extract from the book the maximum amount of meaning intended by the author. One of the chapters in *Luck, or Cunning?* called " The Excised ' My's,' " shows how nearly a hundred passages in which Darwin either directly or by unmistakable implication claimed the theory of descent as his own by speaking of it as " my theory," were gradually altered in subsequent editions of the *Origin*, the " my's " being changed into " the," " our " or " this." Butler believed it was important that this unpleasant task should be performed. More interesting, however, is a paragraph which shows how Darwin would have written explaining his " theory " had he been no longer Darwin but some other disinterested person, another Samuel Butler, perhaps, into which he was suddenly changed.

" I should point out," says the transformed **Mr** Darwin, " that, according to the evolutionists of the last century, improvement in the eye, as in any other organ, is mainly due to persistent, rational employment of the organ in question, in such slightly modified manner as experience and changed surroundings may suggest. You will have observed that, according to my system, this goes for very little, and that the accumulation of fortunate accidents, irrespectively of the use that may be made of them, is by far the most important means of modification. Put more briefly still, the distinction between me and my predecessors lies in this :— my predecessors thought they knew the normal cause or principle that underlies variation, whereas I think that there is no general principle underlying it at all, or that even if there is, we know hardly anything about it. This is my distinctive feature. . . . If you ask me in what my discovery consists, I reply in this ;— that the variations which we are all agreed accumulate are caused—by variation."

Whether this or Darwin's own account of himself is the more satisfactory readers of the various editions of *The Origin of Species* must decide.

We have already, in this chapter, mentioned the impossibility, in Butler's view, of drawing a hard and fast line between the living and non-living ; the same also applies to *ego* and *non-ego*, which touch and meet at countless different points. Butler speculated a good deal on these questions, and in the middle of *Luck, or Cunning?* there are two chapters that bear on them. It must always be remembered that everything he wrote on biological subjects was a development of the sections in *Erewhon* dealing with the livingness of machines—of which Huxley's " conscious automata " theory referred to above is the complete converse. Machines, as we have seen, are extensions of the personality of those who use them. And the same is true, in a wider meaning, of property generally. " It is the last of *ego* and the first of *non-ego*." And so a man's body, with its concomitant organs which he has been making and perfecting for countless ages, is " property carried to the bitter end." Hence we speak of " organic wealth." Our stomach is thus only a living purse in which we keep our food or " petty cash in its handiest and most reduced form." From all this we may see the frequent union between *ego* and *non-ego*, and in what Butler calls " incorporate tools," like the eye or the tooth, there is not a little of the *non-*

ego element.   Just as *ego* and *non-ego* are inseparable,
so life and death cannot be distinguished from one
another as two distinct principles.   The common basis
underlying both of them is change, as Butler somewhere remarked.   Neither life nor death is the greater
miracle ; each lurks within the other and is to it as
pleasure is to pain, good to evil and God to the Devil.

" Does any man," asks Butler, " in continuing to
live from day to day or moment to moment, do more
than continue in a changed body, with changed feelings,
ideas and aims, so that he lives from moment to
moment only in virtue of a simultaneous dying from
moment to moment also ?   Does any man in dying do
more than, on a larger and more complete scale, what
he has been doing on a small one, as the most essential
factor of his life, from the day that he became ' he '
at all ?   When the note of life is struck the harmonies
of death are sounded, and so, again, to strike death is to
arouse the infinite harmonies of life that rise forthwith
as incense curling upwards from a censer."

Later in the same book Butler, from a consideration
of this question goes on to ask what are the dividing
lines between the living and non-living.   He agreed
that a hard and fast line between living matter and
inert matter could not be drawn.   And again in the
Notebooks he dealt with these points in several notes
included under the heading " Mind and Matter."
To Butler the criterion of intelligence was never
whether man could understand the business of any
organism whose intelligence was in question, but
whether that organism understood its own business,
which it could best prove by doing it as well as possible.
So, because plants and animals do not comprehend our

affairs, we have no right to believe that they do not comprehend their own ; and the same applies to what we call inorganic matter—though Butler did not believe that the inorganic is wholly inorganic. Indeed he prophesied that before long the division between organic and inorganic will cease to exist, thus taking with it the division between mind and matter. For scientific discovery has tended to break down dividing barriers to an increasing extent.

Luck, or Cunning? concludes with some considerations on vegetable intelligence which had been the intended subject-matter of the book. Already in *Erewhon* he had written on " The Rights of Vegetables," and in *Alps and Sanctuaries* there is a passage which ingeniously distinguishes the two important departments of the organic world according to their temperament. Animals and plants are respectively examples of the wandering disposition which seeks opportunities for itself, and the stay-at-home habit that waits quietly for whatever happens to turn up. But he recognised that it is plants who are the heretics ; since, therefore, ours is the orthodox belief we are perfectly justified in devouring them—an argument he might have used in *Erewhon* in attacking those philosophers who made it their business to defend the rights of vegetables against the cruelties of those who would eat them. The fundamental difference in form and habit between animals and plants shows that difference of opinion was so strong that there was an early subdivision of primordial life. There might very well have been six main divisions of life ; but here we have evidence of only two. And the one question on which, at an early stage in evolution, opinion was likely to be divided was just this question of staying at home or wandering abroad. Although Butler had decided that plants were schismatics in this matter, he knew that for live people who can move about if they want to, the balance of advantages between staying still and looking about for things was very even ; in one of his notes he described how, acting on the former principle, two Rembrandts—and all his life he had wanted a cheap, " well-preserved, forty-shilling Rembrandt "— came his way. " People talk as though the making the best of what comes was such an easy matter," he added, at the end of this note, written in 1887, " whereas nothing in reality requires more experience and good sense. It is only those who know how not to let the luck that runs against them slip, who will be able to find things, no matter how long and how far they go in search of them."

The concluding passages of *Luck, or Cunning?* have a very direct application to the place in life occupied by plants and animals, and the distinctive phenomena they exhibit. " Bodily form," says Butler, " may be almost regarded as idea and memory in a solidified state." Further, these words contain his view of evolution—that it is the cunningest fittest rather than the luckiest fittest who survive. With the intelligence that is within the organism he coupled a memory of what it had done in the past, both of which aided it in reaching the goal it aimed at through will and desire and sense of need. That, quite shortly, was the position he held against the influential naturalist of the nineteenth century whom he so strenuously opposed.

We have spoken already of *God the Known and God the Unknown* as summarising Butler's philosophy in a convenient form. The view which it put forward was a natural result of the theories set out in *Life and Habit.* Butler mentions God often in all his books ; but the thorough-going materialist was at times no doubt puzzled as to what exactly he meant by the term. Quite briefly it may be said that he believed, though in no mystic sense, that we are all co-members of some undetermined principle which he was unwilling to describe in any other way than " God." Thus some of the terminology of the Psalms and parts of the New Testament were true for Butler in a perfectly literal sense. " What convention or short cut," he says in *Luck, or Cunning ?* " can symbolise for us the results of laboured and complicated chains of reasoning or bring them more aptly and concisely home to us than the one supplied long since by the word God ? What can approach more nearly to a rendering of that which cannot be rendered—the idea of an essence omnipresent in all things at all times everywhere in sky and earth and sea ; ever changing, yet the same yesterday, to-day and for ever ; the ineffable contradiction in terms whose presence none can either ever enter, or ever escape ? " We have had many definitions of God, some in woolly mystical terms, others in a geometrical form which must be infinitely amusing to the person who is being thus described. So He has been likened to a circle whose centre is nowhere but whose circumference is everywhere—or vice versa. How God must smile at these picturesque descriptive attempts ! Butler aimed at no such direct definitions, because to him God was involved and bound up with the whole of life. In the passage quoted above he speaks of God as a convention, and later on as a hieroglyph by which

L

we can most conveniently acknowledge the depths of our ignorance of the universe in general.

None the less *God the Known and God the Unknown* is concerned with the existence and nature of God. Here Butler set out to perform two things : firstly to show that there does exist a single spirit, " whom we cannot think of under any meaner name than God " ; and secondly to show something more of the bodily expression, the outward mask of this vast living Being. His system, however, was not pantheism, the belief of " those who hold that God is everything, and everything is God "—which Butler found to be a contradiction in terms—but a panzoistic conception—the conception, that is, of God comprising all living units in His own person, which comes much nearer to Fechner's philosophy than to pantheism. Or as Mr R. F. Rattray put it in his paper, " The Philosophy of Samuel Butler," already referred to, Butler sought to show that consciousness extends infinite in area through the universe even in the apparently smallest things. As each cell in the human body is an intelligent soul, so are we in ourselves combined to form some vaster being. " As the myriad organisms are parts and processes of us," Butler wrote, linking his thought on to the chapter in *Life and Habit* which deals with those parasites that live and have their being within our bodies, " so are we parts and processes of life at large."

Much of this is analogous with Fechner's speculation —though he is often mystical where Butler is entirely literal. Fechner believed that the whole earth on which we live must have its own collective consciousness, and that there is a place in the universe for every kind of spiritual being between man and God who

includes all things. His view of human consciousness is also interesting : William James thus explains
it in his lecture, " Concerning Fechner," in *A Pluralistic
Universe*. We know that although neither the skin
nor the eye is immediately aware of any of the sensa-
tions of the other, yet both meet and combine in the
inclusive consciousness we call *self*. " Quite similarly,
then," says Fechner, " we must suppose that my consciousness of myself and yours of yourself, although
in their immediacy they keep separate and know
nothing of each other, are yet known and used together
in a higher consciousness, that of the human race, say,
into which they enter as constituent parts." For
" the human race " Butler would substitute " life at
large," or God, as we may conveniently call it, in which
all the constituent units meet. Fechner's theory of
immortality has also some analogy with Butler's—if
again we reduce the rather symbolic terms of the
former to a more practical meaning. He believed
that the death of one of us is as the closing of an eye
of the world. Yet the memories that have eddied
about us remain in the vaster " earth life " and " form
new relations and grow and develop throughout all the
future." [1] Butler also had a distinct theory of immortality to which we have already called attention
in the remarks on *Erewhon Revisited*. As with
Fechner, Butler's immortality was of a vicarious type,
though different in nature from the former. In a
future existence, as we commonly understand the
words, Butler, of course, did not believe. " We offer
immortality," he said, " but not resurrection from the
dead," meaning thereby that everyone, according to

[1] See William James's lecture on Fechner.

the measure of his worth, will achieve a new life after
death in the thoughts and lives of others.   Of the life
we live in others he thus wrote :

" A man should spend his life, or rather does spend
his life, in being born.   His life is his birth throes. . . .
Still the life we live beyond the grave is our truest
life, and our happiest, for we pass it in the profoundest
sleep, as though we were children in our cradles.   If we
are wronged it hurts us not ; if we wrong others we
do not suffer for it ; and when we die, as even the
Handels and Bellinis and Shakespeares sooner or later
do, we die easily, know neither fear nor pain, and live
anew in the lives of those who have been begotten of
our work and who have for the time come up in our
room."

There is a calm and dignified paganism about this
passage, a little reminiscent of Swinburne's lines thank-
ing whatever deities may be

> " That no life lives for ever,
>   That dead men rise up never,
>   That even the weariest river
>   Winds somewhere safe to sea."

It may perhaps be said that Butler's clinging to the
notion of vicarious existence simply arose from the
desire of a lonely bachelor to be remembered, and who
therefore, as he grew older, formulated for himself a
creed to satisfy his own desire.   However much his
theory may be criticised as embodying a different
use of the word " life " from that to which we are
accustomed, there can be no doubt that it entered very
intimately into his thoughts during later years.   It
was another tribute to intelligence and consciousness

—although *quâ* the dead person consciousness was neither here nor there—as the things that really matter. So a good deal of his essay, " How to Make the Best of Life," is concerned not with the conscious life of an individual but with the life he may live in others after his death,

" Where dead men meet, on lips of living men."

Here, then, we have Butler's view of immortality which he put forward in *God the Known and God the Unknown*. As we have seen, the word God is in part an expression of our ignorance of the ultimate nature of ourselves and the universe, except that we know ourselves to be a part of the continual flux and reflux of Nature. Thus in respect of God the Known and Unknown, as Butler would have agreed had he seen William James's analogy, we are not unlike the cats and dogs in our libraries, who see the books in the cases and hear the conversations but understand little of the real meaning of it all. We certainly understand something, though the Unknown God is the expression of our ultimate ignorance. Butler conceived of such a Being —vaster and more remote—who called the God of this world into existence. His system, therefore, is one of concentric phases of life—the innermost of which, perhaps, is the cells that comprise us ; we ourselves are the second concentric sphere ; the God of this world forms the third, and beyond this the imagination can wander after that God the Unknown in whom all the constituent units meet.

Thus in Butler's scientific books there are three main threads which are easily traceable from one to another ; at times they touch and meet ; at others they emerge as distinct pieces of subject-matter which, it may be said without exaggeration, were the most important questions that Butler dealt with in view of the energy and concentration he focused upon them and the significance they had for him.　His theory of memory—which he always modestly spoke of as the Heringian theory, though he was perfectly independent, and therefore original, in formulating it ; his recognition of the value of the doctrines of the older evolutionists as against the mindless, purposeless view of the universe which was being put forward in the middle of the last century ; and lastly, the panzoistic philosophy which grew naturally out of his biological writings—these are the most important of the distinctive features, with, of course, much else that he paused and lingered over in passing, that emerge from the scientific books.　And of these three the Darwin controversy must rank as the first in Butler's eyes.　The last words he wrote on this thorny evolutionary subject were in *The Universal Review* in 1890, subsequently published, with the rest of Butler's essays, under the title *The Deadlock in Darwinism*.

It was doubtless in order that no ambiguous flavour might remain in the mouths of those who had read his books on evolution, that he inserted at the beginning of this essay a short and timely tribute to the work of Messrs Wallace and Darwin.　We quote this passage, in conclusion, as an instance of the clearness with which a well-understood meaning can be conveyed, although the subject may be difficult and the ground worn with the rough and tumble of a long contest.

" I would in the outset," says Butler, " and with the utmost sincerity, admit concerning Messrs Wallace

and Darwin that neither can be held as the more
profound and conscientious thinker ; neither can be
put forward as the more ready to acknowledge obliga-
tion to the great writers on evolution who had preceded
him, or to place his own developments in closer and
more conspicuous historical connection with earlier
thought upon the subject ; neither is the more ready
to welcome criticism and to state his opponent's case
in the most pointed and telling way in which it can be
put ; neither is the more quick to encourage new truth ;
neither is the more genial, generous adversary, or has
the profounder horror of anything even approaching
literary or scientific want of candour ; both display
the same inimitable power of putting their opinions
forward in the way that shall best ensure their acceptance ; both are equally unrivalled in the tact that tells
them when silence will be golden, and when on the
other hand a whole volume of facts may be advan-
tageously brought forward. Less than the foregoing
tribute both to Messrs Darwin and Wallace I will not,
and more cannot I pay."

It is on this note, as showing Butler's attitude
towards his scientific contemporaries—an attitude
from which he never wavered as long as he lived—
that we may, perhaps, best close the chapter on his
scientific books.

CHAPTER V

ITALY

PERHAPS the book of Butler's which forms the best introduction to his work is his travel book, *Alps and Sanctuaries of Piedmont and the Canton Ticino*. It is impossible to resist the charm of the writing or to feel uninterested in the scenes and places and people he describes. There are many diversions, too, as the narrative goes on ; the opinions of the author thrust themselves forward in the pleasantest way possible, for the author of whom we thus catch so many glimpses is in holiday mood. He allows his thoughts to go their own way, to follow up chance hints or suggestions from the scenes he has been describing : the result is one of the happiest imaginable combinations of humour and philosophy and pictures of those Italian places which he knew well.

We are apt to think that topographical description, to be most useful, had better be done by the professional guide-book writers. They will be more impersonal than those to whom a country has come to mean very much, who are interested in particular places because they have a particular and individual appeal. The compilers of a guide-book, as a rule, can tell us about the most comfortable hotels, for ordinary people are pretty well agreed as to what constitutes a comfortable hotel, and which are the views approved by the great majority. This, from the utilitarian

point of view, is a reasonable attitude. No doubt
Butler himself used these guide-books ; but he wrote
one for himself also that was not intended to be so
much a guide-book as a record of his favourite recreations, of his adventures among the Italian people and
the painted statuary in the Alpine sanctuaries, which
are never so much as mentioned in the " useful "
directories to hotels and views. The value of Butler's
book is that it is a live, personal record set down by
one who was a first-rate observer, who had an eye for
character and a tremendous sympathy with the people
of the country. These last, above all, were natural, and
understood their own business ; and they liked the
genial Englishman who remembered them from year
to year, asked about their children and grandchildren,
as Mr Jones says, and " never forgot to inquire after
the son who had gone to be a waiter in New York."
We know that Butler was little likely to go into
ecstasies over the conventionally accepted " sights,"
the pictures and picture galleries of Italy, unless there
was something in the work which definitely appealed to
him. Even then the emotion would hardly extend to
ecstasy. We know, too, from his description of Mr
George Pontifex's foreign travels in *The Way of All
Flesh*, what he thought about prigs like Mendelssohn,
who are perfectly acquainted in advance with what
they ought to admire, and have calculated exactly
how long they must sit contemplating certain pictures
in order to be considered people of " taste and culture."
There are quite as many reputations founded on traditional sentiment in Italy as in England.

It is impossible to neglect the Italian associations
when forming an estimate of Butler's personality ;

they played a most important part in his work. And
the Italian people, with their fresh and unself-conscious
talk, were often providing him with material for his
Notebooks, which he reproduced—such is one of the
particular flavours of those notes—with just that
twist of manner which makes commonplace things
worth telling. There are numerous instances of this.
Again in his extraordinary essay, "Ramblings in
Cheapside," which is a sort of inventory of reincarna-
tion cases which have come under his own observation, and which describes how figures from the past
are continually bodying themselves forth in the most
unlikely places and most unlikely people, there is a
passage about his meeting Socrates in the person of an
old Italian muleteer. The piece is full of the typical
Butler humour, his alertness, and readiness to find
in the most apparently prosaic people at a chance
meeting something interesting which would awake in
him a humorous recollection. Here is the passage :

" I met Socrates once. He was my muleteer on an
excursion which I will not name, for fear it should
identify the man. The moment I saw my guide I
knew he was somebody, but for the life of me I could
not remember who. All of a sudden it flashed across
me that he was Socrates. He talked enough for six,
but it was all in *dialetto*, so I could not understand him,
nor, when I had discovered who he was, did I much
try to do so. He was a good creature, a trifle given
to stealing fruit and vegetables, but an amiable man
enough. He had had a long day with his mule and me,
and he only asked me five francs. I gave him ten, for
I pitied his poor old patched boots, and there was
a meekness about him that touched me. ' And now,

Socrates,' said I at parting, ' we go on our several ways,
you to steal tomatoes, I to filch ideas from other
people ; for the rest—which of these two roads will
be the better going, our father which is in heaven
knows, but we know not.' "

Nor is this all. Very frequently an Italian or
Sicilian character or a chance word in *dialetto* suggested
to Butler something which he was able to link on to
the past, just as the words of a song sung by two small
boys at Trapani suggested Nausicaa's speech to
Ulysses when they first met in the *Odyssey*. Perhaps
it is not fanciful to compare Butler's constant habit
of looking for the past in living men with his love of
revealing the work of older artists in a modern light.
He did this in his translations of Homer and Nausicaa's
Odyssey, and was disposed to regard Shakespeare in
a similar spirit. " We are too fond of seeing the
ancients as one thing and the moderns as another,"
he wrote, for to Butler it was more interesting to show
how near to the moderns the ancients are on the
common ground of human nature than to preserve
them unsullied by the world of to-day in a far-off
idiom unintelligible to ordinary people. Even Scott
realised this, in a different connection, and explained
it in the introduction to *Ivanhoe*.

Not the least interesting parts of *Alps and Sanctuaries*—the two essays, " A Mediæval Girl School "
and " Art in the Valley of Saas," are notable for the
same reason—are the descriptions of the painted
statuary which appealed very directly to Butler.
They were off the beaten track ; and the representa-
tions of the sacred subjects, so near to the hearts
of the artists and the country people, gave many

opportunities of showing the life and habit in the particular localities in which they were found. Butler's descriptions, written, as someone has said, in terms of Mrs Beeton's Domestic Economy, are nevertheless far more graphic and readable than ordinary, accepted dissertations on pictures and statues. Here there is no trace of the academic or deferential attitude. The whole thing would have shocked Ruskin, for instance, and he would have looked in vain for that respect and dignity of utterance which is due to art—although, of course, he might have been very doubtful whether the statues in question were art at all. In the first part of the essay on the chapels at Oropa, Butler mentions his lack of seriousness in these matters from another point of view. He asks whether, after all, these chapels make us wish to speak with bated breath. That is not their atmosphere in the least ; nor are the Italians themselves a people who cannot see seriousness and laughter in the same picture. " We, as is well known, love to take even our pleasures sadly ; the Italians take even their sadness *allegramente,* and combine devotion with amusement in a manner that we shall do well to study, if not imitate."

And then follows Butler's inimitable picture of the schooldays of the Virgin Mary from one of the chapels of Oropa. Everything is highly respectable, except, perhaps, that one of the under mistresses has about her a rather *mondaine* look ; the Virgin herself, who is sitting near the lady principal, is doing a piece of embroidery, although her attention to the work appears to be intermittent. In fact she is represented as quite an ordinary young woman.

In this we have the very *raison d'être* of the statues

in the Alpine sanctuaries. They are intended to bring before the people in the vividest way possible the chief events in Christ's and the Virgin Mary's life as set forth in the New Testament. And their appeal often lies in the homely ordinariness of the details. Just as in England we teach people natural history by encouraging them to contemplate stuffed birds in a convincing habitat of artificial grass, rock or tree, so the Italian peasants learn the mysteries of their faith from painted statues as realistic as the artists knew how to make them. The Roman Catholics are perfectly logical in this ; they believe that in matters of religion, the most important thing that touches man here in this world, no pains should be spared to produce a definite, comprehensible image of sacred events. Naturally, therefore, these subjects are removed from their Eastern settings and transferred into pictures which reproduce their spirit in terms of Italian life, or even that of quite small localities having particular customs of their own. The Virgin Mary, in these painted images, is presented as an ordinary person. The reason of this, perhaps, is that the masses will feel infinitely nearer to the miracles associated with her if they are first made aware that she was not so very different from themselves. In fact, the more the Roman Catholics can make these events enter into the lives of the people and become an intimate part of them the better are they satisfied.

As Butler saw, we are little able to understand this view in England. He admired the Roman Catholic priests, because he thought their faith did not sit so ponderously upon them as was the case with English Protestants. Just as religion is more a part of their

ordinary lives than we have ever been able, or even
wish, to make it, so it enters into and blends with the
humours as well as the seriousness, the small amusements no less than the small troubles of every day.
It is the same at the great *feste*—the people come out
to enjoy their religious exercises with no intention of
being bored. Butler describes the Sacro Monte at
Varese as " a kind of ecclesiastical Rosherville Gardens,
eminently the place to spend a happy day." And he
notes, as an indication of the lack of humbug in the
Italian Catholics, the concluding words of a short
account of the Sacro Monte which is sold in little tin
boxes containing pictures of all the chapels there.
The description winds up with the words : " Religion
and the magnificent panorama attract numerous and
merry visitors."

" Our people," Butler comments, " are much too
earnest to allow that a view could have anything to
do with taking people up to the top of a hill where there
was a cathedral, or that people could be ' merry '
while on an errand connected with religion." Indeed
in such cases as these there is little sense of the intimacy
of religion, and the step from earnestness to hypocrisy
becomes a not very wide one. Moreover, it follows
that the Italians are far less self-conscious in their
religious duties than we are—and this is a noticeable
trait with almost all Continental Catholics. Butler
has somewhere noted that unshakable faith and
unselfconsciousness were also characteristics of his
grandfather, Bishop Butler.

The Italian priests could not help being a little suspicious of English people—they knew so well their tract-
distributing habits. Butler, no doubt, would remark

mildly that this was no hobby of his. And indeed, misbehaving in this way in other people's countries always annoyed him. As soon as an earnest-minded Englishman or Englishwoman appeared, good-bye to peace and quiet. They possessed to a supreme degree the gift of making themselves unpleasant. The Italian priests, when they saw such people tampering with the faith of their flock, could not look at them so disinterestedly as Butler; their one object was to get rid of them as soon as possible.

In other things, too, there were evidences of this carping unimaginative temper, as when an earnest Englishman pretended to be scandalised because the eyes of a figure of St Francis outside a church door were turned ecstatically towards an insurance plate which had been let into the sky precisely at the point towards which he was gazing. The Englishman soon got the plate removed. And the episode gives Butler an opportunity for deriding " earnestness," " intenseness," " æstheticism " and " culture "—all those things we are in danger of carrying about with us as we carry our luggage.

A large proportion of *Alps and Sanctuaries*, as we have seen, is devoted to the Alpine chapels and to the character of the Italians as it showed itself in their religion. But the book also abounds in humorous anecdotes, and the personal opinions of the author are continually peeping out in amusing asides suggested by a chance context. Italy was Butler's hobby and his holiday; he was in a country—his " second country," he called it—that he loved, among people who never failed to interest him. And then there were the sanctuaries themselves, a further recreation when he wished to get away from people altogether. He knew what appealed to him in Italian landscape, and frequently he quotes something from Handel which he considered appropriate, to illustrate his feelings about it. In the chapter on Piora, which should be read in conjunction with the passage about living under grace which we have already quoted from *Life and Habit*, he introduced " Venus laughing from the skies " as expressing precisely what he felt. This chapter stands out rather remarkably from the rest of Butler's work because by its very manner it is doubtless intended to convey a romantic and mysterious quality in the moonlight scene he is describing; and the dream that follows, in which Handel, " smiling and pluming himself like a bird," sits at the great organ thundering forth a giant fugue, is admirable in its realistic detail. Butler knew exactly what he could do with detail without destroying the broad effect of his picture. There are many other memorable passages in the book, as the dissertation on lying, which proves quite conclusively that there is no justification in Nature against telling lies, since the lower animals and even the innocent flowers themselves are many of them habitual liars; we cannot think that God is angry with them because of it—we know definitely He was quite agreeable that the lying spirit should go forth from heaven to breathe lying prophecies into the hearts of Ahab's prophets. *Alps and Sanctuaries* contains also the amusing description of the religious festivities at Locarno, which again shows the sensible attitude of the Italians and of the high dignitaries of their Church on these occasions. We see in this Butler's love of the comic and the beautiful in one setting; he liked to have the

illuminated effigies of Madonnas, saints and angels in
an *ensemble* with advertisements of Richmond Gem
cigarettes and Wheeler & Wilson's sewing machines,
just as he confessed that he would like a picture of the
Holy Family with the Monday wash hanging in the
background. Because the Italians found no incongruity in such things, he felt that their religion was
strong and healthy within them. Those who are never
submitted to tests like these are unaware of their own
weakness or their strength. In the same way Butler
approved of the days when the spiritual saturnalia
was in vogue, for we cannot always or often be religious all through without any alloy of worldly temptations ; and he described appreciatively the feasts at
Graglia because there was so much of the pagan element
in them. Handel and Milton were often pagan enough,
though no one was ever sceptical about their religious
convictions. " The attitude assumed by these men,
and by the better class of Romanists, seems to have
become impossible to Protestants since the time of
Dr Arnold." This is no doubt true ; and the reason of
it is that in religious matters people are little ready to
admit that " blessed inconsistency " which everywhere
else plays such an important part. Religious theory, of
course, is never consistent with worldly practice ;
what Butler wished for was a greater humanity within
the structure of religion itself : it must have a place
for the comic as well as the beautiful, for the grotesque
no less than for the ordinary, for the human equally
with the divine. Butler, who was a humorist, felt the
uselessness of those hard and fast lines with which we
endeavour to mark one subject off from another. Just
as the frontiers between religion and philosophy are

M

vague and ill defined, so in religion itself it is impossible to say that there is a definite water-tight compartment which exists without any reference to what is going on outside it. But this is what we try to do. There is plenty of room for more religious give and take, in fact; when we are dull and cannot forget ourselves, are unimaginative and conscious—like the conscious English ritualist who goes dissipating from one high church to another—we can apply Butler's standard and soon discover that there is no grace in us.

Alps and Sanctuaries, on its first appearance, as might be expected, found most favour from the Roman Catholic newspapers; the author's sympathetic attitude to the Italians was warmly appreciated, and one prominent Catholic periodical went so far as to describe it as " a book that Wordsworth would have gloated over with delight." The less said about Wordsworth perhaps the better, where Butler was concerned, having regard to his remarks about the poet in the essay, " Quis Desiderio . . .? " Mr Streatfeild is disposed to connect a good deal that Butler wrote in *Alps and Sanctuaries* with the chapter " Rome and Pantheism," in *Evolution Old and New,* in which there are some suggestions as to a *rapprochement* between Rome and the particular section of the English Church to which he belonged. It is true that at this time Butler was as dissatisfied with Protestantism as he was disgusted with English so-called scientists, but he never really felt at home with the Romanists, as Mr Streatfeild afterwards adds. To have found himself on too intimate terms with the Roman Catholics would have been an excessive break with the past ; it would have involved a step that was insufficiently

led up to by anything that had gone before it, and one
which seemed little likely to be justified by anything
that was to come after. The whole notion of identifying Butler with the Romanists in any serious sense may
sound absurd—yet not too absurd. For it is no doubt
true of faiths as of ideas : either " can be changed to
almost any extent in almost any direction, if the
change is brought about gradually and in accordance
with the rules of all development." This was pre-
eminently Butler's view of change. The forward man,
the innovator must not be too far in front of other
people, otherwise he will be entirely isolated from
them ; there will be no connecting links by which to
attach himself to those he would lead after him. And
so it is when we contemplate any change for ourselves
—we must not make too violent a discord with our
own past. As in music, every discord, to be pleasing
in its effects, must be prepared beforehand and resolved
afterwards. And if a discord is too violent our power
of assimilation must inevitably fail. And this, after
all, was the case with the advanced wing of the Broad
Church party to which Butler belonged, and the
Roman Catholic Church ; the gulf between them was
too wide for any reasonable settlement. Butler,
among the Roman Catholics, would have been an
inconsistency greater than he could bear, in spite of a
good deal that he admired in their religion, in spite of
their common-sense, their love of beauty and the useful
everyday feeling about many of their beliefs and
practices.

Alps and Sanctuaries, after all, is not a book to be
read about, but a book to be read. It is an intimate
causerie, in which the writer discourses freely on very

many of the subjects that interest him most; after considerable difficulty we have selected for quotation the following brief and vivid description of a *festa* on the Sacro Monte at Varese—to which reference has already been made—as containing in a small compass the spirit of the whole book. Butler understood people in a crowd; and he liked to see a crowd enjoying itself.

" The processions," he says, " were best at the last part of the ascent; there were pilgrims, all decked out with coloured feathers, and priests and banners and music and crimson and gold and white and glittering brass against the cloudless blue sky. The old priest sat at his open window to receive the offerings of the devout as they passed; but he did not seem to get more than a few *bambini* modelled in wax. Perhaps he was used to it. And the band played the *barocco* music on the *barocco* little piazza and we were all *barocco* together. It was as though the clergyman at Ladywell had given out that, instead of having service as usual, the congregation would go in procession to the Crystal Palace with all their traps, and that the band had been practising ' Wait till the clouds roll by ' for some time, and on Sunday as a great treat they should have it.

" . . . I would as soon take an English bishop to the Surrey pantomime as to the Sacro Monte on a *festa*.

" Then the pilgrims went into the shadow of a great rock behind the sanctuary, spread themselves out over the grass and dined."

There is a further side to Butler's love of Italy beyond the interest he took in the people and the sanctuaries, the picturesque *albergi*, and the way in which this holiday country stimulated him to his

happiest flights in thought and imagination. In
addition to these things he liked to meet his own
countrymen, to notice what they did, to study them
away from the securities of their ordinary surroundings.
It was all part of the concentrated interest in England
and English people which had come over him after his
return from New Zealand. When he got away to Italy
he certainly left England behind, but not entirely the
English people, whom he was thus often able to
observe in a new light, or perhaps a new setting, as
they perambulated through the peninsula to see
the cathedrals, enjoy the views and miss none of the
important sights. So Butler often came across these
men and women high and dry on a new ground, as it
were isolated, like chemical substances, for purposes
of observation.

But in all his encounters it was the English bishop
who afforded him the keenest delight. He might
himself so easily have been a bishop if the unfortunate
question of infant baptism had not stood in his way.
Bishops fascinated him. In the *Notebooks* there are
frequent references to them—with " Handel " and
" God " they form one of the first noticeable features
of the index. About bishops, at any rate, there is a
professional air. They have as a rule lost the callow,
amateurish qualities belonging to an earlier stage of
their development ; there is a ripe deliberation in their
movements and actions ; even out of their own country
they are authoritative and important, a little dogmatic.
Sometimes Butler saw that they looked cross, like the
one he met at Siena who went into the cathedral with
his daughter or niece, where he observed them " kneeling bolt upright from the knees " on the bare floor.

This particular bishop did not like being looked at, and was anxious to avoid Butler altogether. On another occasion—this also was in Italy, at Faido—he got on very well with an English bishop until the latter, apropos some words of his, said : " That is a very striking remark," and seemed little inclined to continue the conversation.

Often the people he met in Italy knew who he was. It amused him to see the kind of attitude they would adopt towards him, not because he was conscious of himself as in any way " queer," or as holding all sorts of subversive opinions with which they might radically disagree, but because he had laughed at certain types of English people often enough in his books, and was interested to know how they felt about it. He does not appear to have met any of those who spent their time in distributing religious tracts. Apart from these people, he generally knew pretty quickly whether he could get on with an Englishman or not—certainly he knew in the case of an Italian priest, and the Italian priest knew no less promptly. " I am no sooner in a diligence or railway carriage with an unsympathetic priest, than he curls himself round into a moral ball and prays horribly—bristling out with collects all over like a cross-grained spiritual hedgehog." No English bishop, or layman for that matter, could show his disapproval so unmistakably as this spectacle of outraged sympathies.

Butler contemplated a sequel to *Alps and Sanctuaries,* but it was never made. He left, however, a good deal of material for the proposed book, from which we have gathered some of the foregoing. There is a long note called " Sunday Morning at Soglio," which is a

sort of scenic and human panorama of the place. It
shows, as well as anything we know, how much Butler
could extract from an apparently commonplace picture.
The description is alive with sound and colour and
movement and children and grown-up people. And
Silvio was there, the small boy of ten or twelve who
could repeat " How doth the little buzzy bee," and
liked *Uncle Tom's Cabin*, was interested in Darwin,
and had taught all the boys in Soglio to be noisy.
" And presently the Devil came up to me. He was a
nice, clean old man, but he dropped his h's, and that
was where he spoiled himself—or perhaps it was just
this that threw me off my guard, for I had always heard
that the Prince of Darkness was a perfect gentleman.
He whispered to me that in the winter the monks of
St Bernard sometimes say matins over night."

This living piece of description, which in miniature
is what Butler looked for and found all over Italy, is a
sample of the second *Alps and Sanctuaries*, which, unfortunately, was never completed. It shows also his
method of work, how the notes and thoughts that he
captured, the things he heard and saw, were woven
into the texture of what he wrote. When the details
of a scene were set down in this way they formed a
background for his thoughts and might at any time be
worked up into another picture with all sorts of new
things inserted which suggested themselves to him
later. His conversation with Silvio, for instance, was
secured as a permanent possession partly because the
precocious Italian child was so lovable, partly because
what he said appealed intimately to him. And more
than all this, he possessed the magic secret of reproducing for his readers at times the thrill, at others

the quiet, peaceful flavour—but always the reality—
of what he saw. His writing is thus an admirable
instance of the impossibility of separating matter and
treatment without impairing the whole effect. That
is where people who write about " style " as an ideal
in itself mistake the whole business of writing. " Le
style c'est l'homme," wrote Buffon. But by style he
meant much more than the outward trappings in
which a man clothes his thoughts—he meant, as he says,
the whole man. When people set out laboriously to
acquire a " style "—by which they mean a way of
saying something—without first taking thought about
what they have to say, we may be sure that there is
little health in them. They are like the young man
from the Midlands we heard of recently, who went to
Oxford to learn to write poetry.

The second of Butler's Italian books, *Ex Voto : an
Account of the Sacro Monte or New Jerusalem at Varallo
Sesia*, is largely concerned with the work of Tabachetti
and the other artists who did the paintings and
sculpture on the Sacro Monte. In August 1887, says
Mr Jones, the people of Varallo gave Butler a civic
dinner on the mountain—before this he had been well
known to the townspeople, having frequently visited
the sanctuary. After being thus entertained by the
Municipio—" an honour far greater than any I
have ever received among those who know me better,
and are probably better judges of my deserts "—
he decided that he must write his book about the
Sacro Monte chapels as he had promised in *Alps and
Sanctuaries*.

One of the earliest writers on Varallo, from whom
Butler made frequent quotation, was a certain Canon

Torotti (*c.* 1686). He gives many sprightly descriptions of the life of the place, and speaks of the spirit of "holy cheerfulness" (*allegria spirituale*) that pervades it.

"Assuredly," he adds, "it is one of the wonders of the world to see here, amid the amenities and allurements of the country, especially during the summer season, what a continuous *festa* or holy fair is maintained. For there come and go torrents of men and women of every nation under heaven. Here you shall see pilgrims and persons in religion of every description, processions, prelates, and often princes and princesses, carriages, litters, calêches, equipages, cavalcades accompanied by trumpeters, gay troops of cavaliers, and ladies with plumes in their hats and rich apparel wherewithal to make themselves attractive ; and at intervals you shall hear all manner of songs, concerts, and musical instruments, both civil and military, all done with a modest and devout cheerfulness of demeanour, by which I am reminded of nothing so strongly as the words of the Psalmist in the which he saith ' Come and see the works of the Lord, for He hath done wonders upon earth.' "

We have already spoken of the realism of the painted statuary in the Italian sanctuaries ; and for a proper appreciation of what the artists aimed at we must try and realise the spirit in which they worked. It may be said of Tabachetti that he was too downright, making the greatest contrast, for instance, with Michelangelo's over - subtlety and refinement. But it must be remembered that the realism he practised was a mediæval realism, with which we cannot help feeling somewhat out of touch, for " ages thwart and play at cross purposes with one another, as parents do with children." An analogy with the work of the Sacro Monte artists might be made to-day if living sculptors could be persuaded to deal with the sacred subjects in a modern spirit, keeping closely to our present-day costumes.

There is a further point, says Butler, in regard to these artists which should not pass by unnoticed. It must not be expected that at first, after the mediæval revival of art, they worked with anything else than extreme difficulty. Realism, therefore, was as much as they could manage ; and their work gained to a corresponding extent because they were not over-weighted with too much " knowledge." An excessive facility, in art as in everything else, is dangerous ; it carries a man too far beyond himself, it directs his attention overmuch to the technique of his craft rather than to the spirit trying to manifest itself by means of it. It was for these reasons, or something like them, that Butler objected to Michelangelo. His paintings of religious subjects were conscious and deliberate utterances. He had no eye for everyday things. But the work of Gaudenzio Ferrari and Tabachetti is in striking contrast with Italian idealism in art. They only worked with great trouble, " treating nature as though she were a stuffed set piece, getting her to sit as still for as long a time as she could be persuaded to do, and then going all over her touch for touch with a brush like the point of a pin." And so incompetence often has a certain charm of its own, which is looked for in vain in the pretentious work of artists who have become fashionable and prosperous. If Butler found that an artist had plenty of life and go in him, was taking proper pains, and did not know too much, he was satisfied.

Further, the plastic art in the Sacro Monte chapels is based on a convention. It is artificial just in the same way that the stage is artificial. The dramatic scenes are intensified in order that their effect may be felt more vividly across the footlights. Thus, in a sense, the realism of the work is tempered by a vague melodramatic spirit, of the stage, stagey, which pleased the people much in the same way that exaggerated villains and caricatured sweetness and innocence please us in the theatre to-day. Besides all this none of the chapels has anything like the same freshness and splendour of decoration with which it left the hand of the artist. So imagination is required in viewing the sanctuaries if we are to form any adequate conception of what they once were.

Butler's imagination was always alert in more senses than one as he went through the Sacro Monte chapels. He looked out eagerly for anything that reminded him of what he had written in the past. Thus, while describing the chapel of " The Crowning with Thorns " he relates amusingly an old legend which was current in Varallo. A Flemish dancer was said to have been healed in this chapel. One night a ball was going on at the house of one of his ancestors, and at the same time the Sacrament was being carried through the street under the window. The host refused to stop the dancing, and by-and-by a message was discovered by the priest under the chalice, sent, no doubt, by the Madonna, to the effect that the dancer was cursed because he would not stay his dancing. Therefore shalt thou " dance for nine generations." And so it actually happened. He and his descendants went on dancing until the ninth in descent was cured of his embarrassing infirmity. The story interested Butler because it reminded him of, and supported, his theory of personal identity between parent and offspring set out in *Life and Habit*, " Thou shalt dance for nine generations " was exactly as he himself would have put it.

On the whole Butler's descriptions of the statuary at Varallo lean less towards the diction of the Mrs Beeton school than many of the other descriptions—the essay on " The Sanctuary of Montrigone," for instance. And the reason for this, no doubt, was that there is less humour in the subjects themselves which are represented there. He never felt any kind of irreverence in any of the sanctuaries, only a certain homeliness, and lightness of treatment. In what he wrote, therefore, he tried to preserve the spirit in which they were originally made—just as Tottenham Court Road English was the most suitable medium for preserving the spirit of Homer. *Ex Voto*, however, has its humour too ; in the Presentation chapel at Crea he was a good deal struck with the diminutive size of the Virgin— she was scarcely more than two feet six. " The Chief Priest is holding up his hands, and seems a good deal surprised, as though he were saying : ' Well, my dear, I must say you are the very smallest Virgin that I ever had presented to me during the whole course of my incumbency.' Joachim and St Anne seem very much distressed, and Joachim appears to be saying, ' It is not our fault ; I assure you, sir, we have done everything in our power. She has had plenty of nourishment.' " This is a more or less typical example of his method of describing the Italian shrines ; and although there may often be some exaggeration of certain elements in them, such treatment lends at any rate a distinctive colour. He found that subjects which were treated usually with so little affectation, with such competent disregard of academism and everything pertaining to it, could be dealt with most satisfactorily in this spirit. Besides, it never would have occurred to him to do it in any other way. Butler felt very strongly that the achievements of these artists ought to be commemorated. His research was most diligent and painstaking, especially in the case of Tabachetti, whom he succeeded in identifying with the Flemish artist, Jean de Wespin. Dinant had to be visited in order to establish this fact, but it was only done after the publication of *Ex Voto*.

It was not without reason that Butler inscribed on the title-page of his book the words of L'Abbé Mabillon (1698) : " If n'y a que deux ennemis de la religion—le trop peu, et le trop ; et des deux le trop est mille fois le plus dangereux." So *Ex Voto* closes on one of the keynotes of Butler's religious convictions—it is the spirit and not the letter which must be insisted on. And Butler saw that as the " good churchmen " of Varallo were abandoning their story of the Flemish dancer and superstitions generally, so at home the bishops were discarding all sorts of beliefs, which hitherto were considered as integral items of Christian faith. He warns his readers, however, to beware of the new faith—science, in short—which is manifesting itself with more " Lo heres " and " Lo theres."

The same note, in fact, is struck at the conclusion of *Ex Voto* as at the conclusion of *Erewhon Revisited*.

Butler had now finished all his scientific books, but he felt so strongly the value of the position he was defending that he could not help continually referring to it. He lived, after all, a lonely life, and consequently the only way of making himself heard was by an insistence on the same theme, although he was well aware that his generation took little notice of what he said. But the importance of that theme was certainly a justification for any repetition of argument.

Ex Voto, with certain shorter essays on the Valley of Saas, Montrigone and the Girl School at Oropa, mentioned already, marks the end of Butler's Italian writings. Viewed as a whole, the Italian books, in their range of interest, their humorous freshness and the diversity of subjects and characters with which they deal, are completely unlike anything else in English. Only a man with the deepest human sympathies could have written *Alps and Sanctuaries*; and *Ex Voto*, less wide in its appeal, is the book of an enthusiast off the beaten track of art never knowing for a moment what he may find there. Necessarily, we gather from these two volumes a good deal of Butler's opinions about art, but some fuller consideration of this must be left for a later chapter.

Anyone who reads the introduction to *Alps and Sanctuaries*, and this introduction might well serve as a model of clear straightforward writing unsurpassed in any modern prose, must realise the zest and energy with which Butler entered on his travels and discoveries. Those who are approaching Butler for the first time would do well to begin with this piece, which is a complete expression of himself. Apart from the remarks on London which Butler loved for its life and

movement, and the feeling of mystery about it that
forbids one ever knowing it altogether, there is a concluding passage in which we have a momentary glimpse
of the writer in his week-end holiday mood at home,
as he walks within a thirty-mile radius of Charing
Cross through the villages of Kent, Surrey or Sussex.
From the *Notebooks* we have several records of meetings in these English by-ways. He encountered many
Mrs Quicklys and not a few other worthies of a
distinctively English flavour. And they were generally as communicative as the people he used to meet
in Italy—sometimes embarrassingly so with details of
intimate ailments or family history. They always
liked Butler, and he never forgot them from one year's
end to another, just as he never forgot his Italian
friends.

Thus, although he wrote so much about Italy, and
although he spoke, in the very last lines of *Alps and
Sanctuaries*, of "the science-ridden, art-ridden, culture-
ridden, afternoon-tea-ridden cliffs of old England" he
had the warmest possible place for her in his heart.
He himself was utterly English in his sympathies and
instincts. Had it been otherwise he could never have
written about Italy as he did.

CHAPTER VI

HOMER AND NAUSICAA

At one of the recent Erewhon dinners, held in memory of Samuel Butler, a speaker described himself as puzzled that a man with Butler's sense of humour should think the *Odyssey* written by a woman. Was he serious about it ? Mr Jones said that he was quite serious, and went on to explain how he first turned his attention to Homeric questions. After he and Butler had written the Handelian Cantata *Narcissus*, Butler wished it to have a musical successor also in the Handelian manner. He happened one day to read something about the *Odyssey*, which suggested that the poem might be a good subject for the new oratorio, which Jones and Butler began to write as a collaborate work. The oratorio was called *Ulysses*, and while doing it Butler thought it just as well to look at the original poem to make sure they were not being led astray. He did this, and became so fascinated with the *Odyssey* that he was unable to leave it. His translations of the *Iliad* and *Odyssey*, the lecture on Homer, and finally his book, *The Authoress of the Odyssey*, were the results of the fresh and delighted interest with which he came back to Homer.

In his lecture on " The Humour of Homer " Butler describes the *Iliad* as a divine comedy of gods and men. It was characteristic of Homer, also, that he made his gods entirely in the likeness of men. They are subject

to the same emotions; they feel, only more intensely,
the same passions of love, hatred and jealousy. For
the most part they are a virtueless galaxy of loud-
voiced, squabbling men and women, lazy and promiscuous in their domestic and family relations—and
humorous in their conversation and behaviour. Butler
gives several quotations from the *Iliad* to show the
shrewd and humorous point of view of its author.
But it is difficult to suggest any figure in the poem in
which the writer reveals himself; Butler conjectures,
however, that in Astyanax, Hector's infant son, he is
showing what his own position was. Probably the
author of the *Iliad* was a Trojan, forced to extol the
virtues of his captors, and consequently there is an
undercurrent of irony in what he wrote; those who
were aware of the real sympathies of the writer would
be able to understand the true meaning of it.

Butler seems to have been greatly amused by the
behaviour of the gods and goddesses in the *Iliad*; their
frankly pagan and anthropomorphic habits appealed
to him. And he had no doubt that such a conception
of the heavenly beings could only have been formed
by a genuinely astute and humorous writer who was
intrigued by the comic elements in everyday life and
so adapted them skilfully to his Olympians. A good
deal of this humorous spirit is due to Homer's attitude
towards women—the divine no less than the human.
Woman as a rule is "drawn as teasing, scolding,
thwarting, contradicting, and hoodwinking the sex
that has the effrontery to deem itself her lord and
master"; and many of the most pleasing effects of
the poem are the descriptions of the odd behaviour
Jove had to put up with from his female relations.

N

He was a kindly father, however, as Butler was fully aware, and in the mêlée towards the end of the *Iliad*, when the gods quarrel bitterly among themselves, Jove acted with becoming dignity. Here is Butler's version :

" Then Latona picks up poor Diana's bow and arrows that have fallen from her during her encounter with Juno, and Diana meanwhile flies up to the knees of her father Jove, sobbing and sighing till her ambrosial robe trembles all around her.

" Jove drew her towards him, and smiling pleasantly, exclaimed : ' My dear child, which of the heavenly beings has been wicked enough to behave in this way to you, as though you had been doing something naughty ? '

" ' Your wife, Juno,' answered Diana, ' has been ill-treating me ; all our quarrels always begin with her.' "

Even more important, however, than his showing some of the Homeric episodes in a more human and truer light, was Butler's conviction that the *Iliad* was entirely the work of a single poet. The importance of this decision will become clearer immediately, when we consider Butler's theory of the origin and authorship of the *Odyssey*. It is sufficient to say that he found in each of the poems a unity of design and purpose which forbade the notion that they were created by large numbers of different poets, and pieced together by various hands at various times.

It may be objected to Butler's remarks on the *Iliad* that just as Homer created his gods and goddesses after his likeness, so has Butler set up the image of a Homer who takes on the lineaments of his own alert and humorous mind and becomes, under his hand, a Butlerian Homer of the most unmistakable quality ;

that Butler's Homer, in fact, is simply a product of
his own imagination. It might be objected, also, that
Butler's habit of seeing people and situations created
by older writers and his instinct to see the writers
themselves, in terms of the life of to-day—Miranda
was an up-to-date young woman, very much all there,
Homer a humorist after his own heart, the authoress
of the *Odyssey* a fascinating, brilliant girl whose conduct
was just what we should expect from one of her kind
nowadays—it might be said that his instinct in these
matters was that of the parodist. We remember very
well hearing a Professor of English Literature who in
his lectures was in the habit of rewriting Hamlet's
Soliloquy in modern journalese or the " English " of
Miss Marie Corelli. This was pure parody. And
perhaps such a system had its uses. Butler's mind,
however, was not the mind of the parodist. In all his
dealings with writers long ago dead his purpose was
perfectly serious and legitimate. He wanted to rescue
them from the clutches of a blighting academism ; for
he knew that the terriblest thing Homer, a vital and
living artist, has to fight against is the fact that his
work has been a school book for over two thousand five
hundred years—and the same is true of the authoress
of the *Odyssey*. And after all, Homer was only a
literary man, though far beyond most of the re-
presentatives of the class to which he belonged—but
still a literary man. Butler thought of him in this way,
not to cast any aspersions on his poem, but in order to
bring him, if possible, into the light of day and make
him more real to himself and other people. And he
did this, not by parodying and ridiculing, nor for that
purpose, but by concentrating his wit and attention

upon him and what he wrote. Butler's view of Homer, too, was remarkably his own view ; he wanted to get to know as much about him as possible, for, as Mr Jones says, " it was always the author, the work of God, that interested him more than the book—the work of man." If, incidentally, his conception of Homer appealed to other people, and thus in any way helped to bring his poem out of the rut in which lies the work of very many dead poets and " classical " authors, so much the better. In laying stress on the humorous side of Homer's personality, he was indicating something that found a response in himself. " If a writer, a painter or a musician," as he somewhere wrote, " makes me feel that he held those things to be lovable which I myself hold to be lovable, I am satisfied." To Butler the humour of Homer was entirely lovable and, also, entirely comprehensible. Nor did the presence of this human quality in any way detract from the dignity or value of his work, however much the generation of Mr Darwin and Mr Tennyson might think to the contrary.

The translations of the *Iliad* and *Odyssey* that Butler made are in accordance with the opinions about them which we have tried to reproduce above. It is difficult enough at any time to make a writer speak in a language other than his own, to convey his meaning from one *tempo* to another, and to obliterate that sense of lesion which belongs necessarily to the process. Even with contemporary writers, who may be expected to deal with things that are " in the air," with ideas that are recognisably of their own epoch, even with them there are difficulties in translation not to be overcome lightly. How much more thickly, then, do not such problems crowd in when we are concerned, not with the present

age, but with a civilisation of the far past in a country
differing widely from our own? Butler was quite
alive to these difficulties in his translations, and he felt
them more particularly in respect of the *Odyssey*
because of the peculiar conditions under which that
poem was written, and also because of the sex and age
of the author. There is a passage in the *Notebooks*
which throws some light on this. After showing that
the difference between his translation and that of
Andrew Lang is the difference between making a baby
and a mummy, for the only way to keep alive the
spirit of an author long dead is to " eat him, digest him
and let him live in you, with such life as you have, for
better or worse," he adds: "They say no woman
could possibly have written the *Odyssey*. To me, on
the other hand, it seems even less possible that a man
could have done so. As for its being by a practised
and elderly writer, nothing but youth and inexperience
could produce anything so naïve and so lovely. That
is where the work will suffer by my translation. If
the poem is ever to be well translated, it must be by
some high-spirited English girl who has been brought
up at Athens and who, therefore, has not been jaded
by academic study of the language." This note shows
very well what Butler aimed at as a translator. His
version of the *Odyssey* was made in Tottenham Court
Road English as a protest against the Wardour
Streetisms of Messrs Butcher, Lang & Co., and because
he felt that that was the right treatment for a poem
so entirely free from affectation. We must, at least,
so admit this spirit of youth and straightforwardness,
even if we are not intrigued by Butler's theory of the
female authorship of the *Odyssey*.

In the lecture on " The Humour of Homer " there is a rough contrast between the two poems, where Butler notes that " The scepticism of the *Iliad* is that of Hume or Gibbon ; that of the *Odyssey* (if any) is like the occasional mild irreverence of the Vicar's daughter." He asks us also to observe the difference between the Minerva of the *Iliad* and Minerva the perfect lady of the *Odyssey*. Again the amazing ignorance of the author of the latter poem on certain practical questions, becomes clear where nautical or farming matters or sport are concerned. It is not without significance that ships are described as having a rudder at both ends, that a lamb is considered to be able to live on two pulls a day from a ewe already milked, and that the games at the house of King Alcinous in Ulysses' honour take place immediately after a heavy meal. Such were the kind of details which arrested Butler's attention ; but they did so only after a great deal of puzzling over the fundamental differences—in spirit and atmosphere and that mystery of personality which every great writer throws around his or her work— between the two poems. Even as a schoolboy Butler was aware of these differences, when he used to say that the *Odyssey* was the *Iliad's* wife and was written by a clergyman.

Butler developed his case with great clearness in his book, *The Authoress of the Odyssey: where and when she wrote, who she was, the use she made of the Iliad and how the poem grew under her hands,* which was published in 1897. In the Preface to the book he points out that though his Odyssean theories have been before the public for six years no criticisms deserving serious answer have reached him on the subject. His aim was not to *épater* anyone, but rather to get to know as much as he could about the poem in question and hence, as a necessary corollary, about its author. During the years he was meditating over the authorship and origin of the poem he had also been engaged on the Life of his grandfather, Dr Butler, headmaster of Shrewsbury School and Bishop of Lichfield, which appeared in two thick volumes in 1896. The more that Butler knew about his grandfather the more was he delighted with the honesty of his convictions, his common-sense, and the practical man-of-the-world knowledge he displayed in discharging his everyday duties. In a letter written to a friend at Cambridge about this time Butler shows this respect for his grandfather and for his grandfather's open-mindedness :

" My translations of the *Iliad* and *Odyssey* are long since completed," he says, " but I can get no publisher to take them. My book upon the *Odyssey* will, I hope, be finished in another three weeks or so, and come what may I shall publish it. I really believe myself to have been duly cautious throughout my arguments. I wish poor old Dr Butler were alive. He would have listened to what I have to say with some attention."

Dr Butler, as far as we can gather, was of the opinion that the *Iliad* was the work of one man ; about the *Odyssey* he was doubtful. Butler, in the Life of his grandfather, comments thus on his opinions : " The *Odyssey* does not appear to have been read at Shrewsbury, and I question whether Dr Butler knew it anything like so thoroughly as the *Iliad* ; he does not seem to have even suspected the Sicilian origin of the poem. How can a headmaster, who has to give boys a bird's-eye view of all Latin and Greek literature, afford time for the close study of a poem so fatally easy as the *Odyssey* generally is ? It is not paradoxical to say that if the *Odyssey* had been harder to understand it would have been sooner understood." Thus Butler got little material support from his grandfather which might have helped his Odyssean theories along ; but he was convinced that if ever those theories had been put before him he would have considered and made up his mind about them, which was more than could be said of the classical scholars of his own day whom Butler confronted and from whom he could get no answer. And here again we may repeat that over these Odyssean questions we cannot doubt Butler's seriousness. Any-one who reads *The Authoress of the Odyssey*, in which he shows certain facts, curious and often incompatible, and pursues them with all the will and purpose that was in him to reach explanations which shall cover them, must recognise his sincerity. It may be, of course, that the main theory took its start in a jesting, paradoxical spirit. But when its originator came to examine it, to test it point by point, to turn it round and round in order to view it as a whole as well as in its parts, he was no longer—if indeed he had ever been —doubtful about it, or amusing himself at its expense. We have no business to conclude, *prima facie*, that because Butler wrote *Erewhon* he could be serious about nothing either in heaven or earth, or in things present or of the past. It is always dangerous to come to conclusions about any man which place him in a simple well-defined category. It is impossible in real life to answer directly the child's question : " Is he a good man or is he a bad man ? " though you may be able to do it in respect of Dickens' characters. So

with Butler it is impossible to find his writing at times
entirely serious in manner, at other times not serious—
either wholly serious or wholly humorous. If, argued
the critics, he genuinely believed that Nausicaa wrote
the *Odyssey*, and that its origin was Sicilian, he should
have written about it in quite a different tone—the
tone, for instance, that we use when putting forward
our discoveries or speculations. But to demonstrate
the changed nature of the Homeric gods by saying that
in the *Odyssey* they no longer live in houses or sleep
in four-poster beds—he had already made Homer's
goddesses in the *Iliad* into little else than angry house-
maids—to ridicule the would-be love story of the
Odyssey by referring to Ulysses as a bald, elderly gentleman with a little red hair, and to Penelope, his supposed
widow, who was no better than she should be, as not
a day under forty, outraged their sense of propriety.
They disliked the incongruities of the poem being
illuminated by a humorous presentation. That was a
new incongruity they were unable to tolerate. So the
Homeric scholars and writers met Butler's theories in
silence. They thought, like Mr Romanes, although
unlike him they did not explicitly say so, that when
Butler "aimed only at entertaining" his readers, as he
did in *Erewhon*, he was in his proper place; but they
resented his entertaining—as they considered it—
those readers on their ground, just as Mr Romanes
resented his writing a book like *Life and Habit* and
pretended to believe that that book was written for
amusement only and without the least serious intention in the world. We must not, then, take Butler's
complaint against the neglect of the critics too much
in the letter. He knew from the first how utterly

unacceptable his opinions would be and that his manner of presenting them must be even more unpalatable. But all the same he was delighted with the rounded completeness of his theory—and all the more delighted because he firmly believed in it.

What, probably, put Butler on the track of his discoveries more than anything else was the remark of Bentley that the *Iliad* was written for men, and the *Odyssey* for women. After this lead Butler goes on to show how with great reluctance he came to his opinion about the authorship of the poem ; how he tried to shake that opinion off, but it stuck to him and refused to be driven away. So he had to settle down with it as best he could. It is easy to see the inference that rose naturally out of Bentley's statement ; since the *Odyssey* was written for women and deals with subjects more interesting to women than to men ; since men are frequently put into ridiculous positions, women never ; since, also, there is throughout *a naïveté* in dealing with certain subjects which contrasts strongly with the feminine knowledge displayed in dealing with others ; since, lastly, there is a tendency to minimise the wrong-doings of the female sex, and even to whitewash it altogether in certain cases—although one would have thought the writer must have been aware of the futility of such a proceeding—for these and other numerous reasons Butler came to the conclusion that the *Odyssey* must have been written by a woman, and identified her with the charming Princess Nausicaa, who suddenly introduces herself in Book VI.

She was no ordinary woman, of course, as he was quite well aware. Her swift boldness and genuine cavalier spirit in attacking some situations told Butler

that she was young and ardent; he concluded further
that she was fascinating and brilliant, unmarried and a
man-hatress. But the fact of her being rather of the blue-
stocking variety did not prevent her youth and ingenuous
charm from peeping out on every page. And when she
introduces herself so discreetly in Book VI., "perhaps
the loveliest in the whole poem," we become more and
more aware of the delicate fineness of the personality
that has made itself felt in the preceding books.

It was no half image that Butler had formed of his
authoress. He had made up his mind where she lived
and why she wrote her poem. Nausicaa was a native
of Trapani on the Sicilian coast, near Marsala.
"Fancy," says Butler, "what the position of a young,
ardent, brilliant woman must have been in a small
Sicilian seaport, say some eight or nine hundred years
before the birth of Christ. It makes one shudder to
think of it. Night after night she hears the dreary
blind old bard Demodocus drawl out his interminable
recitals taken from our present *Iliad*, or from some
other of the many poems now lost that dealt with the
adventures of the Greeks before Troy or on their home-
ward journey. Man and his doings! always the same
old story, and woman always to be treated either as a
toy or as a beast of burden, or at any rate as an
incubus. Why not sing of woman also as she is when
she is unattached and free from the trammels and
persecutions of this tiresome tyrant, this insufferably
self-conceited bore and booby, man?"

Here, then, is a picture of the daughter of Queen
Arete and King Alcinous in the days before the
Odyssey was written. It was boredom and a wish to
make people aware of the importance of her own sex

that caused her to write it. She belonged essentially to the *Intelligentsia* of her own day. But she never allowed mere cleverness to outweigh her human instincts. Her slightly malicious spirit, her mischievous remarks, her indefinable " baffled fury " are always directed against man. She caricatures him admirably as only a woman can do ; though her interests are mainly with her own sex, with Penelope and Helen, who is Menelaus' master, and the goddesses Calypso and Circe. And then there is Minerva no longer the militant woman of the *Iliad* but a wise and dignified adviser whom the authoress adopts as her patron. At times, moreover, there is in Nausicaa's writing all the fierceness of a very young woman who feels intensely and is carried away by her enthusiasm. So she strode buoyantly through all the limitations imposed by her youth, and her work gains immeasurably in charm and freshness for that very reason.

Such a personality as he conceived Nausicaa to be appealed immensely to Butler. Youth always attracted him. It is only those who are young and unselfconscious who can abandon themselves to the work they are doing, oblivious alike of their defects and their excellences. So it was with the authoress of the *Odyssey*—the princess whom Butler rescued in fairytale fashion from the depths of academic dullness. She pleased him no less for the limitations than for the splendid vigour of her youth. She had wit and cunning too, and a fund of irony and an engaging humour which she uses in the interest of her own likes and dislikes. When Minerva appeared to her in a dream and told her that she was to be married soon and that it behoved her to have everything neat and tidy, and all their

clothes washed, Nausicaa immediately prepared to
fall in with these orders ; "thus," as Butler says,
"every preparation is made for her getting married
except the selection of the bridegroom." And this,
no doubt, is an instance of her sly humour at the
expense of the sex she so much despised in her heart.

To Butler, then, the central part of the *Odyssey*
is that describing Nausicaa's meeting with Ulysses.
Here is the episode in his own version taken from the
abridgement in *The Authoress of the Odyssey*—the tale
is taken up immediately after the departure of Minerva
as in the preceding paragraph.

"Nausicaa, on waking, told her father and mother
about her dream. 'Papa, dear' ($\pi\acute{a}\pi\pi a$ $\phi\iota\lambda$'), said she,
'could you manage to let me have a good big waggon ?
I want to take all our dirty clothes to the river and
wash them. You are the chief man here, so it is only
proper that you should have a clean shirt when you
attend meetings of the council. Moreover you have five
sons, two of them married, while the other three are
good-looking young bachelors ; you know they always
like to have clean linen when they go out to a dance.'

"Her father promised her all she wanted. The
waggon was made ready, her mother put her up a
basket of provisions, and Nausicaa drove her maids to
the bank of the river, where were the cisterns, through
which there flowed enough clear water to wash clothes
however dirty they might be. They washed their
clothes in the pits by treading upon them, laid them
out to dry upon the sea-beach, had their dinner as the
clothes were drying, and then began to play at ball
while Nausicaa sang to them.

"In the course of time, when they were thinking

about starting home Minerva woke Ulysses, who was in the wood just above them. . . .

" . . . he began by asking Nausicaa to inform him whether she was a goddess or no.   If she was a goddess, it was obvious from her beauty that she could only be Diana. . . .

" Nausicaa replied that he seemed really to be a very sensible person, but that people must put up with their luck whatever it might happen to be.   She then explained that he had come to the land of the Phæacians, and promised to conduct him to their city.

" . . . the maids came back and gave Ulysses a shirt and cloak ; they also gave him a bottle of oil and told him to go and wash in the river, but he said, ' I will not wash myself while you keep standing there. I cannot bring myself to strip before a number of good-looking young women.'   So they went and told their mistress.

" When Ulysses had done washing, Minerva made him look much grander and more imposing, and gave him a thick head of hair which flowed down in hyacinthine curls about his shoulders. . . .

" The maids then set meat and drink before Ulysses, who was ravenously hungry.   While he was eating, Nausicaa got the clothes folded up and put on to the cart ; after which she gave him his instructions. . . .

" ' When you get near the town drop behind, for the people here are very ill-natured, and they would talk about me.   They would say, " Who is this fine looking stranger that is going about with Nausicaa ?   Where did she find him ?   I suppose she is going to marry him.   Is he a sailor whom she has picked up from some foreign vessel, or has a god come down from heaven in answer to her prayers and is he going to marry her? It would be a good thing if she would go and find a husband somewhere else, for she will have nothing to say to any of the many excellent Phæacians who are in love with her." This is what people would say, and I could not blame them, for I should be scandalised myself if I saw any girl going about with a stranger, while her father and mother were yet alive, without being married to him in the face of all the world.' "

This episode in itself contains many points in support of Butler's theory. Here his authoress introduces herself into the story with wonderful skill and reticence. She insinuates herself into our presence, in fact, with the unpractised naturalness of a genuine artist. We can learn much about her from these passages—that she was a person who took count of domestic duties, and that she loved her home since her father and mother were the most important people in the world to her. Unlike her maids she is quite calm and collected all through the scene—nor is her precious washing forgotten in the flurry of Ulysses' unexpected appearance. Moreover, though Nausicaa may be inexperienced she knows the world well enough to avoid even the smallest pretext for scandal; she tells Ulysses to drop behind on their way back to the town, so that people will not " talk." And then she describes exactly what they would say about her in a short passage which argues a very clear knowledge of the world—on this question, at any rate—even if she is hazy about farming, or the rudders of ships, or the conditions under which sports and games can best be contested. The principal charm of the episode, however, consists in the entire absence of affectation; it is drawn from life as well and as faithfully as the author could draw it ; the details, so clear and actual in their minuteness, are made out of reality, not invented. The whole scene, too, takes on a new significance when we think of it as presenting the hitherto unknown authoress to her readers. Having once introduced herself thus she drops out of the story as suddenly as she has entered it. But to anyone who is able to discern the real character of this Princess of Scheria the narrative always afterwards, as Butler was well aware, must have a heightened interest and meaning.

Many writers have felt the grace and charm of Nausicaa's youth. Dr Mackail, in a lecture on Homer's women,[1] writes as follows :—

" One figure there is in the Odyssey never equalled except by the creator of Miranda and Rosalind, the girl-princess of Phæacia. The poet sketched her in, largely, firmly, beautifully, and then stayed his hand. Perhaps no reader—certainly no modern reader—has not felt a pang of regret when she slips out of the story and out of our sight. Whether the poet felt that he had gone too far, that he had been carried away by the delight of creation beyond what the scheme of the Odyssey could bear ; whether he was himself unconscious of the exquisite beauty of what he had created ; whether, here as elsewhere, the hard, unromantic Greek temper refused to let the picture be completed, are questions which at once invite and baffle discussion : but Nausicaa disappears, and the sunlight seems to go out with her."

This is a fine tribute to the reality of the picture. Butler, no doubt, would have said that in thus weaving

[1] Mackail, *Lectures on Greek Poetry*.

herself into her story Nausicaa was quite " unconscious
of the exquisite beauty " of the resulting picture.
She put herself before the public just as she was, quite
naturally ; and her instincts told her, rightly enough,
that the homely details of the clothes and the washing
would not in any way distort the scene, but rather add
to its value as a lifelike portrait. And yet, after all,
the pages in the *Odyssey* which seem to tell us so much
about Nausicaa do not supply us with a complete and
rounded portrait. Dr Mackail speaks of this figure as
unequalled " except by the creator of Miranda and
Rosalind." We know directly much more of Miranda
and Rosalind, however, than we can ever know of
Nausicaa from her own immediate revelations of herself in the *Odyssey*. There is no doubt the illusion
of knowing very much more than we do, because there
is perhaps no episode in literature which flashes upon
the reader with such convincing simplicity. But the
view of herself which Nausicaa saw fit to give is a snap-
shot rather than a portrait. And doubtless it was a
sense half of reticence, half of artistic fitness that prevented her from obtruding herself unduly, mixed with
a certain love of mystery which both went to making
the elusive picture. This at any rate is the niche
which Butler believed she made for herself in the poem.

So the scenes we have reproduced from Butler's
version made for him the central episode of the poem.
He speaks of the " livingness and enthusiasm "—and
we would add the subtle discretion—with which " the
girl described as Nausicaa " is drawn. " No other
episode," he adds, " is written with the same, or nearly
the same, buoyancy of spirits and resiliency of pulse and
movement, or brings the scene before us with anything

o

approaching the same freshness, as that in which
Nausicaa takes the family linen to the washing cisterns.
The whole of Book VI. can only have been written by
one who was throwing herself into it heart and soul."

Having dealt with the authorship of the *Odyssey* the
second problem which engaged Butler's attention—
though actually it is impossible to dissociate the two
questions—was the topographical origin of the poem.
After much consideration he came to the conclusion
that its origin was Sicilian, and that it was written at
Trapani. He went to Sicily in 1892, the first of many
visits, for the purpose of collecting evidence in support
of his Trapanese theories. It was characteristic of
Butler, as we have before said, that whenever possible
he liked to study every subject that interested him on
the spot and at first hand. Probably it was his life in
New Zealand which first taught him to rely on himself
if he wanted satisfactory results. At any rate there
was nothing of the arm-chair spirit about his Sicilian
investigations, which were of the minutest possible
character. He examined the question of Odyssean
topography with an energy unsurpassed by any
geographically-minded theologian who disturbs himself
over the routes taken by St Paul in the missionary
journeys. So Butler became well known to the
Sicilians, all over the island, and after his death in
1902 a street at Calatafimi was called after him, the
Via Samuel Butler.

From the first Butler felt convinced that Scheria
was a real place, and he set himself to find a locality
on the Mediterranean which should satisfy the required conditions : the town must be placed on a piece
of land jutting into the sea, and there must be no river,

because Nausicaa had to go a long way to wash her clothes; and a notable mountain must be near the town, for Neptune threatens to bury it under a high mountain. Butler had not far to seek before he lighted on Trapani and its neighbourhood, with Mount Eryx, which corresponded in detail with the descriptions in the *Odyssey*. He points out that the counter-argument of Homeric scholars, when they did venture to criticise his geography, consisted in ignoring the cumulative value of the combination of facts he had arrayed in his argument, isolating one of the items of description and asserting that it applied equally to half-a-dozen places which they could name. Butler demonstrated elaborately and in detail that the strength of his argument lay in the combination of resemblances which he was able to establish; and he adds that even Homeric scholars must eventually yield to the opinion of sensible people.

These Sicilian studies are amongst the most striking of Butler's activities, both for the minuteness with which they were conducted and the way in which he fitted together all the evidence to present an over-whelming case in favour of his Trapanese theories. The *Odyssey* was the basis of his work—he steeped himself in it while engaged in his discoveries, and at one time learnt nearly the whole of the poem by heart. He kept his eyes always fixed on the poem until he had completely worked out his theory making Sicily the centre of Odyssean adventure—for the latter part of Ulysses' voyage was nothing but a sail round Sicily, with suitable pauses at certain islands—the topography being easily recognisable adaptations of country which the writer, an untravelled young woman, was familiar with.

Throughout this chapter we have considered the Homeric questions in Butler's own point of view because by this method, we believe, it becomes easier to appreciate what he wrote on these subjects. Mr Cannan, in his " Critical Study," has coupled Butler's work on the *Odyssey* with his search for the Mr W. H. of Shakespeare's Sonnets, whom he identified as a certain William Hughes. These considerations are rather curiously labelled by Mr Cannan as " Fads." They belong, he says, to the period after 1885 when *The Way of All Flesh* was completed, though it could not be published, and Butler's work, now slight and assertive in character, showed signs " of a growing irritation." He describes Butler's Odyssean theories as bricks to throw into the midst of the Homeric scholars, and speaks of Sicily as a new hunting-ground where he could entertain his friends.

In the first place we believe that it is impossible to dismiss Butler's theory as a " fad " or a " hobby-horse." It makes no discontinuity with the rest of his work, and indeed we have no reason to think of it as in a different department from his other writing. Of course it was a solid brick to throw among the professors, yet Butler never deliberately selected it for that purpose. It is true that in the *Notebooks* he speaks of himself as " the *enfant terrible* of literature and science "—he was so in spite of himself—and goes on to say : " If I cannot, and I know I cannot, get the literary and scientific big-wigs to give me a shilling, I can, and I know I can, heave bricks into the middle of them." There were not a few very large bricks of Butler's heaving ; but that was only incidental. Every new theory is a disconcerting intruder until it settles

down and establishes itself ; and Butler's authoress of
the *Odyssey*, as he well knew, was no exception. Indeed,
his statements to prove that a woman wrote the poem
were not more a fad than his conviction that memory
and heredity are inseparable, or that Darwinian
Natural Selection was a retrograde step from the
position of the older evolutionists.

His evolutionary books, in fact, with their insistence
throughout on intelligence as the keynote of the
universe, may be paralleled quite fairly by what he
wrote about Homer and Nausicaa. Both the *Iliad*
and the *Odyssey* to him were respectively the work of
a single hand. Butler was quite convinced of this.
The notion of a confused multitude of poets or poetesses
revolted him ; he felt assured that only a single intelligence could have created each of them. A French
critic, M. Jean Blum, who has grasped very clearly
the unity that lies in Butler's work, stated this quite
shortly in an article. He is speaking of *The Authoress
of the Odyssey*.

" L'unité et la dignité de l'intelligence une fois de
plus est ici son vrai sujet ; une fois de plus il prend
parti pour la conscience contre l'inconscient et pour le
cosmos contre le chaos." [1]

Here, indeed, we have Butler's main subject. He
says more than once in his books on the *Odyssey* that
it does not matter to him in the least whether the poem
was written by a man or a woman. His aim is to get
to know as much as possible about the poem : that
is perfectly true ; but the poem only interested
him as being the work of an artist, a living personality
the spirit of whose intelligence breathed itself on to

[1] See the *Mercure de France*, 16 juillet 1910.

every page. It is not without significance that the mechanical coldness of so-called scientific criticism has endeavoured to take away even from art the direction of a single creative intelligence. The outrageous attempt to ascribe the *Iliad* and the *Odyssey* to numbers of haphazard people sounds rather like, as indeed it is, a wild burlesque, in advance, of the recent and present tendencies to foist impossible new authors on to the literature of the past.

Explicit in Butler's work is a repudiation of such attempts. And even if this aspect of his work lies momentarily hidden under his theories of the origin and authorship of the *Odyssey* it is an aspect which cannot be sufficiently insisted on. When viewed from this point *The Authoress of the Odyssey* falls into line with the evolutionary books and becomes a significant part of those other questions which Butler was concerned to establish. Luck, or Cunning ? again is the query.

Little less important, in this connection, was Butler's recognition of the vitality, the " livingness " of the two poems he translated, which were produced in an age and country differing immeasurably from our own. Hope and fear, love and hatred and jealousy were emotions felt just as much then as they are now. The greatest literature, which exists independently of time and place, makes its appeal through such emotions —for a reflection of the merely passing world of their own day we have to look to lesser poets. Anyone, therefore, who is aware of the vital quality of a dead author, whether of his own language or another, and wishes to preserve him, " must not skin him, stuff him, and set him up in a case, you must eat him, digest

him and let him live in you, with such life as you have,
for better or worse." Such were the claims of the
great ones of literature, music and painting. Butler
knew, however, that it is only those who have passed
into the select company who can claim this curious,
vicarious existence. So, in all art the reader or the
listener has to do his part—he has to revive in himself
the spirit, the intention of the original. And that is
what Butler tried to do in his translations, which are
certainly the most readable versions of the *Iliad* and
Odyssey in the language.

Many people, no doubt, are grateful to what they
call his restless, paradoxical spirit, not because they
are in the least interested in the Odyssean theories it
produced, but because it stimulated Butler, incidentally, to translate the two poems. This most important
work, and his chivalrous rescue of Nausicaa from
oblivion, belong to the latter part of Butler's literary
career. Certainly he had *Erewhon Revisited* still to
write, yet it is true to say that his bold, adventurous
journeys into unexplored countries were coming to
an end. The second *Erewhon* book was, after all, a
revisit.

CHAPTER VII

THE NOVEL

It seems likely that Butler's novel, *The Way of All Flesh*, is the book by which he desired chiefly to be remembered. He was engaged upon it for ten years, and its inception belongs to the same period as *The Fair Haven*. In the Memoir of John Pickard Owen he had already found his aptitude for character-drawing ; but the sides of J. P. Owen's life with which he was forced to deal by the very nature of the earlier book were too specialised to allow of a broader treatment, which Butler would perhaps have welcomed. Besides Owen was a caricatured figure, and his creator could not very well allow him to be anything else.

The humour, the sureness of handling and the resource which Butler showed in dealing with Owen in the Memoir gave promise of his success with a novel of larger scale and dimensions. No doubt Miss E. M. A. Savage, who is introduced as Alethea Pontifex in *The Way of All Flesh*, helped in stimulating him to write it. For the soundness of her criticism he certainly had a keen regard, since he submitted the manuscript of the novel, as he wrote it, for her approval. In his " Sketch of the Life of Samuel Butler " Mr Jones in quoting a few of Miss Savage's letters has given us some foretaste of her wit and originality, characteristics which among others had so much appeal for Butler. Miss Savage, as Mr Jones has remarked, posted her literary

reputation in Butler's letter-box, from which it will
some day be resurrected. In the meantime Ernest's
Aunt, Alethea Pontifex, remains the key to a personality which exercised a very considerable influence on
Butler's literary career.

In his excellent chapter on *The Way of All Flesh*
Mr Cannan has described its theme as "the relation of
parents and children under the shadow of the Church
of England when it had . . . claimed its share of the
virtuous prosperity of the English people." That
indeed is the subject dealt with in the book ; and its
interest and force are heightened by the fact that much
of it is an autobiographical record. The various phases
of spiritual development are presented first and chiefly
as the result of the family relations existing in a quiet
English rectory, and then as they are affected by school
and university life and ordination into the English
Church. The whole study, in fact, traces the hero's
gradual emergence from the influence of a narrow and
distasteful upbringing ; while the author shows, by
the career of Ernest Pontifex, that in a sense no other
than the literal one all things do "work together for
good to them that love God," however incongruous or
untoward those things may be. Thus Ernest's stormy
immaturity is a commentary on that text.

Butler, and therefore Ernest, lived in an age of stern
parental discipline. The younger generation was
hedged in in a variety of curious ways which it is
difficult for us now to realise or appreciate. Perhaps
he was right in thinking that the Church Catechism,
and this especially in a clergyman's family, is very
largely responsible for the unhappy relations between
parents and children. Certainly it was written almost

entirely from the parents' point of view, and is a good example of the kind of weapons which, until lately, they have been in the habit of using against their children. It is necessarily, however, confined to religious households, which, unfortunately, are not the only establishments in which children do not see eye to eye with their parents. In his Preface on Parents and Children Mr Shaw has noted a fundamental difference that exists between parents and offspring which is perhaps *the* most fundamental, except difference of language—namely, a wide difference in age. Yet difference in age is after all not an insurmountable difficulty ; although with parents and children it may well be so. That, no doubt, is what the young Ernest Pontifex felt in a dim and vague way when he was wishing so much that people could be born into the world not as children but grown-up persons. And Butler himself, in one of his notes, pointed out the obvious conveniences of having, for instance, clergymen born full grown, in Holy Orders, and even beneficed —an arrangement which would be at once cheaper and more convenient. We know so very little about our parents, partly because of this broad gulf of years fixed between us. Even the antagonism of sex is less important, and what people call incompatability of temperament must take a secondary place when the wide disparity in the ages of fathers and mothers and sons and daughters is taken into account.

Apart, however, from the direct personal relationship, the age in which Ernest Pontifex lived was a period of repression, or at least of neglect, so far as the newer generation was concerned. It was so all through public life. In politics, which may serve as an index,

Bagehot has noted how, for instance, the long years between the two Reform Bills are the history of the activities of comparatively old men. The convention of a larger world was bound to make itself felt in smaller domestic societies; each reacted upon the other, until, as William Pitt had said a hundred years before, it became almost an accredited fact that youth was a crime, and the sooner it could be expiated by growing old the better. It was indeed characteristic of the middle—and later—Victorian epoch that what is called experience—which can only come with age and wisdom—should be considered the one thing needful. The people of the period, on the whole, were not adventurous. They were too satisfied and complacent, too prosperous, in fact, to bestir themselves into pursuing any other course than the one they were pursuing. In the art of self-satisfaction they had indeed become fully experienced. It was the same both in public and domestic life : the younger generation must be brought up to respect what its fathers had respected, to realise the importance of possessing a good head for business—although it must not know too much about the inner workings of this mysterious thing—to recognise with pride its membership of a very great Empire on which the sun never sets, but above all to love, honour and obey its father and mother, to whom it could never be sufficiently grateful for having brought it into the world, and to practise continually that difficult but truly Christian virtue of self-effacement in the presence of the superior wisdom and judgment of its parents and all grown-up people whatsoever.

Butler knew very intimately the position of a son, especially of a parson's son, in those difficult times.

He knew most by personal experience, and made it his business to show how, from the unrighteousness of narrow and entirely uncongenial early surroundings, his hero emerged into a state of grace. Indeed in this case giving up father and mother for Christ's sake did not prove such a harassing affair as might perhaps have been expected. The relentless descriptions of the life at Battersby Rectory are probably not without some rancour ; and no doubt there are many readers who have been repelled, if not by the matter-of-fact flavour of the family history at the beginning, at any rate by the feeling of bitterness in the author as he discloses the various stages of Ernest's spiritual history until the—to him—only logical and tenable position is reached. It is certain that neither Ernest nor his creator suffered from illusions about his home life ; and it is just because the story is so much an auto-biography that it gains in truth and livingness, neither of which Butler was prepared to sacrifice on any altars of imaginary, sentimental virtue.

The Way of All Flesh is chronologically of the same period as *Life and Habit,* and may be regarded, in fact, as a practical commentary on and illustration of the theory of heredity there propounded. Once or twice Butler quotes passages from his scientific book, as embodying the opinions of an obscure philosopher which may have a good deal of truth in them. Identity of personality between parent and offspring is, as we have seen, one of the contentions put forward in *Life and Habit.* Accordingly in *The Way of All Flesh,* before the birth of the hero, Ernest Pontifex, we are asked to examine and consider him in the person of his ancestors for three generations on his father's side and two on the mother's. Over fifty pages of the book are thus devoted to the vicarious existence he was leading in his various progenitors. His immediate paternal ancestors may be noted in a brief table.

THE PONTIFEXES

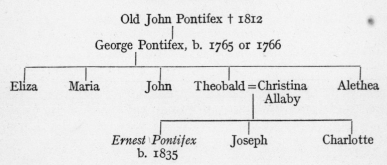

Old John Pontifex † 1812
|
George Pontifex, b. 1765 or 1766
|
Eliza   Maria   John   Theobald = Christina   Alethea
Allaby
|
Ernest *Pontifex*   Joseph   Charlotte
b. 1835

The fact first noticeable about Ernest's ancestors and relations is that, with the exception of two or perhaps three of their number, they were all unpleasant people. Old Mr Pontifex, the village carpenter who married " a Gothic woman " and built himself an organ, is certainly a most attractive character; so also is Alethea, with her dislike of humbug, her straight-forward common-sense supported by those frequent wicked speeches which anticipate Ernest as we know him in later years. But George Pontifex is an un-inviting hypocrite only a little better than Theobald himself, because he had journeyed abroad and seen the conventional sights as a young man, and was more a man of the world than ever Theobald, in any walk of life, was likely to become. Of those characters who live on to the end of the story almost the best is Christina, Ernest's mother. Castles in the air were her chief dissipation; she indulged herself in this

habit until it became almost a vice—if indeed so pious
a woman as Christina could be described as vicious in
any sense of the word—and transmitted it, though in
a very modified form and one which only troubled his
earlier years, to her son Ernest.   Nothing in the book,
perhaps, is so well presented as the prying, pious,
suspicious nature of Christina.   The very fact of Theobald having not only proposed, but even married her,
seems to have thrown her off her balance.   She was
convinced that he was the best husband and consequently the best father in the whole world.   In the
offensive and defensive alliance against Ernest, therefore, she was an indispensable partner : Theobald and
Christina formed an unassailable combination.   In
respect of Ernest and his affairs she was as an insatiable
young cuckoo ; she was ready both in season and out
to pump and molest him on the drawing-room sofa
till the most hidden secrets of his heart were wrung
from him.   And yet she meant well, as we must
charitably believe Theobald did.   What were their
feelings then over the dreadful catastrophe which came
upon Ernest ?

" Poor people !   They had tried to keep their ignorance of the world from themselves by calling it the
pursuit of heavenly things, and then shutting their
eyes to anything that might give them trouble.   A son
having been born to them, they had shut his eyes also
as far as was practicable.   Who could blame them ?
They had chapter and verse for everything they had
either done or left undone ; there is no better thumbed
precedent than that for being a clergyman and a
clergyman's wife.   In what respect had they differed
from their neighbours ?   How did their household

differ from that of any other clergyman of the better sort from one end of England to the other ? Why, then, should it have been upon them, of all people in the world, that this tower of Siloam had fallen ? " The answer to this last question is to be found precisely in their dealings with their son Ernest.

Christina's reveries, as we have said, are among the chief features of *The Way of All Flesh*. And one of the chapters of the book is a chapter of meditations. It occurs much earlier than the passage quoted above, and is occasioned by Ernest's departure to school for the first time. The parents have taken and delivered him safely into the hands of Dr Skinner, the head-master. All of them in their own way are impressed with the commanding presence of Skinner. Theobald and Christina are driving back home in their own brougham. Theobald's meditations, as usual, are disagreeable ; Christina is snobbish and rather feminine, wondering what sort of an impression she has made on Dr Skinner. But Ernest at school sits by the fire in the matron's room and is completely puzzled and troubled about himself. All sorts of questions, of the most far-reaching character, present themselves. It is a fine Tolstoyan orgy of introspection that the small new Ernest is allowed to indulge in, which, however, serves better than anything else to show the trend of his thoughts at that early period.

" ' Grown-up people,' he said to himself, ' when they were ladies and gentlemen, never did naughty things, but he was always doing them. He had heard that some grown-up people were worldly, which, of course, was wrong, still this was quite distinct from being naughty, and did not get them punished or scolded.

His own Papa and Mamma were not even worldly; they had often explained to him that they were exceptionally unworldly; he well knew that they had never done anything naughty since they had been children, and that even as children they had been nearly faultless. Oh! how different from himself! . . . Besides he did not like Sunday; he did not like anything that was really good; his tastes were low and such as he was ashamed of. He liked people best if they sometimes swore a little, so long as it was not at him. As for his Catechism and Bible reading he had no heart in them. He had never attended to a sermon in his life. Even when he had been taken to hear Mr Vaughan at Brighton, who, as everyone knew, preached such beautiful sermons for children, he had been very glad when it was all over, nor did he believe he could get through church at all if it was not for the voluntary upon the organ and the hymns and chanting. The Catechism was awful. He had never been able to understand what it was that he desired of his Lord God and Heavenly Father, nor had he yet got hold of a single idea in connection with the word Sacrament. His duty towards his neighbour was another bugbear. It seemed to him that he had duties towards everybody, lying in wait for him upon every side, but that nobody had any duties towards him. Then there was that awful and mysterious word "business." What did it all mean? What was "business"? His Papa was a wonderfully good man of business, his Mamma had often told him so—but he should never be one. It was hopeless, and very awful, for people were continually telling him that he would have to earn his own living. No doubt, but how—considering how

stupid, idle, ignorant, self-indulgent, and physically
puny he was ? All grown-up people were clever,
except servants—and even these were cleverer than
ever he should be. Oh, why, why, why, could not
people be born into the world as grown-up persons ?
Then he thought of Casabianca. He had been
examined in that poem by his father not long before.
" When only would he leave his position ? To whom
did he call ? Did he get an answer ? Why ? How
many times did he call upon his father ? What
happened to him ? What was the noblest life that
perished there ? Do you think so ? Why do you
think so ? " And all the rest of it. Of course he
thought Casabianca's was the noblest life that perished
there ; there could be no two opinions about that ;
it never occurred to him that the moral of the poem
was that young people cannot begin too soon to
exercise discretion in the obedience they pay to their
Papa and Mamma. Oh, no ! the only thought in his
mind was that he should never, never have been like
Casabianca, and that Casabianca would have despised
him so much, if he could have known him, that he would
not have condescended to speak to him. There was
nobody else in the ship worth reckoning at all : it did
not matter how much they were blown up. Mrs
Hemans knew them all and they were a very indifferent
lot. Besides Casabianca was so good-looking and
came of such a good family.' " The *wurra wurra* of
emotions which his new surroundings awoke in him
was only dispelled by physical sleep.

It is small wonder, with relations such as he had,
that Ernest should be a prig. In his ancestors we can
trace the as yet unmixed ingredients of Ernest : and

P

Butler wished to show how important an influence these ancestors were in his life. He wanted to show, also, that in spite of his having been baptized in water from the Jordan and christened Ernest—the word " earnest " was just then becoming fashionable—his character was not modified to any considerable extent by these things. Butler, moreover, will not allow that conventional fortune, the blind and fickle mother, plays any part in the shaping of men's lives. For fortune is not blind. " She can espy her favourites long before they are born. We are as days and have had our parents for our yesterdays, but through all the fair weather of a clear parental sky the eye of Fortune can discern the coming storm, and she laughs as she places her favourites it may be in a London alley or those whom she is resolved to ruin in king's palaces." Much in the same way Meredith conceived of those imps who " circle and squat " and trim their lanterns, as they wait their opportunity to dog some great house to destruction. So, as both of them showed, Fortune does her work, watching and playing with circumstances. To Butler she is the handmaid of heredity but independent of it. She seizes her opportunities, and gets to business in fairy-godmother fashion to rescue her favourites from the unlikeliest situations. All the same she can work no miracles. Ernest was one of her favoured ones, though she had a difficult time with him. Everything was so much against her —at least most of Ernest's relations were; certainly his father and mother and his early training and consequent priggishness were circumstances she had resolutely to fight against. And in the end she was successful. In all of which Alethea Pontifex, who

left her money to Ernest, was a very valuable
ally.

Ernest, of course, could not dodge his family. Up
to date he was one of the things towards which his
ancestors had been labouring and travailing. And he
left very much to be desired. Mr Salter, as we have
already mentioned, has shown how wide is the difference between Butler's attitude to the family regarded
from the biological point of view and the family as it
actually exists in practice. For the former he had the
greatest reverence. The fact is, that nature in this
respect acts with neither favour nor discrimination;
she metes out the same measure to the unpleasant as
to the pleasant people. In practice, and therefore in
the case of Theobald, Christina and their son Ernest,
Butler saw what an unfortunate expedient the family
was. That is why he always envied Melchisedec, who
was "a born orphan" and "incarnate bachelor."
We should look upon the family, indeed, as a convenient method used by nature for getting us born ;
but any attempt to unite its members for too long by
artificial means and for sentimental reasons, must be
the cause of more unhappiness and positive distaste
than even sentiment can justify.

That, at any rate, was Butler's view of the family,
which in its turn was one of the reasons why he wrote
The Way of All Flesh. Every book, every novel
especially, must contain, ostensibly or not, a portrait
of the author, just as every man's work, whatever it
may be, is always a portrait of himself—the present
Battersby church, which Theobald restored and partly
rebuilt being, as described by the author, the best
extant portrait of Theobald. Ernest Pontifex is

avowedly a portrait of Butler, as Alethea Pontifex
is a picture of Miss Savage and Dr Skinner of Benjamin
Hall Kennedy, who was Butler's headmaster at Shrewsbury. But although *The Way of All Flesh* is, in an
important sense, a life of the author, it must be regarded much more as a spiritual than a material history.
Like his hero, Butler went to a Public School and to
Cambridge, but unlike him, he managed to escape
ordination by the skin of his teeth—as Theobald would
have done had he possessed a little more courage—
nor was Butler ever in prison. Ernest, on the other
hand, never as a young man got away from England
to a freer, more invigorating life in an English colony
as Butler did in New Zealand. Indeed Butler's
sojourn in the Canterbury Settlement did for him, in
a much shorter time, what Ernest's few adventurous
months as a clergyman of the Church of England, his
imprisonment, and subsequent marriage to the unfortunate Ellen did for Ernest. It does not appear
difficult to disentangle from the story the threads of
actual fact. The account of Ernest's relations with
the Simeonites, and the sermon of Mr Gideon Hawke,
for instance, must be based on real occurrences. Dr
Skinner and Gideon Hawke are the most vivid of the
minor characters in the book; and the description of
Edward Overton's quiet game of chess with the headmaster of Roughborough, and the feeling, which the
writer conveys, of an impending Fate, terrible and
silent, that waits somehow upon Skinner's word, are
unequalled anywhere. Hawke and his sermon too
come upon one with a flash of conviction. Indeed
it is just the slight difference of emphasis—Hawke
the prophet of religion and morality, intolerant and

alarming, yet with a certain fascination in his fiery zeal,
Skinner the schoolmaster, on another plane, awe-
inspiring and even terrible, " like the lion in the Bishop
of Oxford's Sunday story "—both of them tormentors
of youth—it is just the difference of emphasis that
makes each of them so admirably supplement the other
and adds to their effect as characters. It was Dr
Skinner whom Alethea in one of her wicked moods
described as having " the harmlessness of the serpent
and the wisdom of the dove." To Ernest he seems
always to have been a terror ; he was acutely aware,
in his presence, of his own insignificance, just as
Gideon Hawke's sermon made him feel his intense
moral weakness. For Ernest was one of that numerous
company who have from their earliest youth been so
impressed with their own potential wickedness that
they approach everything with suspicion. There is
in them an almost morbid feeling that anything that
gives them pleasure must immediately be avoided as
sinful. The fact is that at an early age they have been
made to believe very firmly in the infallibility of their
own conscience—an instrument which has been carefully tuned to that pitch which shall best ensure its
interfering with and repressing them on every possible
occasion. Ernest had to learn a hymn about conscience, which said that if one did not listen to its
voice it would soon stop speaking. " My Mamma's
conscience has not left off speaking," said Ernest to
one of his friends at school; "it's always jabbering."
Though he spoke so flippantly about it, and his
mother, both of them were to be bugbears of his for
a long time yet.

As to Butler's own schooldays at Shrewsbury under

Benjamin Hall Kennedy it is impossible, directly, to
glean very much. Dr Kennedy succeeded Butler's
grandfather as headmaster of Shrewsbury school, and
there is considerable reference to him in *The Life and
Letters of Dr Butler*. In paying a tribute to his
grandfather's work at Shrewsbury, which we know
contained no word more than he deserved, Butler thus
wrote : " Returning to the careers of those whom he
left as his head boys, I would ask, Is it likely that any
other school of the time can show a greater, if indeed
an equal measure of success ? Granted that the
education of these boys was completed by Dr Kennedy ;
but could Dr Kennedy have done what he did if it
had been at any other school than one in which the
spirit infused by Dr Butler was still living ? I mean
no word of disparagement to Dr Kennedy ; I was six
years at Shrewsbury under him, and from the bottom
of my heart can say that he treated me with great
forbearance—far more than I deserved." This is the
only reference to Butler's schoolboy relations with
Dr Kennedy that exists in print, so far as we are aware.

There are numerous other autobiographical periods
in *The Way of All Flesh*. Perhaps the part in which
Ernest follows Butler's life most closely is that
describing his career at Cambridge. We have
noted already the sinister fascination the Simeonites
had for Ernest and therefore for Butler, and how
The Fair Haven marked a revolt from a way of life
of which the doctrines of Simeon may be viewed as
an extravagant parody. Cambridge, however, in a
certain sense started Butler in a literary career, when
he contributed a few pieces to his college magazine.
Ernest also wrote for a university magazine, on the

Greek Drama. Ernest's essay is a little Butlerian at
its close when the writer hints that the Psalms of
David, from a literary point of view, are not all that
has been claimed for them. What is more interesting,
however, is to find the writer in his comments on this
essay reiterating the thoughts which Butler expressed
in his first published piece, " On English Composition,"
written when he was twenty-three years of age. He
again speaks of the uselessness of writing unless there
is anything definite to be said ; and shows how Ernest,
when he had finished his paper, although he thought
he had written himself out, wanted to maintain his
reputation, and so went wildly in search of ideas.
This was Butler's position when *Erewhon* was written
—with the difference that he never went out in search
of material to be converted into books. When
Erewhon was completed he imagined he had written
himself out, and was glad to return uninterrupted to
his painting. But, like Ernest, Butler did not yet know
that it is just when we are not looking for them that
ideas come to us and force themselves upon our
attention. He soon, however, came to realise that,
and like Ernest also acquired the habit of noting down
anything that interested him in a little book which he
carried in his waistcoat pocket. " Ernest had such a
notebook always with him. Even when he was at
Cambridge he had begun the practice without anyone's
having suggested it to him." Here we have the
genesis of Butler's *Notebooks*, which numbered, at his
death, six moderate-sized volumes.

There was no lack of ideas to put into them, although
it took him some time to find out that " ideas, no less
than the living beings in whose minds they arise, must

be begotten by parents not very unlike themselves,
the most original still differing but slightly from the
parents that have given rise to them. Life is like a
fugue, everything must grow out of the subject and
there must be nothing new. Nor, again, did he
[Ernest] see how hard it is to say where one idea ends
and another begins, nor yet how closely this is paralleled
in the difficulty of saying when a life begins or ends,
or an action or indeed anything, there being an unity
in spite of infinite multitude, and an infinite multitude
in spite of unity."

Of the other characters in *The Way of All Flesh* who
may be said to enter the domain of actual fact, Mrs
Jupp is unquestionably the most engaging, inimitable
in talk and behaviour. She may or may not, in Mr
Cannan's borrowed description, be " an old whore's
body with a young whore's mind " ; certainly she is
a triumphant reality, and shows Butler's love of whatever is genuine and unaffected, no matter how
Rabelaisian it may be. There is an Elizabethan
flavour about Mrs Jupp, as there is about Meredith's
Mrs Berry. Her original, Mrs Boss, Butler found in
an English village. " Bravery, wit and poetry," he
says, " abound in every village. Look at Mrs Boss
and at Joanna Mills [a picturesque character in the
early part of *The Life and Letters of Dr Butler*]. There
is not a village of 500 inhabitants in England but
has its Mrs Quickly and its Tom Jones."

Mrs Jupp always said what she had to say in her
own way, illuminating every subject with her vivid
personality. She didn't like hearing that Ernest was
going to be married, though she knew nothing of
Ellen. " But after all," she said, " it ain't you and

it ain't me, and it ain't him, and it ain't her. It's what you must call the fortunes of matterimony, for there ain't no other word for it." To the very end of the story, when she was quite an old woman, she remained the same gay, irresponsible creature, direct and graphic in everything she said, a picturesque, un-repentant ex-member of the oldest profession in the world. Her last appearance in the book is after a very satisfying dinner of cushion of ham and green peas. She is appropriately voluble, as she drifts irrelevantly from one topic to another.

" And there's that Bell, it's enough to give anyone the hump to see him now that he's taken to chapel-going, and his mother's prepared to meet Jesus and all that to me, and now she ain't a-going to die, and drinks half a bottle of champagne a day, and then Grigg, him as preaches, you know, asked Bell if I really was too gay, not but what when I was young I'd snap my fingers at any ' fly by night ' in Holborn, and if I was togged out and had my teeth I'd do it now. I lost my poor dear Watkins, but of course that couldn't be helped, and then I lost my dear Rose. Silly faggot to go and ride on a cart and catch the bronchitis. I never thought when I kissed my dear Rose in Pullen's Passage and she gave me the chop, that I should never see her again, and her gentleman friend was fond of her too, though he was a married man. I daresay she's gone to bits by now. If she could rise and see me with my bad finger, she would cry, and I should say, ' Never mind, ducky, I'm all right.' Oh ! dear, it's coming on to rain. I do hate a wet Saturday night—poor women with their nice white stockings and their living to get."

Mrs Jupp, indeed, keeps the story going, giving as

she does insight into a kind of life which Ernest as a parson knew only from the outside ; later, when he married Ellen and set up his old-clothes shop he saw something of it from the inside. He was impressed with the need of beginning from the bottom, and his great desire was to remain a parvenu in " low-class " society for as short a time as possible. He had ceased to be a prig, was no longer satisfied that he was going hourly towards Christ, while the greater number of other people were going away from Him, nor, consciously, did he " daily gather fresh principles " as he and Pryer, his fellow-curate—who so successfully purloined Ernest's money—were wont to do in the early days of their ministration.

In spite of the fact that the curate attacked his hero in such a vulnerable point as his pocket, he seems, from a glimpse here and there, to be a parson a little after Butler's own heart. He serves admirably as a foil to Ernest in the days of his foolish immaturity. His zeal was all right, but he knew how to temper it with common-sense. Towneley, in *The Way of All Flesh*, is the author's ideal of a successful man of the world : popular, well dressed, with plenty of *savoir faire*. And Pryer is a curatorial man of the world, on an inferior scale. He was not popular like Towneley— Mrs Jupp did not approve of him, which is a point against him—but he did not make mistakes. For instance, he was, of course, far too well informed ever to have made the disastrous mistake about Miss Maitland that Ernest made. At times, too, Pryer is rather Butlerian, and nearly converted Ernest to some of his doctrines before the time was ripe for him to receive them. He fed him with formulæ rather than

instances ; he told him " that no practice is entirely
vicious which has not been extinguished among the
comeliest, most vigorous, and most cultivated races of
mankind in spite of centuries of endeavour to extirpate
it. If a vice in spite of such efforts can still hold its
own among the most polished nations, it must be
founded on some immutable truth or fact in human
nature, and must have some compensatory advantage
which we cannot afford altogether to dispense with."
Ernest was naturally alarmed at this sweeping away of
the distinction between right and wrong ; and his
fellow-curate had to explain to him that the clergy, by
which he meant a new and regenerate clergy, sharply
separated from the laity, without wife or children,
living no longer in what he could only call " open
matrimony," sexless in theory, absolutely, if not in
practice—it is these, the reformed clergy of a better
future, who are to be men's guides in matters of right
and wrong. Such were Pryer's maxims. Perhaps
he is intended as an example of the advanced wing,
broad Church, man-of-the-world curate. Or have we
mistaken him altogether ?

Already, after his parting with Pryer, and his
sojourn in prison, Ernest had given up his father and
mother as a *sine qua non* for reaching that state of
loving God in which all things work together for good.
Much more, however, was yet to follow. And as he
lay in bed in the prison hospital he considered many
things, and "woke up to the fact which most men
arrive at sooner or later, I mean that very few care two
straws about truth, or have any confidence that it is
righter and better to believe what is true than what is
untrue, even though belief in the untruth may seem

at first sight most expedient. Yet it is only these few who can be said to believe anything at all; the rest are simply unbelievers in disguise. Perhaps, after all, these last are right. They have numbers and prosperity on their side. They have all which the rationalist appeals to as his tests of right and wrong. Right, according to him, is what seems right to the majority of sensible, well-to-do-people." And that was about as far as Ernest himself felt disposed to go : the truth that appeals to most sensible and successful people was good enough for him.

He became aware also that he could do very little without faith. Like Euclid, we must begin with an act of faith according to the pragmatist teaching. Ernest came to this conclusion in his disinterested progress towards salvation. Disinterestedness, indeed, remains one of his cardinal maxims—perhaps the only one— after the crisis of his conversion, dating from his unhappy assault on the innocent Miss Maitland. He began to see that professions in support of religion or against it matter very little to anyone if only he possess the gift of charity and is willing to admit that " blessed inconsistency " which is probably the truest charity of all. In the " uncompromisingness of dogma " lies its great and insidious danger.

So Ernest reached some sort of moral regeneration. It ostensibly distressed, but inwardly enraged his father to see him return to his old home—which he did just before the death of Christina—well dressed, healthy, prosperous, enjoying the benefits of his Aunt Alethea's money. There was no precedent, in Scripture or anywhere else, so far as he knew, for such a shameless return of the prodigal. It wasn't in the least what

Theobald had bargained for. " He wanted Ernest to return, but he was to return as any respectable, well-regulated prodigal ought to return—abject, broken-hearted, asking forgiveness from the tenderest and most long-suffering father in the whole world. If he should have shoes and stockings and whole clothes at all, it should be only because absolute rags and tatters had been graciously dispensed with, whereas here he was swaggering in a grey ulster and a blue and white neck-tie, and looking better than Theobald had ever seen him in his life. It was unprincipled." In some obscure way a virtue had been made of wickedness, and the soul of success had blatantly manifested itself in things evil. Theobald was annoyed and puzzled, being naturally quite unable to recognise any other desired salvation than that which he himself had practically already reached. From the very first he had lacked any pretensions to Christian charity, though he was probably entirely unaware of any resemblance to the sounding brass and the other instruments mentioned by St Paul.

Ernest's home-coming, therefore, was a complete success. His mother was the only person in whom the evidences of his new-found prosperity did not cause more than momentary disturbance. In fact they rather pleased her. His good fortune, she thought, quite wiped out the disgrace of imprisonment. And she started off again on one of her exalted reveries. She had never been really able to grasp the fact of Ernest's independent existence, which was one of the reasons of those old, agitating interviews on the drawing-room sofa. She had wanted to know all about his life at school, even down to details which it was

scarcely seemly for a lady to inquire into. She had
never been willing to admit to herself that there was
anything that concerned Ernest that did not also concern herself.   Hence her restless, inquisitive behaviour
towards him.   Christina, moreover, was always in a
highly excitable state of moral fervour. When, years
before, she had become convinced in advance that she
would not survive the birth of her last child, she wrote
a letter to her " two dear boys," which was to be delivered to them when Ernest was sixteen.   It is a
wonderful letter, one of Christina's—and Butler's—
crowning achievements. She enjoined the two boys
to be comforts to their father, to cherish their sister,
to beware of the snares of the world. This letter was
the topmost point that Christina reached in creating
that moral spectacle which seems to have been one of
the chief businesses of her life. She had never been
able to dissociate herself from her children ; and when
misfortune and prison itself yawned over Ernest she
felt doubtless that it was more than she could bear.
On her death-bed she was quite reconciled. And yet, as
Mr Cannan has remarked, it is only in her death that
Christina is a failure. We have accepted her, delighted
in her all through ; and just at the close Butler allows
himself to take her out of the story. That, however,
can have little effect on the intense and surprising
reality of Christina as we have known her throughout
the book.

Apart from this, the account of the prodigal's return
to his home is convincingly done. He found that very
little had changed : the family still prayed night and
morning to be made " truly honest and conscientious " ;
the old water-colours and pictures were just in the same

places; and Theobald stood on the hearthrug as he always used to stand, and whistled, a little imperfectly, the only two tunes that he knew. Ernest's behaviour throughout his visit was quite commendable: only once was he consciously spiteful. It was at family prayers, on the second evening after his arrival, and is like one of those incidents in Butler's notes which he makes worth telling by his way of telling it. " He knelt next Charlotte and said the responses perfunctorily, not so perfunctorily that she should know for certain that he was doing it maliciously, but so perfunctorily as to make her uncertain whether he might be malicious or not, and when he had to pray to be made truly honest and conscientious he emphasised the ' truly.' I do not know whether Charlotte noticed anything, but she knelt at some distance from him during the rest of his stay."

This incident may well be coupled with the earlier description of family prayers at Battersby Rectory, when all the men and maid-servants filed into their appointed places—" they were nice people, but more absolute vacancy I never saw upon the countenances of human beings "—and Theobald read to them about the man gathering sticks on Sunday who was brought before Moses and Aaron. Butler made a sort of pictorial commentary on this, one of the central episodes of *The Way of All Flesh*, when he painted his delightful picture, *Family Prayers*.

Thus Butler's sarcasms at the expense of the Theobalds of this world are always merciless. He makes Ernest wonder how it is that sons ever can, or may even possibly hope to get on with their fathers; and so, lest he should treat his children as his grandfather

treated his father, and his father treated him, Ernest
sent his children away. So alarming an hereditary
taint could not be lightly set aside. Ernest calculated
that " a man first quarrels with his father about three
quarters of a year before he is born. It is then he insists
on setting up a separate establishment ; when this
has been once agreed to, the more complete the
separation for ever after the better for both." It was
almost a law of Nature that it should be so. Ernest
had by this time come to the conclusion that the fewer
people you have to humbug, the better. Least of all
did he want to make a systematic start, as might have
been the case, with his own children. Perhaps, even,
he might have been tempted to exercise " moral
influence " upon them. Probably this would never
have happened ; certainly he would not have tried to
persuade them how indulgent he was, or fed them
" spiritually upon such brimstone and treacle as the
late Bishop of Winchester's Sunday stories," or tried
to convict them of their own original sinfulness, three
cardinal pieces of advice, recommended by Butler,
to those who desire a quiet life. However, it was
dangerous going, and Ernest determined to give the
devil no opportunities. So he sent his children away
to a fine healthy couple, who had several well-grown
children, and others coming on.

From this point, and indeed considerably before it,
The Way of All Flesh becomes much more an unfolding
of the author's own philosophy, through the medium
of Ernest, than a story as such. Butler's opinions
display themselves more and more freely ; we no longer
feel the presence of Theobald, except as a faint shadow
which has done its work ; and the hero devotes himself,

in true Butlerian fashion, to the writing of unpopular
books which told people a good many things they would
rather not have heard—or at least if they were to hear
them they would have preferred them put in a different
way. Like Butler, Ernest's first book was a success, but
always afterwards his work was sneered at by literary
critics as soon as it appeared, although it became
" excellent reading " when followed by a later book.

The various marriage systems of the world engaged
his attention, and he set himself to study them with
complete disinterestedness. He came to the same
conclusion on which Butler had already laid stress in
Erewhon and which later he emphasised more directly
when he spoke of men living in a state of grace. Good
breeding, healthy, well-to-do citizens must be the aim
and end of all healthy societies. " If people require
us to construct," exclaimed Ernest, " we set good
breeding as the corner-stone of our edifice. . . .

" That a man should have been bred well and breed
others well ; that his figure, head, hands, feet, voice,
manner and clothes should carry conviction upon this
point, so that no one can look at him without seeing
that he has come of good stock and is likely to throw
good stock himself, this is the *desiderandum*. And the
same with a woman. The greatest number of these
well-bred men and women, and the greatest happiness
of those well-bred men and women, this is the highest
good ; towards this all government, all social conventions, all art, literature and science should directly
or indirectly tend. Holy men and holy women are
those who keep this unconsciously in view at all times
whether of work or pastime."

So, at the last, when Ernest came into his money

Q

and adopted book-keeping by double entry, Butler did successfully steer him into that state of life where he possessed "good health, good looks, good sense, experience, a kindly nature and a fair balance of cash in hand," which belong to those who obey that difficult precept about loving God.

The Way of All Flesh probably remains Butler's most brilliant work. Nothing he wrote, with the exception of the *Notebooks*, is so free and unfettered an expression of himself. If he put his thoughts into the *Notebooks* certainly the novel was for his friends and other people the memory of whom he wished to preserve in a permanent form. He always said that his books were not made, but rather grew of their own accord and came to him. *The Way of All Flesh* must have forced itself more insistently upon its author than any other of his books. It is intensely sincere, and consequently it is useless to pretend that it can appeal to all, or even the majority of tastes. It is not extravagant to describe it as one of the real novels in English ; and as Mr Cannan has so well shown, it goes back to a tradition almost obscured—that of the most distinctively English writer, Fielding. Butler's novel, moreover, in spite of the devastating nature of its satire, has a note of restraint all through, without which it must have failed in its effect. It is no disparagement to Butler's genius to add that *The Way of All Flesh* is the only novel he could have written, or indeed cared to write, not because he was deficient in creative ability, but because this book expressed for him definitely, and in that form, what he wanted most particularly to say about certain aspects of contemporary life. So it is a merciless exposé of some of the foibles of his own day,

and more directly of the cruelties and ugliness which
so often surround the life of children in a narrow,
evangelical family. And its characters are presented
with a fine ironic force. Here Butler used that kind of
irony which has about it the comic elements, to lead
the characters into strange and undignified positions
and even disasters. A perverse fortune—though she
may be a happy Fate in disguise—plays around
Ernest's head ; he has an infinite capacity for making
mistakes ; and his ordination brings to a culminating
point his aptitude, in sublime self-confidence, for always
just doing the wrong thing. We are disposed to think
that Butler intended his adventurous climax with Miss
Maitland should teach him, more than anything else—
discrimination.

Moreover, the influence of Butler's novel on the
younger generation of writers has already made itself
felt. It stands, of course, quite outside the modern
school of self-analysis and contemplation, yet in some
of the fiction of recent years, which has attempted the
difficult task of portraying a family in its unity and
diversity, its arguments and differences, it is possible
to trace the inspiration of Butler. His influence on
English fiction, though he was only an amateur in the
art, can work nothing but good. He had an eye for
character ; he entered tremendously into the lives of
his best characters, so that they appear in his pages as
living realities who move through the story of their
own accord and not at the bidding of the author ; and
further, he could recognise a distinctively English
figure and present it so that it lost none of its unique
flavour in the process. Just as he had an eye for
character and the gift of presenting it, so he was able,

by the quality of his writing, to bring out the full meaning of an apparently trifling episode or series of episodes as they appealed to him. Often what he treated in this way was by one touch, perhaps, redeemed from the commonplace. Yet more than this, he did not fear what was prosaic and ordinary ; he wrote, in one of his notes on Handel, of the art that is involved in being " easily and triumphantly commonplace." Butler himself also understood that secret.

The Way of All Flesh may be described, then, as one of the remarkable achievements in English fiction— the work of a non-professional novelist. If he had not felt the reality of it all with such intensity he could never have done it so supremely well. The crises through which his hero passed—the dramatised and expanded crises of his own life—are not only real in themselves, but genuinely transforming. No one who has appreciated the wit and irony, the sweeping, irresistible logic of the story, can ever be doubtful about the finely disciplined intelligence of its author. It is a tribute, too, to the imaginative gift he possessed that he was able to weave so coherently into a narrative the scattered realities which he had been absorbing all his life. He called *Erewhon* " A Work of Satire and Imagination," but *The Way of All Flesh* is much more so.

CHAPTER VIII

POSTHUMOUS

By a rather arbitrary classification we have included in this chapter, as its main subject, some consideration of *The Notebooks of Samuel Butler,* which were published ten years after his death. For the *Notebooks* was not the only posthumously published work of his ; *The Way of All Flesh* did not see the light till 1903 ; and yet Butler's notes, perhaps even more than the novel, make in their entirety a more vivid picture of him than it is possible to find elsewhere ; they are the most characteristic of his works, summing up and concluding everything else that he did, and may best be examined as the after-piece to a varied and versatile career. It is only after reading *Erewhon*, *Alps and Sanctuaries*, *Life and Habit* and the novel that the full flavour of Butler's notes can be appreciated.

But although, viewed in this light, they come as an after-piece, they were also, in an important sense, an accompaniment to the rest of his work. It is said that the novelist Charles Reade kept in his study, besides his desk and chair, only one important article of furniture—a series of bound volumes of newspaper cuttings, containing anything that might possibly be useful to him in his work. Each volume had its index, and there was a final index of indices. By the help of these he was able to construct his books, one of which, admittedly, is a masterpiece in English fiction.

245

Butler kept his *Notebooks* much in the same spirit, and during the last ten years of his life spent an hour each day editing and indexing them. But there was this difference : unlike Charles Reade's newspaper cuttings, Butler's notes were his own—his thoughts, the wanderings of fancy, hints and suggestions from all sorts of odd and unexpected sources ; they always had a personal relation, linking themselves on in their own fashion to the various activities of his working life. Primarily they were intended for his own use, and were written in this way because he found that ideas surged in upon him so rapidly and unannounced that the only hope of securing them was to pin them down as we do butterflies or beetles. Or, as he himself put it : " One's thoughts fly so fast that one must shoot them ; it is no use trying to put salt on their tails." So he secured them as best he could, always with the view that some time he would require them, either in their original form or a slightly altered one, to suit the context, for his books. Mr Festing Jones, who has edited and arranged Butler's *Notebooks* with such care and discrimination, points out that " When he had written and rewritten a note and spoken it and repeated it in conversation, it became so much a part of him that, if he wanted to introduce it in a book, it was less trouble to re-state it again from memory than to search through his ' precious indexes ' for it and copy it."

All this gives a very interesting insight into his method of writing. What he most wished was that his work should be compact of thoughts that had been tested, as it were, by the competitive examination of frequent reconsideration. All knowledge, he believed, to be really useful must have passed through

as many people as to become vital and living : and the
same with ideas in so far as it was possible ; he looked
at them and sifted them, and considered them from
as many angles as he could, always with the same aim
—to test their validity and permanence. And after
long practice he became an adept in seizing and select-
ing his ideas.

Samuel Butler's *Notebooks*, moreover, reveal more
clearly than anything else a characteristic we have often
insisted on in these pages. They show how intimate
was the relationship which he had established between
the crowded collection of subjects he was concerned
with. Hence the difficulty of arrangement. When a
man has reached a definite position, has built up for
himself a particular philosophy from which he is little
likely to recede, all the subjects that interest him, no
matter how much they may differ among themselves,
will take a definite place closely related to the main
principles that he has established. It is like a fugue
in music. " The great thing is that all shall be new,
and yet nothing new, at the same time ; the details
must minister to the main effect and not obscure it."
And so when one has grasped the broad outlines of the
Butlerian philosophy by reading his books, the numerous and diverse matters dealt with in the notes fall
into their proper places. Butler, in all his writings,
was entirely consistent. He never receded from a
theory. He says : " The reason why I have discarded so few theories that I have put forward—
and at this moment I cannot recollect one from
which there has been any serious attempt to dislodge
me—is because I never allowed myself to form a
theory at all till I found myself driven on to it

whether I would or no." This we believe to be a true explanation.

The great danger in keeping a series of notebooks, as Butler did, is lest the writer should become a mere gatherer of ideas as ends in themselves, thinking only of how he can best increase the size of his collection, which he takes out day by day to look at, and puts carefully away again. In such a case fantastic, un-related thoughts will do as well as anything else ; a chaos, indeed, often has that special charm which is lacking in well-arranged order. For if one is simply out in search for ideas, their quality and ancestry, and hence their possible offspring, need not be much taken into account. Certainly Butler treated his ideas with great reverence : he tells us in one of the notes that he is most prone to get new ones near the Record Office in Fetter Lane ; but he was never a mere collector. The value of an idea was just in proportion to its ability to stand frequent twistings and turnings— that is to say, he valued it in proportion to what it would do for him. But he knew that inevitably they must often collide. " In the complex of human affairs," he says, " we should aim not at a supposed absolute standard but at the greatest coming-together-ness or convenience of all our ideas and practices ; that is to say, at their most harmonious working with one another. Hit ourselves somewhere we are bound to do : no idea will travel far without colliding with some other idea." So from the beginning he kept careful watch over his ideas, and often found he had to modify them as time went on. But—and this is a further important trait—he acted always disinterestedly. He never clung to anything because he thought he ought

to like it. That an opinion was commonly received
was no reason why it should not be examined and reconsidered ; though, as Mr Jones has said, it is quite
unfair to assert that if a thing was generally accepted
it was sufficient reason to make Butler take a contrary
view. There was nothing of the bigot about him.

Further, Butler's method of making and revising
his notes was an important influence in forming his
style. Although in the early part of his life readings
in the late seventeenth and eighteenth century writers
had made him acquainted with a kind of prose which
appealed to him for its downrightness, he played the
sedulous ape to nobody. Yet Swift's orderliness, his
sobriety must have attracted Butler ; and he himself
came to it by a different method. It was by frequently
re-writing his notes that his style developed its clear,
terse quality. He considered first what he wished to
say, and then expressed it in the simplest possible
manner. Butler was never conscious of style ; *quâ*
style it was an incidental, for the aim of all writing
should be to express the underlying idea as directly
as may be. Hence slovenly thought is revealed in
slovenly, confused writing. Edward Fitzgerald has
put the whole matter into a compact sentence. He
defines style as " the saying, in the most perspicuous
and succinct way, what one thoroughly understands,
and saying it so naturally that no effort is apparent."

And yet, as Butler said in one of his notes, diffuseness has its uses. When a subject is difficult to master
it often helps if a little that is unnecessary is inserted
to give the reader or listener time to digest what has
gone before. There are instances of this in Butler's
own writing. In *Luck, or Cunning ?* much of the

chapter on Herbert Spencer, in which he explains how
ideas, to escape incoherence, must first be led up to and
afterwards resolved as is done with a discord in music,
is an example of this slight diffuseness. In *Life and
Habit*, too, when the exposition was novel and difficult,
Butler consciously wrote at considerably greater length
than he might otherwise have done. It helped him,
moreover. If the argument was new and complicated
a little repetition and multiplying of words enabled
him to see more clearly the ins and outs of what he
was dealing with.

But this manner of writing was an exception, not
the rule, with Butler. His prose was admirably clear
and concise. And he possessed that rare gift of bringing out his own point and meaning when describing the
most apparently commonplace scenes and episodes.
For this reason his writing all through is alive with
his alert, humorous personality. It remains a very
complete harmony of manner and treatment, showing
once more the impossibility of separating these two
elements. His note " My Son," which we have frequently referred to, is remarkable both for its typically
Butlerian philosophy and the humorous twists of
fancy it reveals. Probably nothing can better illustrate the peculiar texture of Butler's writing than this
note :

" I have often told my son that he must begin by
finding me a wife to become his mother who shall
satisfy both himself and me. But this is only one of
the many rocks on which we have hitherto split. We
should never have got on together ; I should have had
to cut him off with a shilling either for laughing at
Homer, or for refusing to laugh at him, or both, or

neither, but still cut him off. So I settled the matter
long ago by turning a deaf ear to his importunities
and sticking to it that I would not get him at all. Yet
his thin ghost visits me at times and, though he knows
that it is no use pestering me further, he looks at me so
wistfully and reproachfully that I am half-inclined to
turn tail, take my chance about his mother and ask
him to let me get him after all. But I should show a
clean pair of heels if he said ' Yes.'

" Besides, he would probably be a girl."

It would be difficult to find anything better than
this self-contained, rather wistful Butlerism. Like all
his other notes, it is perfectly free from affectation.
As a good black-and-white artist deliberately prunes
his work of all superfluous lines, so Butler took out of
his writing those little ornaments and irrelevancies,
and the stereotyped phrases generally signifying ready-
made thought which insinuate themselves so cunningly.
And he did this always with the intention of being
first of all clear to himself as to his own meaning and
then making that meaning as clear as possible to his
readers.

He was well fitted, for these reasons, as a prophet of
very much that was new to English moralists. He
disliked dogma above everything, and was convinced
of the relativity of morality as well as of religion. In
all things there are degrees. " So with light and darkness, heat and cold, you never can get either all the
light, or all the heat out of anything. So with God and
the Devil ; so with everything. Everything is like a
door swinging backwards and forwards. Everything
has a little of that from which it is most remote and to
which it is most opposed and these antitheses serve to

explain one another." Hence Butler's quarrel with
those who, in their attempt to simplify human relations,
endeavoured to find "pure" instances, untainted
with their opposite elements. Such things existed
only as abstractions. Good and evil, virtue and vice,
and their personalised forms, God and the Devil were
thus, in Butler's view, necessary to each other. They
are like Mr Belloc's conception of the Party System,
which is carried on, he says, by collusion between the
two Front Benches. They lived through and in each
other. In cases like these, as we pointed out in the
introduction to this study, the one side was never all
square and independent of the other. Life and progress consist in the continual clash and encounter of
opposing forces ; competition is necessary to them ;
complete virtue and complete vice alike mean stagnation. In Butler's opinion humanity and kindliness
and the charity that St Paul wrote of in the noblest
chapter of the New Testament, are what men and
women should aim at in this world.

"If virtue," says Butler, "had everything her own
way she would be as insufferable as dominant factions
generally are. It is the function of vice to keep virtue
within reasonable bounds." He would have approved
altogether of M. Anatole France's delightful dissertation on the death of the Devil in *Le Livre de mon Ami*.
The tragedy at the Punch and Judy show when the
Devil died awoke rather melancholy thoughts.

"Le Diable mort, adieu le péché ! Peut-être la
beauté, cette allieé du Diable, s'en ira-t-elle avec lui !
peut-être ne verrons nous plus les fleurs dont on
s'enivre et les yeux dont on meurt ! Alors que de-
viendrons-nous en ce monde ? Nous restera-t-il même

la ressource d'être vertueux ?   J'en doute.   Gringalet
n'a pas assez considéré que le mal est necessaire au
bien, comme l'ombre à la lumière ; que la vertu est
toute dans l'effort et que, si l'on n'a plus de Diable à
combattre, les saints seront aussi désœuvrés que les
pécheurs.   On s'ennuiera mortellement.   Je vous dis
qu'en tuant le Diable, Gringalet a commis une grave
imprudence."

Here again effort is the concomitant of virtue ; yet
with the devil dead, boredom would become even more
rife than during his lifetime.   Nor can M. France persuade himself that such an event would not mean the
disappearance of beauty both in nature and the sons
and daughters of men.   And to Butler, who was
brought up in a constricting religious school, with its
stern insistence on the rampaging habits of Satan, and
the close proximity of hell and damnation as its most
vital elements, there was very little beauty in life, as
far as religion revealed it to him.   Such a religion took
its texture from the ugly qualities with which it en-
dowed its chief assailant and its chief supporter.
Satan and the world and the flesh, and the kind of religion which was principally concerned with them, were
all of a uniform unlovely type.   If it is the fact, as
M. France suggests, that Satan is the father of a
kingdom of happiness and of beauty that pleases our
senses, it is none the less a fact that religion, when it
is not the religion of prigs and pedants, may have a
place for these things also.   But Butler never knew
such a religion.   In any case he did not want people
to be too much troubled about it all : he quotes with
relish, in *Alps and Sanctuaries*, the little dialogue he
had with a nice old Italian priest about the Devil.

The priest, referring to a fourteenth - century bridge known as " The Devil's Bridge," told Butler that it was not really built by the Devil. Butler said he imagined not, since he was not in the habit of spending his time so profitably.

" ' I wish he had built it,' said my friend ; ' for then perhaps he would build us some more.'

" ' Or we might even get a church out of him,' said I, a little slyly.

" ' Ha, ha, ha ! we will convert him, and make a good Christian of him in the end.' "

And Butler liked this, because it showed how lightly and happily the old priest's religion sat upon his shoulders. The episode is interesting too as showing the kind of religious atmosphere—where such remarks would have been considered irreverent and unseemly —in which Butler was reared. After all the Devil dead and the Devil converted would come to very much the same thing.

Righteousness was a further question on which Butler " allowed himself to speculate," in Darwin's phrase. He used the word in a broad sense, identifying it with strength and grace and virility. For this reason he was little disposed to agree with those who maintain that the highest righteousness was to be found in the Jewish people. Holiness may be a Semitic character- istic, but it is a professional holiness, which generally results in a goodly outcrop of hypocritical self- satisfaction. Butler saw this as the dominant trait of the entire Hebrew nation, and hence he came to dis- trust professional religion as he was apt to distrust professionalism altogether. He saw ulterior motives in it—a wish to be clever, or socially successful. So he attacked the decorative righteousness of the Hebrews, and in his further remarks upon them develops a criticism of their literature on lines which Ernest Pontifex might have followed in his essay on the Greek Drama had he been a little bolder. The Psalms especially Butler disliked, as being " querulous, spiteful and introspective " ; and he thought that the prayer, " Lord, let me know mine end, and the number of my days : that I may be certified how long I have to live," was of all prayers the stupidest. It certainly is that, looked at from the point of view of a normal, healthy man. But the Psalmist was neither of these : he was always troubled about matters which did not concern him, self-conscious, communing with his own heart. A lady who had been reading in Butler's *Notebooks* confessed that she was so much irritated by his remarks on this verse of the Psalms that she felt inclined to read no more. Of course, she said, the prayer was simply a piece of poetic licence, not perhaps realising that in that case Butler's remarks also might be poetic licence. Yet it seems likely that the writer meant his petition *au serieux* ; indeed it is recited with a circumstance and directness which forbids any other conclusion.

No doubt the Psalmist was being righteous according to his lights when he prayed thus ; and righteousness, Butler was inclined to agree with Matthew Arnold, should be a man's highest aim in life. Yet we should not be conscious of it, just as we can never be conscious of that Unknown God who sums up and includes in himself all the lesser units that compose him. We may be aware of the lesser aims, but not of the highest aim in life.

It is because of this attitude, no doubt, that many

readers have condemned Butler, as throwing cold water on those zealous spirits which know quite well where they are going and are loud in their conversations about it. The kingdom of heaven, however, doesn't come by observation. Yet Butler had great enthusiasm, though he only lavished it where he believed it was well deserved. All sorts of people and opinions that have been accepted by the great majority, he disliked. In this he was perfectly sincere. Unless there was something in the character or work of the man in question that appealed to him, he was not going to pretend that he had any sympathy with him. And when he wrote his dissertation on earnestness it was perhaps intended more than anything else as a warning to himself, because he was apt to be so enthusiastic both in his likes and dislikes. He was earnest only when he saw very good reason for it. Indeed it was all part of that intellectual sincerity which with Butler was far-reaching in its effects. " Sincerity," he said, " is a low and very rudimentary form of virtue that is only to be found to any considerable extent among the protozoa." Although it is a low virtue it is singularly perfect, as it shows itself in them. " The germ-cells will not be humbugged ; they will tell the truth as near as they can. They know their ancestors meant well and will tend to become even more sincere themselves." But inherent in grown men is the desire to hoodwink ; and the general public likes it. Butler had too much of the early, discredited virtue of the protozoa ever to be popular with the general public. It likes being hoodwinked—but in its own way, which it understands and approves of. Butler's irony was something it did not understand. That irony was unduly reasonable. And the method of reducing to an absurdity whatever it happened to be attacking was a too mystifying one to be approved by the general public. Butler, of course, knew that in advance; consequently he made his book, *The Fair Haven*, completely ironical in its method, and let it establish for itself as best it might its own sheep and goats, the two audiences which every genuine piece of irony produces. The general public was, however, quite unwilling to admire the hoax when it discovered how unorthodox it had been.

All of which reveals Butler's seriousness and sincerity. He could not help himself in these respects, for, as Mr Shaw says, he knew the importance of the things he had hit on and would develop them into a message for his age.

In one of his notes he made a list of his finds : none of them was the result of study or research, though he confessed that after he had secured them they generally gave him plenty to do in the way of study. Starting with *Erewhon*, he tabulated these finds which he picked up in the many fields over which he ranged. They make one aware how essentially Butler was a spectator observing the actions of the men on the stage of the world, to use a metaphor suggested in Professor Hering's lecture on Memory. He was a spectator with a remarkable power of shrewd observation and of drawing conclusions from what he saw—but still a spectator. He had no pretensions to being behind the scenes. Hence to the end he remained an amateur—the last of the courageous amateurs—by which we mean a non-professional worker in the various departments that interested him, as well as a lover. He wrote a

R

note on these two classes of people, and though he was
thinking more particularly of painters his words have
a wider application.

" There is no excuse," he says, " for amateur work
being bad. Amateurs often excuse their shortcomings
on the ground that they are not professionals, the professional could plead with greater justice that he is
not an amateur. The professional had not, he might
well say, the leisure and freedom from money anxieties
which will let him devote himself to his art in singleness
of heart, telling of things as he sees them without fear
of what men shall say unto him ; he must think not
of what appears to him right and lovable, but of what
his patrons will think and of what the critics will tell
his patrons to say they think ; he has got to square
everyone all round and will assuredly fail to make
his way unless he does this ; if, then, he betrays his
trust he does so under temptation." Conversely the
amateur is free from all such disabilities. This was
all very well, but in an age which was dominated by
specialists Butler could not expect to find that his
heretical doctrines won much approval. His own
position, moreover, had all the symptoms of instability
about it, and the Victorian age liked stability. The
specialist, too, was the bulwark of the Victorian
system, the mainstay of a period when materialism
was rampant. He gave the public an impression of
security and knowledge, just as the mechanic always
has an air of infallibility to one who is entirely
ignorant of machinery. Here at any rate is the
practical man who knows !

Butler tried to explain to his generation the risks it
ran in being humbugged and deluded by its specialists—

the professional men of science especially. It paid no
attention to him, however, and acquiesced in dullness as
a necessary accompaniment to all this, indeed coming
almost to believe that the importance of anybody or
anything was in proportion to his or its capacity for
creating boredom. That, again, was part of the reason
why it so quickly eliminated Butler from among its
chosen. " Don't bore people," he says. " And yet I
am by no means sure that a good many people do not
think themselves ill-used unless he who addresses them
has thoroughly well bored them—especially if they
have paid any money for hearing him." From the
first rather puzzled pages of *Erewhon* to the triumphant
convictions of *The Way of All Flesh* he attacked
English shams, hypocrisies and humbugs—one of
which was just this delusion in English people that
they liked being bored and deluded. Taken as a whole,
the English are a humorous race, but they dislike a
man's jokes to mean very much—which is quite distinct from their having a double meaning—hence the
prevailing popularity, to take random examples,
of musical comedy and Marie Corelli's novels.

But while Butler was writing his books, there were
two other interests which absorbed him, each in its
own way, and which remain as a kind of background
to the rest of his work. These were painting and
music. After his return from New Zealand he began
life as an artist, and so his remarks on art, which occur
chiefly in *Alps and Sanctuaries, Ex Voto* and the *Notebooks*, have a further interest as being the views of one
who was himself a painter.

We have noted, in the chapter on Italy, that what
Butler chiefly looked for in an artist, as finding the

readiest response in himself, was life and go, a reasonable degree of attention to his work, and the evidence
that he didn't know too much about what he was doing.
If he found these things he was satisfied. One of the
reasons why the painted statuary so much appealed
to him was that its homeliness, which not seldom de-
scended to tawdriness also, was natural and unaffected ;
the statuary was put into its particular form for a
definite purpose, and fulfilled it. This amounts to
saying that there was not much academic flavour
about it ; and in the best work this was so.

Butler's objection to academies, and the current
systems of " art-study," was that they had mistaken
the whole intention of art. An oldish lady who had
received scanty education in her youth once made the
following remark to him :—" You see the world, and all
that it contains, is wrapped up in such curious forms,
that it is only by a knowledge of human nature that
we can rightly tell what to say, to do, or to admire."
It reminded him of an academy picture. The defects
of the academic system are the defects of the old lady :
word-painting and fine phrases which have nothing
more to recommend them than is revealed on the
surface are all, apparently, that is aimed at ; each is
an instance of style devoid of subject-matter.

Further, Butler condemned the academic system
because it did not satisfy the paradox that the way to
learn how to do a thing is to do it, and not be taught
lessons about it. He believed that the only way to
learn how to write was by writing. And the same with
painting. This is what he called the apprentice system
—learning, that is, very slowly, in company with one
who is doing similar work. The great secret, Butler

thought, in painting, as in literature and music, is not
to attempt too much, but to work only at that which
gives pleasure and satisfaction, even if this means
aiming at a lower point than we might have wished for.
Life and Habit taught Butler all it was necessary for
him to know about writing ; here he wanted to create
for himself a clear and direct means of expression ;
he wished everyone to understand what he was saying ;
and as the controversy with Darwin progressed his
writing became even clearer and more incisive. But he
was never conscious in his writing of taking anything
like the same pains he took with his painting. And he
considered that he was weakest in painting : " I am
weakest where I have taken most pains, and studied
most."

In a note on academicism Butler writes thus : " He
who knows he is infirm, and would yet climb, does not
think of the summit which he believes to be beyond his
reach, but climbs slowly onwards, taking very short
steps, looking below as often as he likes, but not above
him, never trying his powers but seldom stopping, and
then, sometimes, behold ! he is on the top, which he
would never have even aimed at could he have seen
it from below. It is only in novels and sensational
biographies that handicapped people, ' fired by a knowledge of the difficulties that others have overcome,
resolve to triumph over every obstacle by dint of sheer
determination, and in the end carry everything before
them.' " Here again the goal that is aimed at does
not come by observation. And when Butler speaks
of looking not upwards but downwards he does not
mean that we are to do so in a spirit of complacency
for what we have achieved, but rather with an air of

dissatisfaction and self-criticism, thinking always how much better we might have climbed. So, looking beyond what lies before us in these respects is a kind of artistic introspection which can do no good. Painting, in fact, must be a development, a becoming, a continual but gradual moving forward : the less it is impeded by theories the better. The beginner can best help the beginner because the gulf between them does not exist as compared with that which yawns between the beginner and the master of technique. After the mediæval revival of art, as Butler said in *Ex Voto*, the first artists " rose as little to theory as children do." They worked with great difficulty. And hence their very incompetence saved them from vulgarity, just as the Eastern peoples saved their good manners until Western culture seized them in its clutches. For an " amiable and painstaking " incompetence has a charm of its own which no amount of technical knowledge can reach by itself.

Butler summed up the secrets of success in painting in a passage which occurs in his remarks on the " Decline of Italian Art." [1] These secrets, he says, " are affection for the pursuit chosen, a flat refusal to be hurried or to pass anything as understood, and an obstinacy of character which shall make the student's friends find it less trouble to let him have his own way than to bend him into theirs. Our schools and academies or universities are covertly, but essentially, radical institutions and abhorrent to the genius of Conservatism, their sin is the true radical sin of being in too great a hurry, and of believing in short cuts too soon." So apart from their function of keeping

[1] See *Alps and Sanctuaries*.

down geniuses, a work valuable in itself and necessary for the welfare of the community, Butler did not see much reason for the existence of universities or academies. The institutions themselves are no doubt little accustomed to the charge of radicalism in their spirit and methods which he levelled against them.

What, after all, Butler chiefly liked in painting was a well-behaved simplicity. When he saw men painting subjects that were unpretentious and commonplace, and hence unattractive to those in search for novelty or loftiness of subject, he knew that their interest was genuine. With others who, like Michelangelo, were always trying to soar, it was at times impossible to make up one's mind on this point. He did not believe, however, that any artist can hope to please very many people. No man who has much inspiration in him and sets out to satisfy himself can hope to satisfy many others at the same time. When Tolstoy said that all art must be tested by that " infective " quality whereby it appeals immediately to the greatest number, he was lowering the dignity of the artist in order to support his theory of the infallibility of the crowd. Butler would have approached this view from another side and condemned it as being subversive of common-sense.

To him a master in any art should be a combination of man, poet and craftsman. The craftsmanship is the least, and the humanity the most, important of the elements that compose him. So in Italian art he found it necessary at times to deprecate the " saint-touch," not because he objected to pictures of Madonnas, saints and angels, but because in the works themselves he very often failed to see any of that inspiration born of a genuine interest in the sacred subjects—only the stereotyped intention to behave nicely and do the proper thing as mechanically as possible. Soaring is all very well when it is done with sincerity and self-forgetfulness, but even then it is not a very human process. Butler tried to imagine Michelangelo contemplating a priest chucking a little boy under the chin ; neither of them could compass such an image. And the inference is that in so far as an artist is thus cut off from a vital side of human life and intercourse—that represented by the priest and the boy—he is an inferior artist.

Just as all art is based on certain delusions so again in one of its departments, notably painting, the man who can lie well will often bring nature more actually and vividly before us than strict accuracy alone can do. In other words, it is by the simplification of details, as Butler explained, and by the emphasising of those relevant to his subject that the artist gives the illusion of reproducing the whole when he only reproduces a part. In writing it is the same here as in painting. And we have touched on this particular point because Butler, in *Alps and Sanctuaries*, himself gives an interesting instance of it. In the chapter on Piora referred to in a prevous section, he records a dream he had in which Handel appears—reminiscent of that other Handelian dream in *Erewhon*. Butler knew what he could do with detail, and here the whole description is illuminated and made alive by his telling us, in one piece of detail, that when the women-singers and the huge orchestra, which Handel was to conduct, had taken their places so that they were massed together to the extreme edge of the mountain, he " could see

underneath the soles of their boots as their legs dangled
in the air." This small item of detail, appearing in
the middle of a description which is purposely somewhat vague and misty in its outlines, gives conviction
to the whole piece. Precisely in the same way Butler
believed a painter should make use of detail in his
pictures.

He himself had learnt this lesson from his painting.
It had trained his eyes, moreover, in observation; had
taught him to look for characters and incidents in
out-of-the-way places as an artist looks for colour in
unlikely nooks and corners. Butler was an incomparable observer. He was always ready to absorb what
was going on, and come to conclusions about it. Anyone at all less observant than he would have passed
by very many of those incidents and characters that
he paused to write notes about. He knew their value
for him. And so the apparently flimsiest things take
on a distinctive light and colour under his hands.
The note he wrote on " Colour " contains very much
that applies to his own faculty for extracting what
appealed to him from a scene or conversation or what
not.

" That we can see in a natural object," he says,
" more colour than strikes us at a glance, if we look for
it attentively, will not be denied by any who have tried
to look for it. Thus, take a dull, dead, level, grimy
old London wall : at a first glance we can see no colour
in it, nothing but a more or less purplish mass, got,
perhaps as nearly as in any other way, by a tint mixed
with black, Indian red and white. . . . There may be
bits of old advertisement of which here and there a
gaily coloured fragment may remain, or a rusty iron

hook or a bit of bright green moss ; few indeed are the
old walls, even in the grimiest parts of London, in
which no redeeming bits of colour can be found by
those who are practised in looking for them. To like
colour, to wish to find it, and thus to have got naturally into a habit of looking for it, this alone will enable
a man to see colour and to make a note of it when he
has seen it. . . ." It was a particular gift of Butler's
that he saw colour in the least expected places—but
only because he looked for it.

The *Notebooks* appropriately conclude with two
sections on " Death " and " The Life of the World to
Come," subjects on which Butler wrote not a little.
His remarks on the life after death are, as it were, an
addendum to what he said in *God the Known and God
the Unknown* and the essay, " How to Make the Best
of Life." Like the French philosopher, Guyau, Butler
wrote about the defeat of death ; and their views,
though dissimilar, are not without interest in their
contrast. Guyau has somewhere spoken of the strange
final irony of Death ; for sometimes, he says, it is our
fancy that perhaps in their last moment the dying will
guess her secret and close their eyes in a quick, clear
flash of light. " Notre dernière douleur reste ainsi
notre dernière curiosité," said Guyau. So the defeat
of death lies in fathoming her mystery even though we
do not afterwards exist to be aware of our discovery.
Butler, however, did not believe there was any secret.
Our dislike of death is instinctive : this dislike is a
quality of life itself, notwithstanding that there are
degrees of death in life and vice versa. Dislike, then,
is not a fear of the unknown and the mysterious, but
quite otherwise. This note on defeating death may

be contrasted with Guyau's view of the "dernière douleur."

"There is nothing," says Butler, "which at once affects a man so much and so little as his own death. It is a case in which the going-to-happen-ness of a thing is of greater importance to the man who dies, for Death cuts his own throat in the matter of hurting people. As a bee that can sting once but in the stinging dies, so Death is dead to him who is dead already. While he is shaking his wings, there is *brutum fulmen* but the man goes on living, frightened, perhaps, but unhurt ; pain and sickness may hurt him but the moment Death strikes him both he and Death are beyond feeling. It is as though Death were born anew with every man ; the two protect one another so long as they keep one another at arm's length, but if they once embrace it is all over with both."

We only defeat death, therefore, by the act of dying.

We can hope for no continuity of life after death, Butler believed, except that life we live unconsciously in the thoughts and deeds of others. It is, however, as impossible to speak with any certainty about the quality or duration of this life we live in others as it is impossible for an embryo to know anything about the life it is to live in its own person. In *Erewhon Revisited* it is all stated in a symmetrical form, almost like a diagram ; the World of the Unborn is thus the perfect counterpart of the World of Vicarious Existence. And as Butler there pointed out, the memories and works of those who are dead to their physical and conscious selves have exactly the same right to force themselves upon living people for that renewed life that consists in being remembered—with its obverse, the complete

death of forgotten-ness—as the unembodied spirits of
the Unborn World have a right, if they think fit in
their misguided ignorance, to pester the numerous
married persons of this world in order to get themselves
born. Sex, therefore, which Butler defined as among
" the first great experiments in the social subdivision
of labour," is, in this view, an afterthought. The
restlessness of those germs which seek a new condition
of life is the primary cause of that human desire to
assimilate something else which is the unvarying
accompaniment of sexual attraction. The wish for
complete assimilation, in the same way, is the key to
eating as of every other appetite.

Exploring among Butler's notes it is thus possible
on every page to find something which demands attention either for its substance or the way it is stated.
The section called " Higgledy-Piggledy," in which Mr
Jones has included those notes which come under no
definite heading, is one of the most attractive. Butler
writes here of the men of science who should be about
God's path and bed, of " Cat-Ideas and Mouse-Ideas,"
of Jones' conscience and Purgatory and the Universities
and David's (the Psalmist's) teachers, of sex and
marriage and the happiness of the devils when they
were cast out of Mary Magdalene, of the triumphant
feeling of superiority about religious " Hallelujahs."
These are a few of the varied dozens of things touched
on in this section alone. And these fantastic thoughts
that moved across his mind, one is tempted to think,
are rather like the erratic progress of the knight in
chess as he moves across the board. They may be
erratic, but they cover a very wide area. They show,
too, that on every subject which came his way he had

something, if not original, at any rate valuable, to say.
And he did not hesitate to make his jokes about the
sacredest things in the universe, because that was his
method of arriving at a truer estimate of them. Of
course now and again there is a spice of perverse
naughtiness; but looking through the *Notebooks,* one
is struck with the high and serious aim of nearly
everything in them.

What he wrote about himself moreover, was, we
believe, the result neither of egotism nor *naïveté.* His
disinterested nature enabled him to exercise a large
measure of self-criticism where his work was concerned.
He criticised his first book, the description of New
Zealand life, as the work of a prig who couldn't help
himself because his Cambridge skin was still clinging
so tightly to him. Perhaps he was right. He knew that
Erewhon was an imperfect book; but he wrote it
entirely for his own comfort, to clear away accumulated
material so that he could get on with his real work and
be a painter. But when the Owen Memoir was written
Butler could no longer help himself; he had discovered
that he could create character, and he went on to write
his masterpiece, *The Way of All Flesh.* The painting
became intermittent, and when the Darwinian affair
demanded attention he knew that his vocation was
literature. It is evident, however, that throughout
the whole of his literary career he never published a
book that was not the result of much careful thought
and criticism. The *Notebooks* throw this much light
on his work. Reference to the note we quoted in the
Introduction, " Myself and my Books," [1] will show
what his position was. He speaks of the necessity of

[1] See page 19.

being " fearless and thoroughgoing " if a writer hopes
to attract a larger and later audience—outside his own
generation.   George Eliot is a person who should point
a moral in this connection.   And he might have added
Tennyson.   But the note was written in 1883, so perhaps he had not yet found out about Tennyson.   Butler
was anything but a reckless writer : when a friend
suggested to him that his manuscript should be " gone
over " by some judicious person before printing, so
that the random passages might be excised, he had
to explain to him that the more reckless they appeared
to be the more carefully had these passages been considered and reconsidered, and submitted for criticism
to personal friends.   So, as he was not able to say the
General Confession altogether without reserve, and as
it had no particular clause which related to this matter,
Butler composed a smaller General Confession, which
explains his own view of himself and his work :

" I have left unsaid much that I am sorry I did not
say, but I have said little that I am sorry for having
said, and I am pretty well on the whole, thank you."

At this point we may leave these considerations of
Butler's *Notebooks*, into which he put the most intimate
and personal part of himself.   The notes are perhaps
the best guide to his complex personality.   Much that
he wrote in his manuscript books may be of no interest
now, and, as Mr Jones says, many of the entries " are of
a kind that must wait if they are ever to be published."
But those entries which Mr Jones has selected and
edited and published in *The Notebooks of Samuel
Butler* are all worth their place, both for themselves
and the light they throw on the live and humorous
mind of their author.

CHAPTER IX

CONCLUSION

WE have attempted in the Introduction to this study to give some rough view of the age in which Samuel Butler lived. And from the foregoing it follows naturally enough, we believe, that he was little likely to be in sympathy with the spirit of his own time, when outlined against the background of contemporary life and thought. He found himself out of touch with it on countless questions, as becomes abundantly clear in reading his books; but it must be remembered that English Victorian life always fascinated him. He wanted to hunt down its deceits and weaknesses, to understand it first from its own point of view, and then draw his conclusions about it. Otherwise he would never have been the satirist he was—merely, perhaps, an amateur in music and painting with a lazy, humorous but never serious interest in the society in which he found himself.

Throughout history, ages, like countries, may in one view be estimated by their great men. Contributions to literature, science and art are the work of the great men of every age. Butler looked round upon the work that was being done in his own day, and found himself, as a rule, utterly unable to appreciate or to understand the praise that was lavished upon his contemporaries. Reference to the *Notebooks* sets his contempts—from the Psalmist to Tennyson—in quite

271

a clear light. Here again we believe that Butler was altogether sincere : there was no jealousy, nor did he dislike the successful man merely because he was successful. Mr Festing Jones has told us that the reason of Butler's contempt for his successful contemporaries was that he so often found that success had been obtained by unworthy means. Hence he got into the habit of approaching it with suspicion unless there was something in the work that appealed to him—much more often the case with painters than with writers. "Whenever we met a celebrated man," says Mr Jones, "Butler assumed that the onus of proving that he deserved his success, was upon the celebrated man ; at any rate Butler was not going to accept it without proof or make it easy for him. Consequently these meetings were apt to be a bit chilly." Then, again, Butler resented the confusion between success and that power of getting on in spite of the work which is characteristic of so many of our arrivistes. A passage in his " Apologia " at the end of the *Notebooks* shows how far he had identified success and opportunism. " If I were to succeed," he says, " I should be bored to death by my success in a fortnight and so, I am convinced, would my friends. Retirement is to me a condition of being able to work at all. . . . Nor do I see how I could get retirement if I were not to a certain extent unpopular."

Tennyson and Darwin were two figures which Butler thought of as particularly representative of his time. He would have delighted, we are sure, in Mr Edmund Gosse's vivid description of Tennyson as he saw him on the first occasion they met. It is no doubt difficult for this generation, as Mr Gosse says, to understand

the awe and reverence with which Tennyson was regarded in the early years of the enthusiastic seventies,
when this writer first met him. The meeting was in
the Sculpture Gallery of the British Museum. Tennyson stood "bare-headed" and "imperial-looking."
At length the party moved on to look at the sculpture.
Tennyson led. "But the only remark," says Mr
Gosse, "which my memory has retained was made
before the famous black bust of Antinous. Tennyson
bent forward a little, and said, in his deep, slow voice :
'Ah! This is the inscrutable Bithynian!' There was
a pause, and then he added, gazing into the eyes of the
bust : 'If we knew what he knew, we should understand
the ancient world.' "[1]   And Mr Gosse has insisted that
nothing could equal the dignity with which Tennyson
made this pronouncement. The whole description
would have delighted Butler; it supports very well
his own conception of the revered Victorian poet.

Darwin, on the other hand, had a curious low-Church
tone about him, quite alien to Butler's temper. His
"May we not believe," and "Have we any right to
infer," which we meet more than once in his books, are
indications of the kind of spirit which lurked behind.
The two men were so fundamentally opposed in
temperament that if there was any opportunity for
it, a collision was almost bound to occur. That the
quarrel was over a vital question in the philosophy of
evolution it is easy to see; later on Butler carried the
matter a step further by showing that his "cunning"
and Darwin's "luck" were to be identified with
free will and necessity respectively. It does not
appear, however, that Darwin ever very carefully

[1] *Portraits and Sketches.* By Edmund Gosse.

S

considered where his " theory " was leading him and
what it actually involved.

It was not much wonder, then, that his contemporaries did not know what to think of Butler. He
refused to be classified in the same uncompromising
way that he flew in the face of their most cherished
beliefs. They were helplessly mystified by one who
would persuade them to abandon zeal and earnestness
when he himself was so obviously possessed by these
things. Equally they were puzzled by a writer who
flatly told them not to believe in him : " Above all
things, let no unwary reader do me the injustice of
believing in *me*. In that I write at all I am among the
damned "—and that he was simply making the best
of a bad job. This kind of temper they were quite
unable to understand. What Butler meant when he
classified himself among the damned was that he was
becoming a prig. " The essence of priggishness is
setting up to be better than one's neighbour." It
means behaving like the sons of Levi who took too
much upon themselves. Everyone is liable to this
fault to a greater or less extent. And every writer,
by the very fact of his writing, tacitly sets himself on
an eminence above his fellows—even if he is unconscious of doing so. He sets out to instruct other
people. Butler could not help this, much as he disliked prigs, who are only a few degrees preferable to
bores. For priggishness can at least exist by itself,
but the bore is a social evil who requires others in order
to realise and complete himself. So Butler took his
chance about priggishness and set out to tell other
people all kinds of things about themselves, and the
world in general, after having plainly warned them

against believing what he said. He knew very well that the race he belonged to was naturally prone to this priggish habit. Also he seems to have been brought up among prigs and virtuous people, and was always meeting them. And the fact that he was more sensitive to detect them than most people —it was the same also with humbugs—made him very much aware of them, as becomes clear in his novel. It follows, then, that Butler's contemporaries could not resolve his apparent inconsistencies. And this was because they never realised the unity in his work. Nor, indeed, did it much concern them to do so.

One small part of Butler's work might have appealed to them—the book that is least characteristic of him but interesting both for its subject and because it is so different from the others. We refer to the biography of his grandfather, *The Life and Letters of Dr Samuel Butler, in so far as they illustrate the Scholastic, Religious and Social Life of England*, 1790-1840. It appeared in 1896 in two large volumes. As Mr Jones says, " he became penetrated with an almost Chinese reverence for his ancestor," and the result was a very full account of his activities given for the most part in letters, diaries and personal notes. We may repeat that the more Butler got to know about his grandfather, the more was he impressed with his knowledge of the world, the solidity of his character and his practical common-sense. In spite of this he did not hesitate to include in *The Way of All Flesh* some descriptions of scenery which he extracted from the diaries of his grandfather's foreign tours, and which he quotes as examples of the conventional priggishness of Mr George

Pontifex. The passages in the two books are identical. Here is the extract from Dr Butler's diary, June, 1819 —a first sight of Mont Blanc was the cause of the writer's raptures :

" My feelings I cannot express. I gasped—yet hardly dared to breathe as I viewed for the first time this monarch of the mountains. I seemed to fancy the genius seated on his stupendous throne far above his aspiring brethren, and in his solitary might defying the universe. I was so overcome by my feelings that I was almost bereft of my faculties, and would not for worlds have spoken after my first exclamation, till I found some relief in a gush of tears. With pain I tore myself from contemplating for the first time, ' at distance dimly seen ' (though I felt as if I had sent my soul and eyes after it), this sublime spectacle."

On his later foreign tours, Dr Butler was much less a rhapsodist than on his first, though on one other occasion, when contemplating Rome, from the tower of the Capitol, he allowed himself to indulge in a further gush of tears. His biographer gives many quotations from the diaries; in fact, all through he lets his grandfather speak for himself where possible. Butler obtrudes himself very little. Personal opinions, his own likes and dislikes, appear rather by suggestion and inference, though there are one or two references to the authoress of the *Odyssey*. And in one place, after quoting his grandfather's impression of the Lake of Como, he cannot resist setting side by side with it a few meditations of Dr Arnold suggested by the same lake in the same year, 1829. The latter thought how delightful it would be to live there always with his family ; but he remembered that that would mean

" abandoning the line of usefulness and activity "
which he had in England.   Such scenes for Englishmen
are only designed " to gild with beautiful recollec-
tions our daily life of home duties," for England's
destinies are different from the destinies of these
countries. Then he considered her immense power
for good in the world—" her full intelligence, her restless activity . . . her pure religion and unchecked
freedom." And he closes on that thought which was
never far distant in the earlier part of the last century,
when the French had been overcome—the thought of
England's material prosperity.   " Therefore these
lovely valleys and this surpassing beauty of lake and
mountain, and garden, and wood, are least, of all men,
for us to covet ; and our country, so entirely subdued
as it is to man's uses, its gentle hills and valleys, its
innumerable canals and coaches, is best suited as an
instrument of usefulness."

We have summarised this passage because of its
evident interest for Butler—otherwise he would not
have quoted it in full in its particular context. It is
to be regretted that the two illustrious headmasters,
Dr Butler and Dr Arnold, never met, though they
corresponded in later years.

While writing this Life, Butler came upon two or
three epitaphs composed by his grandfather which
appealed to him both for their dignity and vigour.
He knew how difficult they are to write. As the art
of composing prayers went out with the Tudors, so it
was in later times in the making of epitaphs. And
when Butler was doing the *In Memoriam* passage to
the old lady in *Erewhon Revisited*,[1] he was, no doubt,

[1] Quoted, p. 95.

thinking of that epitaph on Dr Butler's parents which
Dr Butler wrote in 1822, and which is reproduced in
The Way of All Flesh in memory of old John Pontifex
and his wife. It is worth quoting again, however,
for its quiet dignity and straightforwardness. After
setting out the names and ages of the departed
Butlers, it runs as follows :—

> "They were unostentatious but exemplary
> In the discharge of their religious, moral, and social duties.
> This monument is erected by their only son,
> SAMUEL BUTLER, D.D.,
> Archdeacon of Derby and vicar of this church,
> In veneration for the memory of his beloved parents,
> And in humble thankfulness to Almighty God,
> Who vouchsafed to grant them
> Length of days, esteem of friends, content of mind,
> And an easy, gentle passage to eternity."

As we have shown, however, it was not only as a
descriptive writer of this kind that Butler admired
his grandfather. In the concluding chapter to the
Life he notes a virtue—the uncommonness of which,
in Butler's experience, can be judged by reference to
Erewhon Revisited—that his grandfather happily possessed : he was without any fear of giving himself
away. " Those who indulge themselves in this fear,"
adds Butler, in an interesting and illustrative passage,
" are probably quite unaware that he who shrinks from
expressing an opinion which may be reasonably asked
will ere long shrink from forming one that he should
reasonably form." Nor can he resist some further
exposition : " Nothing conduces to indolence and
timidity of thought like indolence and timidity of
expression. Expression is to the mind what action
is to the bodily organ."

In an anonymous pamphlet on University Reform we find many sceptical opinions which Dr Butler did not hesitate to put forward, though it was treasonable for him in his position to do so. One or two of the extracts that are given might have been written by his grandson. He criticised university examinations, for often the examiners, like Samson or the Queen of Sheba, were doing little else, in their misdirected ingenuity, than setting riddles to the candidates.

" But there is one melancholy fact. It is a certain sign of incipient decay in any people when their refinements begin to be excessive. As soon as the true and legitimate standard of taste and judgment either in morals or science is exceeded, it is even more difficult to retrograde towards perfection than it was before to ascend to it. It is hard indeed to save ourselves when, having climbed up the mountain on one side, we have begun to topple down the precipice on the other."

Butler himself had not much sympathy with the ultra-refinements which are the marks of an over-civilised people. To him it meant that too little attention was being given to the essentials of living, too much to the unimportant details. A reasonable degree of refinement is, of course, necessary to the pursuing of art or letters, but only so much as shall not obscure what is vital and human. So Butler never lived in the over-civilised, rather self-conscious world of Meredith or Henry James. He knew that world only as a region, rather to be avoided, where affectation and a certain convention of enlightenment—which was taken for granted—were unfailing accompaniments.

In literature it was character and livingness that appealed to him, and a faithful rendering of contemporary life, as he said in *The Way of All Flesh*. It was these things that he found notably in the *Odyssey*. A satirist is always on the look out in literature for pictures of the past, for satire is concerned with the wider social life rather than with individuals—with social rather than individual evils—and hence the spirit of the time must breathe itself into the pages. Homer, of course, cannot be called a satirist; but Butler, who was one, looked for those attributes, oftenest to be found in the satiric writers. Romance had small place in his work, though he knew that every artist, to be worthy of the name, must possess a poetic gift without which everything he does is flat and empty. In one case, however, in the Memoir of John Pickard Owen, we do discover Butler intrigued by the romance of his story, led on by it to the weaving of fantastic images gathered from the Apocalypse and elsewhere, until Owen and especially his mother emerge as romantic figures. The unpleasantness of Owen, and our knowledge that the author too dislikes him intensely, should not blind us to the delightfully romantic fancy of much that is in the Memoir.

When Butler settled in Clifford's Inn, at the age of twenty-nine, he meant painting to be his profession. Soon, however, he became involved in literary work. But it was always a matter for congratulation that he had his painting and music to fall back upon, at least as recreations, during the twenty-two years of ups and downs, when his financial embarrassments were considerable and anxieties pressed upon him, before the death of his father. Even then, however, when money matters ceased to worry him, he made very little change in his mode of living, except, as Mr Jones says, that he bought a new pair of hairbrushes and a larger wash-hand basin, and engaged Alfred Emery Cathie as his clerk and factotum, " the best body-guard and the most engaging of any man in London," in Butler's description.

Butler's music was no small item of his work. It was in 1885 that he began to write music with Mr Festing Jones, and in that year they published a book of short piano pieces, *Gavottes, Minuets, Fugues*, composed as nearly as possible in the manner of Handel. A few years later, Butler and Mr Jones, in collaboration, issued *Narcissus: A Dramatic Cantata*, also written in the Handelian manner. The subject of the Cantata arose from the authors' wish to deal with the Money Market, a theme that Handel never touched. The Argument is simple : a young shepherd, Narcissus by name, and Amaryllis, a shepherdess, with their companions, have left their pastoral life and embarked on a course of imprudent speculation on the Stock Exchange. The result is a loss of one hundred pounds, on which Narcissus and Amaryllis had hoped to marry.

In the second part Narcissus' aunt is discovered to have died worth one hundred thousand pounds, the whole of which she has left to her nephew. So all obstacles are overcome. Narcissus at first wishes to invest the money in speculative ventures. He is overruled by Amaryllis, however, and eventually agrees to place the whole sum in Three per cent. Consolidated Bank Annuities. The Cantata closes with the congratulations of the Chorus on this happy consummation.

The opening is a Chorus of Shepherds and Shepherd-esses setting out their rash resolve :

> " No more upon the mountain's brow
> We'll tend our tedious flocks ;
> 'Tis smiling commerce charms us now
> And fluctuating stocks."

This is followed by a five-finger exercise, as being the most tedious thing that Butler knew of. So the work proceeds : Speculation is discovered to be a fiend in disguise, and it seems likely that Narcissus and his sweetheart will be compelled to separate. But, as we have seen, fortune smiles upon them, and all ends happily with the Chorus :

> " How blest the prudent man, the maiden pure,
> Whose income is both ample and secure,
> Arising from Consolidated Three
> Per cent. Annuities, paid quarterly."

Narcissus was followed by another collaborate work, *Ulysses : A Dramatic Oratorio*, which was published

by Mr Jones after Butler's death. The Oratorio is
concerned with Ulysses' wanderings—his sojourn on
Circe's island, his adventures in Hades and the return
to Ithaca—and, owing to its subject, is necessarily very
different from the former composition. The narrative
in the *Odyssey* is followed closely, and *Ulysses* is on a
larger scale than *Narcissus*; there are a greater number
of characters, the entire scheme is more ambitious,
and the humorous elements are naturally absent. It
might have been expected that Nausicaa would make
an appearance in the Oratorio, but evidently no place
could be found for her. Circe and Penelope are the
two principal female characters. Nothing is added to
the usually accepted version of Circe, but her greeting
to Ulysses shows the spirit of the composition.

> "What glorious presence greets mine eyes
>   And takes my fluttering heart by storm ?
> Art thou a king in some disguise
>   Or god concealed in human form ?
>
> . . . .
>
> "Say from what distant land you sail,
>   What name your royal father bore,
> What wind unkind or favouring gale
>   Hath borne you to our friendly shore."

As to Penelope, there is no hint that she is anything else than the dutiful wife, waiting for her husband's return—though Butler himself did not feel very confident about her.

" From morn to eve, the whole day long,
My web I weave and sing my song,
And I pray that heaven will send him home,
For he tarrieth long but he yet will come.

" And I ply my loom while the sun rides high
With threads of silver and threads of gold ;
And the days pass on and the years roll by,
But the tale I weave is still untold."

Both *Narcissus* and *Ulysses* are written in the fugato style ; in each of them the authors show an unusually full knowledge of the rules of harmony and counterpoint, and while *Ulysses* was being composed they studied mediæval counterpoint under William Rockstro. To Butler, Handel was the greatest of all musicians, and the two musical compositions were intended as a tribute to him. At the end of *The Authoress of the Odyssey* he wrote as follows about Handel and his own Cantata :—

" Those who know the cantata *Narcissus* . . . will admit that there are people who are fully aware that there is no music in this world so great as Handel's, but who will still try to write music in the style of Handel, and when they have done it, hardly know whether they have been more in jest or earnest, though while doing it they fully believed that they were only writing, so far as in them lay, the kind of music which Handel would have written for such words had he lived a hundred years or so later than he did."

This was the spirit in which Butler embarked on his music. It did not matter to him in the least that people thought he was laughing at Handel because he had written *Narcissus*. The question whether he wrote in jest or earnest never troubled him, because

he knew how deep-rooted and unshakable his affection
for Handel was. There are few books of Butler's
which do not contain some reference to him—illustrations and lessons drawn from the greatest of all artists.
But great as Handel was, Butler knew that there were
moments and glimpses which he could not reproduce ;
it must be the same with all great poets—they can only
catch a part of what is put within their reach. Dignity
and playfulness, solemnity and happiness, an infinite
variety of lights and shades, all enter into Handel's
music. The range of his powers Butler tried to express
in one of his sonnets called " The Life after Death."

> " He who gave eyes to ears and showed in sound
>   All thoughts and things in earth or heaven above.
>   From fire and hailstones running along the ground
>   To Galatea grieving for her love ;
>   He who could show to all unseeing eyes
>   Glad shepherds watching o'er their flocks by night,
>   Or Iphis angel-wafted to the skies,
>   Or Jordan standing as an heap upright—
>   He'll meet both Jones and me and clap or hiss us
>   Vicariously for having writ *Narcissus*."

Butler's miscellaneous work, in which his poems and
sonnets may be included, was not large in extent. The
essays, less than a dozen in number, form the most
important part of it. A few of them deal with art in
out-of-the-way Italian valleys—descriptions of painted
statuary and records of Tabachetti's work in various
places. But the most interesting are the two essays,
" Ramblings in Cheapside " and " Quis Desiderio . . . ? "
The former is a picturesque narrative of cases of
physical transmigration that have come under the
writer's notice. It is a delightfully personal item of

the Butler philosophy—vivid and humorous. There
is no doubt left in our minds about the reality of this
varied procession representing so many of the best-
known figures of the past. Butler noted them all.
There was Mary Queen of Scots, who wore surgical
boots and was to be seen in Tottenham Court Road,
and Michelangelo appeared on board a steamer to
Clacton-on-Sea, a most surprising commissionaire;
Raphael's model for the well-known Madonnas, Butler
observed in a Montreal confectionery shop; Socrates
was an old, rather dilapidated muleteer on an Italian
excursion. And there were many more. In this way
Butler met most of the people that he disliked, and he
often found that their new dispositions contrasted
very favourably with what we know of their past
histories; for they were all quite unconscious as
to who they really were. "Ramblings in Cheapside,"
which is compounded of stray thoughts and suggestions
such as the writer could get into twelve pages of *The
Universal Review*, closes with a few remarks about
that co-operation which exists throughout nature, and
is one of the principles through which the universe is
carried on. He again insists that the universe can
live by faith alone—the faith which you can do little
with, but nothing without—for " it is based on vague
and impalpable opinion that by some inscrutable
process passes into will and action, and is made
manifest in matter and in flesh."

In " Quis Desiderio . . . ? " Butler indulged in the
happiest and most attractive humour. He wanted to
show—and he succeeded quite convincingly in doing
so—that one of Wordsworth's poems about a certain
Lucy conceals a darker secret than has perhaps been

dreamed of.　The poem in question is very short, only
three stanzas, in fact, and in the Oxford Wordsworth,
to which we have referred, is classified under the
heading, "Poems founded on the affections."　Butler
did not believe it was founded on any affection at all,
but rather the contrary.　"What right have we,"
he exclaims indignantly, "to put glosses upon the
masterly reticence of a poet, and credit him with
feelings possibly the very reverse of those he actually
entertained ? "　The poem runs as follows :—

> " She dwelt among the untrodden ways
> 　　Beside the springs of Dove,
> 　A maid whom there were none to praise
> 　　And very few to love.

> " She lived unknown, and few could know
> 　　When Lucy ceased to be ;
> 　But she is in her grave, and, oh,
> 　　The difference to me ! "

The chain of Butler's reasoning is conclusive.
Wordsworth was always accurate in his statements,
and in the second stanza of the poem, which we have
omitted, he hints in no uncertain terms, for those who
can penetrate the smallest distance below the surface,
that Lucy was "ugly and generally disliked."　He
particularly refrained from defining the exact nature
of the difference occasioned by Lucy's death.　We can
only presume, therefore, some entanglement with the
young woman which had become irksome to the poet,
from which he was glad to break loose by murdering
her, probably in concert with Southey and Coleridge.
　All this is a sermon on the text that we cannot
be too careful in the interpretation we put upon the

words of every great poet. And the same applies to
Moore's poem about the lady and the gazelle.[1] Butler
used to say that Lucy and Moore's heroine were
" probably the two most disagreeable young women
in English literature "—and to their number he would
no doubt have added Ernest's sister Charlotte in *The
Way of All Flesh*.

These essays show Butler's humour in its freest and
most unrestrained form. There is a light-hearted
irony in them, and a freshness which he never surpassed. The personal element shines through unmistakably in each of them. In the second of the
essays he again resorts to his favourite intellectual
exercise of turning familiar propositions or conventional
interpretations inside out, on this occasion not so much
for the new discoveries he might make about the works
in question as for the amount of fun he was going
to get out of the process. Incidentally and quite
casually you would become aware that the Wordsworth and Moore poems were only at all tolerable for
the little amusements of this kind which could be
extracted from them. He liked " stuff " of this sort
" to vie strange forms with fancy."

There is a further trait, already mentioned, in
Butler's writing which is vividly illustrated in the
paper " Thought and Language "—namely, his capacity
for describing things, however apparently trifling they
may be, so that their significance for the writer may
be conveyed, as accurately as possible, to the reader.
Here there is a three-page description of a cat playing
with a fly on a window-sill. Butler was a spectator
of the game from the other side of the glass. It is all

[1] Moore's *Fire Worshippers*.

T

of the intensest interest because he makes it so,
because he shows us the meaning of the cat's game
as he interpreted it for the cat, and the conclusions
that he himself drew from it.   It is only a few writers,
whose attention is not distracted always by themselves, who can achieve this perfection of balance
between the subject in hand and the expressing of it.
Such a writer possesses the imagination which enables
him to place himself in the position of a second person
and consider what he has done from that new point
of view.   Butler understood this so well because he
could manipulate incomparably a much more difficult
method of writing—that which in its dual meaning
appeals differently to two different classes of readers.
As " a lord of irony that master spell " he learnt many
lessons.

All this, in fact, is an indication of his disinterested
nature.   Mr Clutton-Brock, in a recent correspondence
about Butler, after insisting on his seriousness, which he
concealed by dissertations against earnestness because
" he did not want to be laughed at by the frivolous,
and protected himself with a kind of mimicry . . . and
by making fun of them when they thought themselves
serious," goes on to describe his attitude as conspicuously disinterested.[1]   " What Butler was really
always preaching," says Mr Clutton-Brock, " and
trying to practise, was disinterestedness in every job
that a man may undertake ; and his own work is so
good because it is so profoundly disinterested.   He
wasn't going to quarrel with the world because he
happened to be unworldly.   Or rather, when he had
his own personal quarrels with things, he knew that

[1] See *The New Statesman,* 15th May 1915.

they were personal, and indulged himself in them as a relaxation. So he enjoyed his haughtiness, knowing that it was haughtiness. He doesn't pretend that his likes and dislikes are those of God also ... they are a holiday from his seriousness, which he thinks he deserves. What he cannot endure is the people who think that their own likes and dislikes are those of God ; that when they are irritable God is angry. That is the cause of most of the cruelty in the world ; and it was the cause of Theobald's cruelty in *The Way of All Flesh*. He had no disinterestedness whatever. His morality is poisoned by his self ; and therefore Butler hated him. But even so he didn't insist that God hated him. He lets you see that he has a personal quarrel with Theobald, and doesn't want you to make it your quarrel."

If his utterances against earnestness were a kind of protective mimicry, there seems to have been no ambiguity in his endeavour after disinterestedness— even though he was unconscious of it. Butler had a certain conception of salvation, or, as Mr Clutton-Brock says, a conception as to how " you could put yourself right with the universe." *The Way of All Flesh* thus records, in Ernest's career, the chequered process of being saved. Although Ernest is a partial portrait of the author, it must not be concluded that what was good for Ernest was necessarily good for him. *The Way of All Flesh* is Butler's key to the text about loving God which is quoted on the title page ; the key to the novel may be found in a note which we have already given.

Butler's profound seriousness is seen again in his mysterious poem, " A Psalm of Montreal." It has

always seemed mysterious to us, this dialogue—
" perhaps true, perhaps imaginary, perhaps a little
of the one and a little of the other "—between the
writer and that grotesque old man who stuffed owls
and was in such dubious relationship to Mr Spurgeon.
It is a vivid picture of certain aspects of Western
character, and of that vulgar irrelevance and ludicrous
pose of respectability which, however, are confined
to no one quarter of the globe. It must have been a
memorable experience to hear Butler recite it. But
there is another most mysterious thing in connection
with " A Psalm of Montreal " : it was published
originally in *The Spectator*. It is difficult to realise
how anything that Butler wrote could ever find a place
in that reckless print which, it is said, still has a
dangerous vogue in some country rectories. This
poem in its seven stanzas shows very well the cast of
his mind ; it displays many of those virtues on whose
account he suffered neglect.

" Stowed away in a Montreal lumber room
The Discobolus standeth and turneth his face to the wall ;
Dusty, cobweb-covered, maimed and set at naught,
Beauty crieth in an attic and no man regardeth :
          O God ! O Montreal ! "

The piece has now been reprinted with Butler's
Notebooks ; before it was so readily accessible we have
heard of people making pilgrimages to the Fitzwilliam
Museum at Cambridge, where one of the manuscripts
is to be found, to copy it.

Like Lord Beaconsfield, Butler succeeded fairly well
in veiling his own earnestness. So, often, did Swift,
with whom Butler has probably more affinity than any

other English writer. Swift's earnestness, and hence his orthodoxy, was considerably blown upon in his own day. As a clergyman of the Church of England, he was, however, much more fully aware of the difficulty of his position than many others of his own time. He was convinced of the truth of what he was called upon to believe, but honest enough to admit that doubts did assail him at times. " I am not answerable to God," he says, " for the doubts that arise in my own breast, since they are the consequences of that reason which He hath planted in me, if I take care to conceal those doubts from others, if I use my best endeavours to subdue them, and if they have no influence on the conduct of my life." His attitude here, in fact, was the same as Butler's over his own fictitious clergyman. Butler imagined an earnest clergyman who was forty-five years of age, with a wife, five children and a living in the country worth four hundred pounds a year, but no private means. The clergyman had ceased to believe in the dogmas that he was called upon to preach. Was he to go on with his present life, or abandon holy orders, thus plunging himself and those dependent upon him into poverty ? This was an extreme case, of course, which Swift was never called upon to face. But it interested Butler, and he manufactured a correspondence about it. Butler, and from the foregoing quotation we cannot doubt that Swift would have agreed with him, settled the question on grounds of expediency. Provided the clergyman concealed his want of faith from others, and behaved as he always had done in the past, no harm would be done. This conclusion on Butler's part may sound like a lack of appreciation of the

serious difficulties of another person. Although the
case was purely imaginary, we believe that the decision
he arrived at was sincere and genuine. Because he
admitted the absolute necessity of compromise in
certain cases, no doubts need be thrown upon his
earnestness. He had too much common-sense to follow
any doctrine to what was plainly a disastrous climax.
The words that he put into the mouth of one of the
correspondents in this controversy over Truth and
Convenience apply very directly to those serious convictions of his, which he tried to conceal from the
rest of the world.

" There is that irony in nature," he says, " which
brings it to pass that if the sayer be a man with any
stuff in him, provided he tells no lie wittingly to himself and is never unkindly, he may lie and lie and lie
all the day long, and he will no more be false to any
man than the sun will shine by night ; his lies will
become truths as they pass into the hearer's soul."

The great sin then is self-deception : Butler might
deceive others about his earnestness, but he never
deceived himself. In this matter Dr Arnold was an
example and warning. There was no real objection
to his being earnest-minded ; the error lay in not being
able to hide it more successfully than he did.

Samuel Butler emerges, then, as a writer quite alone
in the later Victorian age. Mr Shaw has described
him in general terms as a man who saw the importance
of things : hence his genius. Butler wasn't very fond
of the word, but probably it is the one that best suits
him. It has nothing to do with knowledge, the γνῶσις
which he so often mentions. Rather it consists in
the intimacy of the relation which is established

between all the ideas and thoughts that possess a man.
Thereby he sees the relative meaning of things.
Coupled with the extraordinary quickness with which
Butler arrived at his conclusions—however novel the
methods of thus arriving might be—was a great aptitude for detail. No labour was too great, which would
in the slightest degree enhance the value of the final
result. He worked in the British Museum library
untiringly, during the whole of the period he was
engaged in writing. Almost he might have been a
man without ideas dependent on other people's books.
But facts were all he wanted from the British Museum
books. His own library was probably the smallest of
any literary man in London.

In following Butler's literary career we have noted
his gradual emancipation from the influence of unsympathetic early surroundings. Throughout his life
it seemed that the capricious fates were keeping careful
watch over him. To paraphrase his own words, they
can spy out their favourites long before. These
favourites may be as days having parents for their
yesterdays, but through all the bad weather of a stormy
parental sky the fates that are keeping guard over them
can afford to laugh because they discern the fair
weather yet to come. It is interesting to notice what
they did for Butler : the few adventurous years in
New Zealand gave him a new insight into English
life, and the fact that he was never recognised, that
he reaped no success in his own time, enabled him to
continue his work and mould it as nearly as possible
according to his own taste and not that of other people.
In any case, however, it is difficult to think that he
could have been successfully got hold of by any one

section of the community because of anything he wrote that was useful to them. He would have been a little disappointing in his new position. Just before his death he spoke of " the pretty roundness " of his literary career. With *Erewhon* at its beginning and *Erewhon Revisited* at the close, it was a compact and symmetrical achievement. And perhaps it is not fanciful to see in it a replica of the mental orderliness of Butler himself.

The dignity of the human intelligence was one of the lessons he tried to teach in most that he wrote. Man's will and his intellect are the strongest things in the universe. He was a humanist in the sense that other-worldliness did not much concern him except in this : that although he did not believe in a spiritual world, he recognised a world of the unseen and the unknown, which certainly existed, as God the Unknown existed, though there was nothing mystical about it. The transiency of everything in nature forbade him to believe that man alone should be selected for a personal life after death. He saw, as more than one philosopher has done, that that involved a certain conception of pre-existence, and hence as a sort of parody—a parody that was at once jesting and serious—he created in *Erewhon* his World of the Unborn. In a note on Religion, Butler spoke of that Unknown World which we can never expect to comprehend. " There never was any man," he says, " who did not feel that behind this world and above it and about it, there is an unseen world greater and more incomprehensible than any-thing he can conceive, and this feeling, so profound and so universal, needs expression." But since the un-seen world is so incomprehensible that we can never hope to know anything of it, we had better concern ourselves with this present world for its own sake. Man continually improving himself towards higher states of physical comeliness and physical grace was one of Butler's ideals. And it is no mere accident that good breeding and good births are again and again insisted on as the aim of all religious and social institutions whatsoever.

Those who knew him have spoken of Butler's kindness and sympathy, his consideration and generosity. And even when we have all his works before us it is a difficult task to sum up his complex personality—although in his books he revealed himself unselfconsciously and without reserve. He was before everything else a satirist : to this end he used his scorn and hence the fierce gibes at the humbugs and deceit of modern life and conventional customs, his irony, that deadly instrument used with such precision when exposing his age to the merciless light of common-sense, and the " cool enormity of sarcasm," as a recent writer has called it, which continually leaps out from his pages. And behind it all is the feeling of a sane, vivid and attractive personality. *Alps and Sanctuaries*, the genial holiday book, shows us the author in his freest, happiest mood ; so do several of his essays.

Perhaps he may be best summed up as the last of the adventurous English amateurs, interested in so many things that even at the end of his life he hardly knew what his true vocation was, though he would have called it the making of books. In the vulgarity of modern life he found no satisfying means of expression, since he hated publicity and self-advertisement,

and in these matters would admit no compromise. He
was well fitted, therefore, for his " outside " position,
the shrewd spectator of an extraordinary drama who
levelled his jokes and criticisms on the various phases
and situations of the play as they were unfolded to him.

A friend has described him as " kind in heart,
curiously obstinate, good-humouredly prejudiced ; inscrutable in a laughing way ; absolutely careless of
public opinion, full of quaint fancies in art and literature." No doubt he was all these things. But his
fancies, like his humour, were the components of a
well-ordered system. He had real imagination, which
sees where it is going. For this reason also he knew
so much about the people in his novel, and was so
appreciative of any characters he happened to meet
in real life. He has told us about these characters in
his own way, not distorting them, but with the touch
of his own imagination, so that we perhaps can see
them as he did.

We should look upon him chiefly, however, as a
writer with an unusually disciplined intelligence. It
was this that prevented him from fitting comfortably
into his own age. He was an intellectual, but one
tremendously aware of what was alive and picturesque,
and human in human affairs. Perhaps the best
concluding description of Samuel Butler is to be found
in the words of one who knew him well : " Il sait
tout ; il ne sait rien ; il est poète."

BIBLIOGRAPHY

Contributions to *The Eagle*, the magazine of St John's College, Cambridge. 1858-1861.

Contributions to *The Press*, N.Z. 1862-1865.

A First Year in Canterbury Settlement. 1863.

The Evidence for the Resurrection of Jesus Christ as contained in the Four Evangelists critically examined. Printed privately. 1865.

Erewhon, or Over the Range: a Work of Satire and Imagination. 1872.

Erewhon. Second edition, revised and corrected. 1872.

Erewhon, translated into Dutch. 1873.

The Fair Haven: A Work in Defence of the Miraculous Element in Our Lord's Ministry upon Earth, both as against Rationalistic Impugners and certain Orthodox Defenders, by the late John Pickard Owen. With a Memoir of the Author by William Bickersteth Owen. 1873.

The Fair Haven. Second edition, disclosing Butler's authorship. 1873.

Life and Habit: an Essay after a Completer View of Evolution. 1877.

" A Psalm of Montreal," published in *The Spectator.* 1878.

Erewhon, translated into German. 1879.

Evolution Old and New: A Comparison of the Theories of Buffon, Dr Erasmus Darwin and Lamarck with that of Charles Darwin. 1879.

A Clergyman's Doubts: a series of letters in *The Examiner.*

God the Known and God the Unknown: a series of articles in *The Examiner.* 1879.

Unconscious Memory: A Comparison between the theory of Dr Ewald Hering, Professor of Physiology at the University of Prague, and *The Philosophy of the Unconscious* of Dr Edward von Hartmann, with translations from these authors, and preliminary chapters bearing on *Life and Habit, Evolution Old and New,* and Charles Darwin's edition of Dr Krause's *Erasmus Darwin.* 1880.

Alps and Sanctuaries of Piedmont and the Canton Ticino. Illustrated by the author, Charles Gogin and Henry Festing Jones. 1881.

Evolution Old and New. Second edition, with a short preface alluding to the recent death of Charles Darwin, an Appendix and an Index. 1882.

Selections from Previous Works. With " A Psalm of Montreal " and " Remarks on G. J. Romanes' *Mental Evolution in Animals.*" 1884.

Gavottes, Minuets, Fugues, and other short pieces for the piano by Samuel Butler and Henry Festing Jones. 1885.

299

Holbein's *La Danse* : a Note on a drawing in the museum at Basel. 1886.

Luck, or Cunning as the main means of Organic Modification ? An attempt to throw additional light on Charles Darwin's theory of Natural Selection. 1887.

Ex Voto : an account of the Sacro Monte or New Jerusalem at Varallo-Sesia, with some notice of Tabachetti's remaining work at Crea, and illustrations from photographs by the author. 1888.

Narcissus : a Cantata in the Handelian manner. Words and music by Samuel Butler and Henry Festing Jones. 1888.

" Quis Desiderio . . . ? " and other papers contributed to *The Universal Review.* 1888-1890.

The Humour of Homer : a lecture delivered at the Working Men's College, Great Ormond Street. Reprinted with preface and additional matter from *The Eagle.* 1892.

" L'Origine Siciliana dell' Odissea." Extracted from the *Rassegna della Letteratura Siciliana.* 1893.

" On the Trapanese Origin of the *Odyssey*." Translated, with additions, and reprinted from *The Eagle.* 1893.

" Ancora sull' origine dell' Odissea." Extracted from the *Rassegna della Letteratura Siciliana.* 1894.

Ex Voto, translated into Italian by Angelo Rizzetti. 1894.

The Life and Letters of Dr Samuel Butler [his grandfather] in so far as they illustrate the scholastic, religious and social life of England from 1790-1840. 2 vols. 1896.

The Authoress of the Odyssey, where and when she wrote, who she was, the use she made of the *Iliad* and how the poem grew under her hands. 1897.

The *Iliad* rendered into English prose for the use of those who cannot read the original. 1898.

Shakespeare's Sonnets reconsidered and in part rearranged. With Introductory chapters, notes and a reprint of the original 1609 edition. 1899.

The *Odyssey* rendered into English prose for the use of those who cannot read the original. 1900.

Erewhon Revisited twenty years later, both by the Original Discoverer of the Country and by his Son. 1901.

Samuel Butler : Records and Memorials. A collection of obituary notices, with a note by R. A. Streatfeild. Privately printed. 1903.

The Way of All Flesh : a novel. 1903.

Essays on Life, Art and Science. Reprints of some papers from *The Universal Review*, together with two lectures not previously published. 1904.

Seven Sonnets and a Psalm of Montreal. Privately printed. 1904.

Ulysses : an Oratorio. Words and music by Samuel Butler and Henry Festing Jones. 1904.

Diary of a Journey through North Italy to Sicily in the Spring of 1903 undertaken for the purpose of leaving the manuscripts of three books by Samuel Butler at Varallo Sesia, Aci Reale and Trapani. By Henry Festing Jones. Privately printed. 1904.

Extracts from *The Notebooks of Samuel Butler* in *The New Quarterly Review*. 1907-1910.

Essays on Life, Art and Science. Reissue. 1908.

The Way of All Flesh. Second edition. 1908.

Erewhon. Reissue. 1908.

Erewhon Revisited. Reissue. 1908.

God the Known and God the Unknown. 1909.

Unconscious Memory. New edition, with a note by R. A. Streatfeild, and an introduction by Professor Marcus Hartog. 1910.

Life and Habit. New edition, with preface by R. A. Streatfeild and author's addenda. 1910.

" Samuel Butler," in *The Encyclopædia Britannica.* 1910.

Charles Darwin and Samuel Butler : a Step towards Reconciliation. By Henry Festing Jones. 1911.

Evolution Old and New. Reprint, with prefatory note by R. A. Streatfeild. 1911.

Essays on Two Moderns [Euripides : Samuel Butler]. By W. H. Salter. 1911.

The Notebooks of Samuel Butler. Selections, arranged and edited by Henry Festing Jones. 1912.

" Samuel Butler " in *The Dictionary of National Biography.* Second supplement. By Thomas Seccombe. 1912

Alps and Sanctuaries of Piedmont and the Canton Ticino. New edition, with an introduction by R. A. Streatfeild. 1913.

The Fair Haven. New edition, with an introduction by R. A. Streatfeild. 1913.

The Humour of Homer and Other Essays [*Essays on Life, Art and Science,* with the addition of *The Humour of Homer*]. Edited by R. A. Streatfeild ; with a biographical sketch of the author by Henry Festing Jones. 1913.

" Parody of a Simeonite Tract," written by Butler at Cambridge in 1855, and discovered by A. T. Bartholomew among the Cambridge papers of the late J. W. Clark. Printed in *The Cambridge Magazine,* 1st March. 1913.

A First Year in Canterbury Settlement, with Other Early Essays. Edited by R. A. Streatfeild. 1914.

Samuel Butler : A Critical Study. By Gilbert Cannan. 1915.

The Notebooks of Samuel Butler. Reissue. 1915.

All Samuel Butler's books that are not out of print are published by Mr A. C. Fifield.

INDEX

[The Bibliography is not included in the Index.]

Redwood Library

:TIONS FROM THE RULES

ree volumes may be taken at a time
three on one share. Two unbound
of a monthly and three numbers of a
ublication are counted as a volume.

oks other than 7-day and 14-day ones
ept out 28 days. **Books cannot be
d or transferred.**

ooks overdue are subject to a fine of one
ay for fourteen days, **and five cents a
r each day thereafter.**

Neglect to pay the fine will debar from
of the Library.

o book is to be lent out of the house of
to whom it is charged.

erson who shall soil (deface) or
book belonging to the Library
ch fine as the Directors may
the value of the book or of
of a set, as the Directors
ing or any marking or
or turning down the
or tearing any matter
belonging to the Library, will be con-
d defacement and damage.